MOST
VALUABLE

MOST VALUABLE

How Sidney Crosby Became the Best Player
in Hockey's Greatest Era and Changed the Game Forever

GARE JOYCE

VIKING

VIKING

an imprint of Penguin Canada, a division of Penguin Random House Canada Limited

Canada • USA • UK • Ireland • Australia • New Zealand • India • South Africa • China

First published 2019

www.penguinrandomhouse.ca

LIBRARY AND ARCHIVES CANADA CATALOGUING IN PUBLICATION

Title: Most valuable : how Sidney Crosby became the best player in
hockey's greatest era and changed the game forever / Gare Joyce

Names: Joyce, Gare, author.

Identifiers: Canadiana (print) 20190102896 |
Canadiana (ebook) 20190101113 | ISBN 9780735237926

(hardcover) | ISBN 9780735237933 (HTML)

Subjects: LCSH: Crosby, Sidney, 1987- |
LCSH: Hockey players—Canada—Biography. | LCGFT: Biographies.

Classification: LCC GV848.5.C76 G37 2019 | DDC 796.962092—dc23

Book and cover design by Five Seventeen
Jacket image: Mike Ehrmann / Getty Images

Printed and bound in Canada

10 9 8 7 6 5 4 3 2 1

 Penguin
Random House
VIKING CANADA

In memory of Mark Giles, my best buddy in a room
full of talented friends at *ESPN The Magazine*

CONTENTS

CHAPTER 1

ROUGH TREATMENT

Pittsburgh, April 2017

It was a too-familiar scene and a recurring nightmare: Sidney Crosby lying face down and motionless on the ice after landing on the wrong end of a shot to his helmeted head; teammates standing around him and then waving to the Penguins bench; a trainer running out to see if he was okay when everyone knew he wasn't; the Penguins star helped to his feet, to the bench and down the hallway to the dressing room, disappearing from sight.

In those awful couple of minutes, my mind raced. Of course, like anyone who was watching this in real time, or soon after on replay, I thought of the immediate fate of a 29-year-old. I had met him just days after his 16th birthday; over the years, I had come to know people in his inner circle, those who had been there since the beginning, and I had worked dozens of his games, with the

Penguins and on the international stage. I had been around for his first game as a junior player, and I was wondering (and not for the first time) whether I had just watched the last shift he'd ever play in the National Hockey League.

When I say that my mind raced, understand that, for the matter of my profession, there was little time. The inciting incident went down six minutes into Game 3 of the Eastern Conference semifinal against the Washington Capitals at the PPG Paints Arena. The Caps had won the Presidents' Trophy with the league's best record but the Penguins had swept the first two games in Washington and it looked like, once more, Crosby and company would own Alexander Ovechkin and company, a hero-and-nemesis thing that seemingly always came out in Crosby's favour. With Crosby off the ice and receiving attention from the team doctors, there was still going to be a game story to write a couple of hours down the line. Still, before the puck would be dropped, there was time enough to do at least a preliminary taking of stock.

From its routine beginnings to the gloomy end point, the sequence was replayed in the arena: Crosby had been skating down the left side of the ice on a two-on-one with his winger, 21-year-old rookie Jake Guentzel, carrying the puck. The defenceman back was Matt Niskanen. Ovechkin was skating furiously in Crosby's wake, but still a step or so behind, with Crosby bearing down on the Capitals net. Guentzel found Crosby with a pass and Crosby crashed the net. Ovechkin swung his stick in a desperate and reckless attempt to break up the play and clipped Crosby's helmet. Crosby went into a speed wobble and his knee seemed to give. He went bailing by goalie Braden Holtby, where Niskanen was waiting, the shaft of his stick not quite six feet off the ice, ready to intersect with either the side of Crosby's helmet or anything unguarded from the neck up. In real time—and even more on replay—it seemed to me that Niskanen intended to drill Crosby with a cross-check, maybe intending to hit his torso, but he wound up connecting with head and neck. Niskanen stood over the Pittsburgh captain like a hunter over his kill. The refs saw it the same way I did and handed him a five-minute major for cross-checking and a game misconduct.

While Crosby was being helped off the ice, I did a quick search of Niskanen's history: a 10-year pro who signed with the Capitals in the summer of 2014. At an unimposing six foot one and just over 200 pounds, Niskanen wouldn't really throw a scare into opposing forwards. He had never been suspended by the league and could never be accused of being a thug, much less a headhunter. In fact, you wouldn't even think of him as a particularly physical defence-man at all—in 78 regular-season games, he had 32 penalty minutes. By position, that qualifies him as relatively peace-loving and risks him getting labelled as soft. A curious footnote here: Niskanen had played in Pittsburgh for three full seasons prior to jumping to the Caps. Was there anything to read into that, any hard feelings? Without any record or even hint of previous animus, you'd have to have a predilection for intrigue to read anything into that. Niskanen would be no more likely than anyone in the league to commit some sort of heinous act against any player, never mind the most decorated star of his generation. In fact, given all the aforementioned reasons, you'd presume he'd be less likely than most.

In the immediate aftermath of the felling of Crosby, the fans reflexively booed Niskanen but that only lasted a beat or two. When Crosby didn't move, the booing gave way to a hush. In that split second, the world inside the arena was upended—as should have been expected, because it was very much an arena, and a world, created by the player who was lying on the ice. When Crosby arrived in Pittsburgh in the fall of 2005, he was billed as a franchise player, a centre that a team could be built around. No one quite billed him as a saviour, because whether the Penguins franchise could be saved was an open question.

Even though it doesn't have an NBA franchise and the Pirates have been perennial MLB doormats for more than two decades, Pittsburgh is among the first to be mentioned whenever discussion turns to the best sports cities in North America, but five years into the new millennium the Penguins were running a poor second to the Steelers. They always have, and to some extent always will: the city's demographics and history just skew towards football and really, the Steelers' four Super Bowl wins in the '70s simply represented a midpoint in Pittsburgh's love affair with the gridiron game, which dates back to the era of leather helmets. During the early '90s, when the Pens won a couple of Stanley Cups and the Steelers were a middling team, hockey had cachet in the market. But by autumn of 2005, that was ancient history.

Eighteen months before, the Penguins were tearing down the franchise, selling off parts in an effort to dump salary and tank to land the first pick in the 2004 draft. After a tremendous downward struggle the Penguins finished with the league's worst record, but their bad luck held and they wound up losing the lottery to Washington. The prize in the 2004 draft was Alexander Ovechkin, who went to the Capitals. The second-best prospect in the pool was another Russian, Evgeni Malkin, whom the Penguins selected. Malkin was not remotely close to being hyped up as much as Ovechkin — it was the difference between superstar and elite talent, a more substantial difference for a struggling franchise than it might seem at first glance. Malkin made it clear that he was in no rush to leave his team in Russia's Kontinental Hockey League, and given the state of the Penguins, his recalcitrance was understandable. He and goaltender Marc-Andre Fleury, the team's first-overall pick in the 2003 draft, were seasons away from making meaningful contributions.

That said, the future of the roster was less cloudy than that of the franchise itself. Before Crosby's arrival, the franchise had been at least rumoured to be relocating to Kansas City or Hamilton or elsewhere for almost a decade, on and off. How real were the threats? Well, most aren't. Usually owners will float the possibility in hopes of extracting better leases, tax breaks, venue upgrades or, if they're really lucky, a new arena entirely. In Pittsburgh, those threats had really never paid in a big way. The Penguins were still playing out of the Civic Arena, their original home, a quirky but tired place—the venue had a retractable roof that had rarely, and never fully since '85, been opened. In the upper bowl, fans could literally peer through seams in the roof a yard wide and see the night sky.

The Penguins' situation can be best summed thusly: in 1999, when the ownership group headed by film producer Howard Baldwin could no longer pay the then-retired Mario Lemieux and were about to default on the terms of his contract, they negotiated a settlement and handed him the keys, making him the proprietor. When Lemieux came out of retirement a year later, he may well have been motivated, at least in part, by a desire to increase the value of his investment, or at least improve the bottom line. By 2004, as he neared his 40th birthday, Lemieux could no longer carry the team on the ice—or, possibly, on the spreadsheet.

Of course, the Penguins weren't the only NHL team whose precarious finances kept them from competing with the Tiffany franchises—the Detroit Red Wings and New York Rangers, among others—and for this reason, commissioner Gary Bettman and the owners of the NHL's teams dug in their heels for 12 months of collective bargaining that would sacrifice the 2004–05 season as collateral damage. Not even World War II had caused a major North American sports league to cancel a full season, but a battle to the death over a salary cap did. This was uncharted territory—there was no way of knowing how the fans would respond after their good faith had been breached. That said, things were so bad in Pittsburgh that a cancelled season might not have qualified as bad news, just a way to stem seven- or eight-figure financial losses and avoid further alienating fans with another indifferent campaign.

And yet, after owners and players finally forged a collective agreement in the spring of 2005 and the Penguins won a special draft lottery that gave all 30 NHL teams a chance at the No. 1 pick, interest in hockey surged in Pittsburgh. GM Craig Patrick went to the market and signed veteran free agents, spurred more by the desire to give Lemieux a shot at winning a Cup before he retired than by the arrival of Crosby. It was a quixotic gambit: Lemieux would retire in midseason with a heart arrhythmia, the veterans had trouble adjusting to the loss of a season away and to new NHL rules and the Penguins missed out on the playoffs once more. Crosby represented the team's lone bright spot in his rookie campaign—he scored more than 100 points and was runner-up to Ovechkin in Calder Trophy voting. That was even more impressive, given that Ovechkin was almost two years older than Crosby. The following season, Crosby won the Hart Trophy as the league's most valuable player, and that spring the Penguins ownership managed to negotiate a deal with the city and state to build a new arena. Two years after that, while the arena was under construction, Crosby raised the Stanley Cup after Pittsburgh beat the Red Wings in Game 7 in Detroit. When the Penguins moved into the PPG Paints Arena in the fall of 2011, they had two banners from the '90s to raise to the rafters, a nod to history, and the one from 2009, which promised more down the line.

The turnaround of a franchise that had seemed beyond salvaging was complete, but more fragile perhaps than might have been anticipated. That was the takeaway from Crosby's struggles with post-concussion syndrome, which caused him to miss more than 100 regular-season games in total between January 2011 and the spring of 2012. During that stretch, hockey fans not only wondered if they would ever see Crosby again at the peak of his abilities, but also whether they would ever see him again at all. Those fears were renewed when Crosby lay at Niskanen's feet.

If you had wanted a sense of the NHL as it entered its second century in operation, you could have learned a lot over the 24 hours after Niskanen's takedown of the league's best player.

During the game itself, there was nothing really meaningful in the way of retaliation. Perhaps if he hadn't been ejected, Niskanen might have been slashed and speared and elbowed, or even jumped. Perhaps there would have been some rough justice. Or not. Like virtually every NHL team in recent seasons, the Penguins carried no designated tough guy, no enforcer, no goon to protect their star players—players who fit the policeman's profile have gone from endangered-species status to extinction, simply because they could not keep up with the pace on the ice and contribute meaningfully. With the salary cap in effect since that 2004–05 lockout, money spent on a tough guy just didn't make sense, offered no useful return on investment. Through 82 regular-season games, the Penguins had but 12 fighting majors, six of which were meted out to three minor-leaguers who had been called up for a combined 36 games, earning the NHL's minimum salary (Tom Sestito with three, Steve Oleksy with two and Cameron Gaunce with the other). All three were watching the playoffs from the sidelines. Evgeni Malkin had a fighting major after tangling with Winnipeg's Blake Wheeler a few weeks earlier, but there'd be no goading an all-star into a fight, not with a game on the line and Crosby *hors de combat*.

You might have expected the Penguins to target the Capitals' star players — say, Ovechkin and Nicklas Backstrom — in something of a tit-for-tat. Didn't happen either. Running the massive Ovechkin is probably more likely to hurt you than him. Maybe Backstrom would present a more accessible target, but again, it would've been counterproductive to the Penguins in the short run, sending someone to the penalty box and/or out of a crucial game with the outcome still hanging in the balance. After an overtime goal by defenceman Kevin Shattenkirk, the Capitals escaped with a win and without physical payback for Niskanen's shot on Crosby.

In the immediate aftermath of the game, Niskanen pleaded his case, although, if he had been in court, he would have benefited from a lawyer's advice. He admitted that he had meant to cross-check Crosby but "didn't mean to knock him out of the game." That was something less than a denial, something closer to a plea bargain to a reduced charge with an expression of meaningful, if tempered remorse. It goes to the point that, in a league where hooking, holding and interference are called tightly, refs condone a lot of slashing and cross-checking, considering it incidental contact. The cross-check was simply everyday business.

That was the party line in the Capitals camp. Said coach Barry Trotz, "I thought it was really a hockey play. Crosby is coming across, [goaltender Braden Holtby] throws his stick out there and [Crosby] sort of gets split . . . and he just sort of ran into Niskanen."

The league effectively concurred. The next day, the NHL's department of player safety announced that Niskanen wouldn't be called in for a hearing, and thus he escaped any suspension: the major penalty and misconduct were going to be his only punishment. It's not the act alone, but the actor too that influences league decisions on matters like these. Niskanen's record—his penalty minutes and the fact that he had no previous suspensions—factored into the decision not to investigate the matter further. Seemingly, though, no consideration was given to the player who took the brunt of the blow. Of all the players on the ice, it just happened to be Crosby's helmet that Ovechkin clipped with his stick. It just happened to be Crosby who took the blow from Niskanen's cross-check. The Penguins' franchise player. The winner of the Conn Smythe Trophy the season before. And a player who had missed more than a season in his prime with post-concussion syndrome. You'd hardly need to be a conspiracy buff to believe that this was no coincidence.

Neither did you have to be an expert in public relations or executive management strategies to wonder about the league's messaging as it gave Niskanen a pass. After all, the NHL was embroiled in litigation with alumni, from journeymen to stars, who claimed to have had their careers shortened or ended, and even their lives ruined, by brain trauma that had gone undiagnosed or poorly treated, if treated at all. The league was enduring a spate of bad-news stories that landed with clockwork regularity: the premature retirement of players with post-concussion syndrome (Marc Savard and Crosby's former linemate Pascal Dupuis, among others) and the cognitive and psychological issues that led to the deaths of Derek Boogaard and Steve Montador. Under commissioner Gary Bettman, the NHL had taken various programs, including in-game protocols on head shots and mandatory examination of players dazed by blows. Still, the efforts often came off as lip service to the physical, psychological and, in particular, neurological toll the game takes on its players. The league's official stand seemed to be founded on magical thinking: CTE might abound elsewhere — in boxing, in football — but somehow you gain immunity once you put on skates, or perhaps an NHL sweater grants the wearer a super-recuperative power. If Sidney Crosby's career were to end with a concussion, no matter whether on a dirty hit or an accidental play, it would seem hard for Bettman and the owners to keep their blinkers on.

Over the 2016–17 season, the NHL celebrated its 100th anniversary. As the league enters its second century, the brand of hockey is more dynamic and more dangerous than ever before. It's not that it bears no resemblance to the scenes captured in black-and-white film footage from bygone days, or even that it looks nothing like the game I covered when I started writing about the league 30 years ago, when Wayne Gretzky was in his prime and the Edmonton Oilers looked down on the rest of the league; the fact is, it looks utterly unlike the game that was played even 13 years ago.

In terms of entertainment value, it's hard to pinpoint the league's nadir. Some would point to one of New Jersey's runs to its three Stanley Cup championships over an eight-year stretch, beginning in the mid-'90s. The Devils were reviled for clogging the neutral zone like an ancient drainpipe and slowing games to a crawl. Compounding the damage, the Devils became the template for coaches looking to preserve their NHL jobs—if you can't compete on skill, take the flow out of the game and pray for some puck luck. Across the league, scoring fell into a steady, measurable decline, and skill could be neutralized by clutching and grabbing. Making matters worse was the dilution of the talent pool by expansion, from 21 teams in 1990 to 30 by the year 2000.

It wasn't evident at the time, but the tipping point came in the spring of 2004, when the Tampa Bay Lightning beat out the Calgary Flames in a Stanley Cup final that went the full seven games. The series was not without suspense and drama—at its worst, it would be better than the best of the Devils' Cup runs. Nonetheless, the hockey played in those seven games is noticeably different from what we see today, in terms of pace. Some of it is a function of rule changes, such as the elimination of the rule barring two-line passes, while enforcement of existing rules (for example, referees ceasing to overlook the sort of hooking and holding once seen on every shift) also played a role.

Watching Game 7 from 2004, you're left to wonder: How many in the NHL's showcase event, if somehow transported ahead in time, could play in the league now? And keep in mind that the players on those two teams had won 15 NHL playoff games that spring for the right to play one single game to have their names engraved on the Stanley Cup.

Said one veteran NHL executive whose career stretched back into the 1980s, "Set aside the stars—[Vincent] Lecavalier, [Jarome] Iginla, [Martin] St. Louis. At least half the players on the ice that night couldn't take a regular shift with an average NHL game. They wouldn't be nearly fit enough. Others would struggle. But some guys, like [defencemen] Mike Commodore or Krzysztof Oliwa, there just isn't a place for them in the game anymore except on the fringe of a roster. They couldn't skate well enough to keep up. For Tampa, they had Andre Roy and Chris Dingman, tough guys who just don't have a role in the league anymore. And even for Lecavalier, Iginla and St. Louis, players who were in the top 20 in the whole league, they would have to adapt their games." (By 2017, the last holdovers from that 2004 final, Lecavalier and Iginla, were out of the league—Lecavalier retired that summer, while Iginla, a free agent, was unable to land a new contract.)

Said Matt Duchene, who entered the league in 2008, "Just in the time that I going from peewee and bantam to junior, there was a whole other game before and after. I don't know that [Crosby] reinvented the game, but he invented a way to get ready to play, and you didn't have a choice really—you had to adapt and adopt the way he did things or get left way behind."

Maybe it only stands to reason that the league's most dynamic player is also its most endangered. Fans go to arenas to see Crosby play knowing that, given his history, given the way the game is played, this might be their last chance, if the game were to claim its best as it has claimed others. The thinking: *it might end right here, on the ice tonight.* The underlying irony: the game that he basically forged in his design will be the game that takes him down, and perhaps not without awful and lifelong effects. And if that most awful of scenarios were to play out, the game would not only lose its best player—the very face of the league—in his prime, but the NHL would have to undertake another reinvention of the game. Too late for Sidney Crosby. Hopefully in time for the next Sidney Crosby.

CHAPTER 2

HIS PLACE AMONG THE GREATS

By the time this book is in your hands or on a screen, Sidney Crosby will be 32 years old. If he remains relatively healthy he'll be less than a season away from the 1,000th regular-season game of his NHL career. He'll be roughly two years away from scoring his 500th goal. He got a head start on the field, given that he played his first NHL game just two months after his 18th birthday, making him the youngest player in the league that year. He has won the Art Ross Trophy as the NHL's leading scorer twice, in 2006–07 and 2013–14, and was well on his way to winning another before injury cut short his bid. He has finished in the top three in points five other times, and on a sixth occasion he tied Alexander Ovechkin for third in points, but his Washington rival knocked him off the podium based on the tiebreaker, goals scored. There's seemingly little or no drop-off in his game, what you'd expect of an average player in his demographic; he's coming off a 100-point season, 13 seasons after he hit that benchmark for the first time.

As impressive as those statistics might be, his numbers in the NHL playoffs are even more so. He is sitting 10th all time in postseason points, and only Hockey Hall of Famers rank above him, all having played deep into their 30s or early 40s. It doesn't seem likely that anyone in our lifetime will make a run at the postseason records set by Wayne Gretzky and Mark Messier, who both benefited from playing on the powerhouse Edmonton Oilers in the NHL's highest-scoring era. In the 2019 playoffs, the Penguins were swept by the New York Islanders and Crosby registered just a single point, which was enough to move him past Steve Yzerman. Nonetheless, there's every chance that a couple of playoff runs will allow Crosby to pass two other former Oilers, Jari Kurri and Glenn Anderson, who are in third and fourth place. Nor is any active player a threat to chase him down. His teammate Evgeni Malkin is 18 points behind, and you'd have to go another 41 points down the list to find the next one (Toronto's Patrick Marleau, who turns 40 in September 2019). To find a player younger than Crosby on the list, you'd have to flip the page to find Chicago's Patrick Kane—63 points behind. If Crosby's career continues to unfold as he hopes, he will have separated himself from the pack of his generation—unless, say, Crosby chooses to walk away from the game early and Malkin plays deep into his 40s, as Jaromir Jagr did.

No matter what the sport, the assessment of a star in mid-career is a risky—if not suspect—proposition. No matter how fair and accurate, it paints an incomplete picture, akin to a review of an epic novel based on only a reading of the first 200 pages. So it is with Sidney Crosby in 2019.

There's no way of knowing whether we've seen his best, though you would have to suspect that his peak seasons are behind him. (According to a University of British Columbia study published in the *Journal of Quantitative Analysis in Sports*, the performance of forwards peaks between the ages of 27 and 28; defencemen, a year later.) Crosby would have to be the exception to a mercilessly iron-clad rule, but then again he has always been an outlier, one who breached convention. You might bet against a sustained late-career bloom fuller than any before, but you'd do it at your peril. Worth remembering: Wayne Gretzky has long maintained that he played his greatest game in the 1993 Eastern Conference final. He scored three goals and added an assist in Los Angeles's 5–4 victory over Toronto in Game 7 at Maple Leaf Gardens. Gretzky was 32 years, four months and three days old. So there could be more Cups for No. 87, perhaps even with another team. Maybe more Olympic glory.

And as for Crosby's farewell, it could be one that provides a lasting image, like Jean Beliveau exiting with one last Stanley Cup in 1971, or Ray Bourque raising the Cup in Colorado, finally ending a 22-year quest for a championship. For Crosby, there might be a farewell tour, a glorious exit that will play out as if it were scripted. These are the storybook exceptions, of course, and not the way things played out for Orr, Gretzky or Lemieux, Crosby's mentor in Pittsburgh. A slow fade to black remains a possibility; perhaps even a sharp cut. Borrowing from Donald Rumsfeld, "unknown unknowns" await.

So let's leave the hard statistical measures aside and leave the projections to those for whom a game of flesh, sweat and blood is reducible to so much fodder for spreadsheets. Let's leave the guesswork to the psychics. Let's consider, rather, Sidney Crosby's place in the great sweep of history.

———

Ranking those in hockey's pantheon is the game's most subjective and speculative exercise. The more that you dig into it, the sillier it can seem. Of all the greats, who's greater than who? And what do you mean by "great"? Greatest in a single game? Greatest across the span of a career? Most dominant in his era? Most talented? Such differentiations start to matter less, the closer you get to the top of any list, I suppose. There's open debate about who belongs at Nos. 1 and 2, whether it should be Gretzky over Orr or vice versa, and disagreements are bound to cascade thereafter. That said, the same names tend to occupy the upper ranks time and again.

In 1997 the *Hockey News* put together a panel of 50 experts, including NHL executives, veterans in the media and hockey historians, and came up with a list of the top 100 players of all time. In a close vote, Gretzky, owner of every major NHL scoring record, ranked No. 1 and Orr, whose single-season numbers for a defenceman have never been threatened, placed second. Rounding out the top 10, in order, were:

3. Gordie Howe, the 12-time NHL First Team All-Star at right wing, who scored 975 goals in 2,168 games in the NHL and World Hockey Association.
4. Mario Lemieux, the Pittsburgh centre who won the Art Ross Trophy as the league's leading scorer six times and the Conn Smythe Trophies as the most valuable player in the Stanley Cup playoffs twice.
5. Rocket Richard, the Canadiens right winger whose 50 goals in 50 games stood as the NHL's single-season scoring record for 21 years.
6. Doug Harvey, the seven-time winner of the Norris Trophy as the league's best defenceman.

7. Jean Beliveau, the centre of the Canadiens' five consecutive Stanley Cup teams in the '50s and member of five other championship teams through 1971.
8. Bobby Hull, the 10-time NHL First Team All-Star at left wing, who broke Rocket Richard's single-season record for goals.
9. Terry Sawchuk, the four-time Stanley Cup–winning goaltender whose 103 career shutouts stood as an NHL record for 39 seasons.
10. Eddie Shore, the Boston Bruins defenceman who won the Hart Trophy four times, a record for a blueliner.

Steve Dryden, the editor of the *Hockey News* in '97, moved over to TSN a few years later, and there he put together a new list in 2017, this one ranking the top 25. Again, a comprehensive panel of experts voted. The top seven slots remained unchanged from the *Hockey News* poll, but Crosby claimed the No. 8 spot, behind Beliveau and ahead of Hull and Sawchuk. (Shore dropped all the way to No. 14, overtaken by great Howie Morenz, Guy Lafleur and Mark Messier. Jacques Plante was No. 15.) Two of Crosby's contemporaries made the top 20: Ovechkin at No. 16, and Nicklas Lidstrom at No. 19.

Some will argue that Crosby was moved up the list too high or too soon. Others will claim that the TSN survey underrates him. Jim Rutherford, the Penguins' GM since June of 2014, is in the latter camp. Rutherford has called Crosby "one of the four greatest players in NHL history," leaving him in the company of Gretzky, Orr and Lemieux and placing him ahead of Howe, with whom Rutherford played in his rookie season in Detroit back in 1969–70. But, for the sake of argument, let's just go with the *Hockey News* and TSN lists.

If we look at these rankings, or even just contemplate players who have come to define their eras, we get a sense history folding over on itself—that is, a great new player arrives just as another leaves. When a legendary star begins to fade, an heir becomes apparent. TSN's top 15 features players who played their first NHL games in the 1940s (Richard, Howe, Harvey and Sawchuk), the '50s (Plante, Beliveau and Hull), the '60s (Orr), the '70s (Lafleur, Gretzky and Messier) and the '80s (Lemieux). Thus, through the back half of the 20th century, the NHL never lacked for star quality. But then comes a curious void: the decade of the '90s. Lidstrom made his debut with Detroit in 1991, and if you shuffle farther down the list, you'll hit three others from that decade, in slots 21 through 25: Dominik Hasek, Jaromir Jagr and Martin Brodeur, who began their careers in 1990 or 1991. Now consider: of the hundreds of players who made their NHL debuts between 1992 and 2004, none landed on this list. In fact, the gap between Lidstrom, Hasek, Jagr and Brodeur and the two stars of the new millennium, Crosby and Ovechkin, is the widest on the list. Further, consider that of the four who did come along at the start of the '90s, two are goaltenders (Hasek and Brodeur), while Lidstrom was a ruthlessly effective defenceman who could shut down the league's most creative players. Jagr was the only one who often made magic happen with the puck on his stick, but his career featured peaks and valleys, not to mention a stretch of four years spent in self-imposed exile in Russia's KHL.

In the '90s, the NHL undertook an aggressive expansion, generating greater demand for talent, but at the same time it gained access to pools of players previously unavailable—namely those in Russia and Eastern Europe. Even with this influx, as well as hockey's expanding footprint at the grassroots level in the US, there was a seeming dearth of unique, transcendent talent. It's true that no shortage of players who began their NHL careers in the '90s have been voted into the Hockey Hall of Fame on the first ballot, including all of the aforementioned, along with Peter Forsberg, Chris Pronger and others. Give them full credit for their achievements. And yet they fell short, probably far short, of greatness, no matter how you define it. Gretzky vs. Forsberg or Orr vs. Pronger —even a hardcore contrarian would have a hard time taking up such a debate with a straight face.

There was but one player who seemed to be on track for the upper reaches, at least by virtue of talent: Eric Lindros, who at 18, before he played in an NHL game, played alongside Gretzky et al. for the Canadian team at the 1991 Canada Cup. Even in his teens, Lindros possessed a physical force and an inclination towards violence that, for spectators, evoked the memory of Howe and that struck fear into opponents. Many middle-tier NHLers looked like schoolchildren when they skated beside (or in fact, under) the six-foot, five-inch, 230-pound Lindros, who hit his peak in 1995 when he won the Hart Trophy with the Philadelphia Flyers. The line he centred between John LeClair and Mikael Renberg deserved its nickname, cribbed from professional wrestling: the Legion of Doom. I remember working a game when, for an awful minute or so, I feared that Lindros had killed an opponent on the ice—that night, he ran Ottawa Senators forward Andreas Dackell into the plexiglass and left him in a pool of blood, with every juror in the arena convicting him of attempted murder with their boos.

The Era of Eric never really came together, though. His career was ultimately star-crossed, his peak short-lived. A series of injuries, including eight too-awful-to-watch concussions, first diminished his game and ultimately shortened his career. At age 27, at what should have been the peak of his game, Lindros spent an entire season on the sidelines, recovering from two concussions in quick succession the year before. While his points-per-game numbers placed him among the greats, he was limited to 760 NHL regular-season games.

Thus, with Lemieux walking away from the game in 1997, with Gretzky's retirement two years later and with Lindros in early decline, the NHL entered the new millennium with "a greatness void." For the first time in almost six full decades, nobody on that list of the 10 greatest players was active. Think of as it as an indefinite interregnum. Lemieux would return in December 2000, in time for a few great moments, including leading the Canadian team to Olympic gold in 2002. Still, at that point, it felt very much like we'd never see his like again. And there was seemingly no one who could pick up where he would leave off.

I'm just a writer by trade and a listener by nature, one who worked hundreds of NHL games in the '90s and into the next century, one who bent an ear towards hundreds of those who worked in the league, on the ice, behind the bench or in the executive office. I'd balk at being labelled an authority but I think I toiled long enough and just barely hard enough to be allowed an opinion or two.

I definitely had a sense that a pall had fallen over the game at its highest level in the mid-'90s. If I were looking for someone to second the opinion, I could have submitted Lemieux's own estimation when he hung up his skates the first time. Reports varied —some said he derided the NHL as "a garage league," others were sure he intended to say "a garbage league"—but either way, he couldn't be bothered to conceal his contempt. At that time,

Lemieux was still the game's most singularly skilled player, having come back from lymphoma and career-threatening back injuries to lead the league in scoring. He was no less than the fourth-greatest player in the league's history. So it was the worst possible message for the NHL to receive: the sport couldn't sustain the interest of its best player.

How did the NHL get to that awful place? There wasn't necessarily a turning point, nor a catalyst. It was the by-product of evolution rather than a revolution.

In the '80s, when I first wrote about hockey, there was a significant stretch when nearly eight goals were scored in the average NHL game. Scoring reached its peak in 1981–82, with the rise of Gretzky's Oilers, when the average climbed fractionally above eight goals. This isn't to say that the game was better, and it certainly doesn't imply that the *players* were better. It only suggests that you couldn't leave your seat in an arena or look away from the television without risking missing something meaningful.

Across the next 13 seasons, though, scoring ebbed dramatically. In 1995 the average dropped below six goals. You had to go back a quarter century, to the 1969–70 season, to find the last time a moderately gifted team was as hard-pressed to come up with three goals a night. Back in '70, mind you, the NHL was only three years removed from an expansion that had doubled the number of teams, adding dozens of career journeymen—honest but limited pluggers getting their chance to skate in the spotlight—who would've been buried in the minor leagues a few years before.

By the late '90s, the average had dropped to barely over five goals. The numbers don't lie, but neither do they tell the whole story. Lower scoring doesn't necessarily correlate to a lower skill level but it was undeniable that the NHL's brand of hockey in the late '90s and the early 2000s, the era of Mario Lemieux's "garage/garbage league," offered less entertainment value. Some would again blame the expansion that took place throughout the decade, and yes, there were too many teams in need of infusions of talent. But expansion alone, even if it did create a dramatic imbalance in talent—even within the context of individual lineups—couldn't have been enough to so limit scoring on a leaguewide basis.

I don't know if the 1994–95 New Jersey Devils were simply a symptom of the malaise or represented the nadir—which seems unkind to say of any team, but particularly in this case, given that they were Stanley Cup champions. In 1994 the NHL enjoyed a spike in publicity when the heritage team in the biggest media market, the New York Rangers, ended their long championship drought behind a stirring performance from Mark Messier, among others. A year later, though, it felt more like a dead-cat bounce. First, NHL owners locked out the players until mid-January. Then, the abbreviated and highly compressed season produced a championship team that was, let's face it, hard to watch. The '95 Devils' motto could have been *Reductio ad Absurdum*. They weren't wholly lacking in talent—their lineup featured three future Hockey Hall of Famers, but they were two defencemen and a goaltender. Under the direction of coach Jacques Lemaire, the Devils followed a game plan based on passivity and nullification. His antidote for offence was the neutral-zone trap, which sounded far more intriguing and entertaining than it proved to be. Lemaire's team only engaged in forechecking only sporadically. They didn't just prefer to let the game come to them, they were fully committed to that ethic. The Devils clogged the neutral zone with skaters, and they would have used concrete barriers if available. They aimed primarily—perhaps only—to pounce on the other team's mistakes, to make their opponents pay for their overwillingness to make something happen. It was effective but hardly entertaining. As in boxing, a counterpuncher may win fights without ever making the heart race. The Devils played in a style that could only be loved by a coach whose job security hangs in the balance.

I remember covering a Devils visit to Ottawa in the late '90s, a stretch when the Senators rivalled New Jersey in terms of caution. The game ended in a 1–1 tie and could have easily been scoreless, given that neither team managed 20 shots on goal through 60 minutes. Afterwards, Senators defenceman Jason York perfectly captured the "action" when he described the game as "a real chess match." That always stuck with me. When NHLers step on the ice, they're doing so at no small physical risk and are defending their jobs just about every game—in the heat of battle, York recognized how little entertainment value there must have been for the fans in the stands.

The Devils won three Stanley Cups over a nine-year stretch and did so despite having a payroll in the league's bottom half throughout. Not all Stanley Cup winners adopted the Devils' approach, but it did spawn imitators—teams with lesser talent could give the big dogs a world of trouble, just by taking the pace out of the game (for example, Florida made the Stanley Cup final just three years after joining the league as an expansion franchise). If this style of game didn't pose an existential threat to the NHL, it certainly didn't augur well for its growth. Hard to see how it would attract new fans when it too often bored diehards and even the players.

The NHL needed to evolve or risk fading into irrelevance. It had to figure out a way to reward skill, talent and creativity. And more than that, it needed star value—names that could be featured at the top of the marquee, the way Orr and Gretzky and Lemieux had.

Instead, it stared down into the abyss.

The decades-long battle between the owners and the players had stolen the first half of what should have been the 1994–95 season. (All the NHL games that season were played in the latter calendar year, beginning January 20.) That, however, was just a prelude to the 2004–05 season, an empty space in the NHL record books. While the 17-year-old Crosby was playing his second and last winter in junior, the league and the NHL Players' Association dug into their positions during collective bargaining, leading at first to a lockout and then to the outright cancellation of the season. Franchise owners were bound and determined to institute a cap on team payrolls based on a percentage of league revenues. The NHL had stayed open for business through World War II, but not through the last battle between commissioner Gary Bettman and the NHLPA director at the time, Bob Goodenow. The owners got their way but exhausted the goodwill of the fans. As Gretzky said, "At the end of the day everybody lost. We almost crippled our industry."

Into this unpromising situation was thrust Sidney Crosby, skating in his first NHL game just weeks after his 18th birthday. He was not going to get a free ride. In many ways he was set up to fail, and some seemed to delight in the prospect of watching him crash and be exposed as pure hype—not a phenomenon, but an illusion, or perhaps even a fraud.

It may be forgotten at this point, but a healthy degree of skepticism and even hostility greeted Crosby upon his arrival. He had been a frequent topic of discussion over the past couple of years, during which he was named the top player in major junior hockey in back-to-back seasons. But what made the criticism remarkable was that few had actually seen him in action. Other than in highlight packages, he had only appeared on television at a couple of world junior championships and the Memorial Cup.

At that time, I was writing a book about Crosby's run through junior hockey to the NHL draft—I'm reluctant to call it a biography, simply because there's no "life story" per se to tell about a subject when the manuscript must be submitted before his 18th birthday. It was more of a study of a phenom and his transition from boy to man; less of a life so far than a look at the game at a level below the NHL, with maybe a bit of crystal-ball gazing thrown in. On TSN's *The Reporters*, a weekend television sports-talk show, Steve Simmons brought up the book I was writing and called it "absurd." I'd have had no problem if Simmons had come to this conclusion the old-fashioned way, by reading the book. But the *Toronto Sun* columnist couldn't have read it. It hadn't yet been published, and review copies had yet to be shipped.

Even when Crosby burst onto the scene, the media remained determinedly unconvinced. *Sports Illustrated*, not exactly a bastion of hot-take flamethrowers, took shots. In Crosby's rookie season, *SI*'s Stephen Cannella wrote that "opponents have taken to manhandling the league's alleged savior in an effort to throw him off his game." This acute observation was offered at the midpoint of a season in which Crosby would record 102 points.

Crosby didn't have the benefit of seeing firsthand how the other greats looked after their business the way that, say, Orr had with Hull and Beliveau, or Gretzky had with Howe in the World Hockey Association. Because of that "star deficit" in the '90s, Crosby's overlap with the others in the all-time top 10 was incidental—he would play barely two months in Pittsburgh with Lemieux before the latter's retirement. Other than that, well, you'd have to go back to the time when, at age 14, he was joined in an on-ice workout by Gretzky in Los Angeles.

Continuity now seems to have been fully restored. The bridges from one era to the next seem secure. For players on the rise, those who will await the torch passed from Crosby's hands, it's a clearer picture. Connor McDavid has been able to go to school on Crosby's experience, and likewise Auston Matthews. Whoever comes after them — Rasmus Dahlin, Elias Pettersson or Jack Hughes — will have grown up watching him and then moved on to face him. If there was a deficit of star talent in the '90s, it seems abundant now. If the game of hockey seemed to stall in that dreary period of dumping and chasing and the neutral-zone trap, it has fully regained momentum over the course of Crosby's career. The league he will leave behind will be healthier than the one that coldly greeted him back in 2005.

It will be years yet before Crosby's ultimate ranking among the game's greatest players can be fairly determined. And it'll still be possible to make a case that others were better — it's a never-ending debate, one in which Orr and Gretzky will have their supporters, and you'll even be able to find contrarians like Hockey Hall of Fame coach Pat Burns, who told me he thought Mario was the best, but that he'd deny it if I quoted him directly. But what can be stated categorically, even though he's just past the seeming mid-point of his career, is that no NHL player has ever single-handedly influenced the way the game is played to the degree that Sidney Crosby has.

Crosby came along at the time of the NHL's most desperate need. When he was dubbed "the Baby Jesus" or described as "a saviour," it wasn't completely facetious; his team, the league and, at a fundamental level, the game itself needed saving.

As unseen as he might've been before breaking into the NHL, Crosby as a pro has been seen much more than any of the game's great players. It's simply a function of the times and technology: he also came along at a time when his games would never be "dark." Richard and Howe's games in the '40s were seen by only those in the arena. The stars of the '60s and '70s were seen on national television in Canada only on Saturday nights, and in the US barely at all. Players might get some exposure in their local markets, but then there were players like Bobby Hull of the Blackhawks, whose home games weren't televised in Chicago. By the '80s and '90s, television's reach was extended, but nowhere near to the extent it is today. It's no overstatement to say that any NHL game can be seen by anyone, anywhere in the world, at their convenience, live or on playback. In the old days, Howe, Hull and Orr's heroics played out in grainy black and white on a small screen, while Crosby skates as big as life on wall-sized high-definition units with stereophonic sound. Fans in the last row of the arena can read the expression on his face on high-def Jumbotron screens. From the '40s through the '70s, we had some sense of the legends—their faces, the sounds of their voices—but their stories were told at second and third hand. Now, you can summon up Crosby's life story on Google.

And not only has Crosby been accessible to the world, but he has been able to take his game to the world stage. For Richard and Beliveau and others, the idea of international hockey was a fever dream. Their best hockey was played in the confines of a six-team league, or in an expanded league in which only six teams mattered. Further, this league was made up almost entirely of Canadians. The NHL had a provincial outlook. Orr and Hull had an opportunity to play against international teams, but this was a case of the world coming to them, very late in their careers, giving everyone just a taste of what might have been. Gretzky and Lemieux had their chances to go up against the world's best, although in their primes they skated only in the Canada Cup and World Cup of Hockey, in-house affairs that provided some historic moments, along with many other moments that were less so. Only in their last years were Nos. 99 and 66 able to play in the Olympics, Gretzky with crashing disappointment, Lemieux with a more satisfying, if not fully resonant, swan song.

Of those in the all-time top 10, only Crosby has had a chance to take his game to the world: two appearances in the world junior championship and two in the Olympics, as well as a World Cup and an IIHF World Championship tournament. The NHL's decision to pass on the 2018 Winter Games in South Korea denied Crosby the chance to take a Canadian team to a third straight Olympic gold, but it's not beyond the realm of belief that he might return to the big stage. If so, he will be doing it in Beijing, before a domestic audience of up to a billion. Gretzky is credited with helping to grow the game of hockey in California, but Crosby could have a chance to do the same in China, an exponential difference in terms of scale. At a time when the game is growing internationally, Crosby is a figure known and seen worldwide.

When Gretzky passed to Lemieux for the overtime goal that won the 1987 Canada Cup, the International Ice Hockey Federation's world tournaments at four different levels featured teams from 28 nations; in 2019, nearly twice as many nations—52—competed, and others are vying for the federation's sign-off. Crosby is the face of the game; to an extent, he's an ambassador—not a role he aggressively pursues, but that he has accepted. It seemed fitting that, when a Kenyan hockey team came to Canada in 2018, Crosby and Nathan MacKinnon skated with the novices in a pickup game—a bit of promotional wizardry engineered by Tim Hortons, one of the corporate interests that bought into Crosby Inc. on day one.

Think about Maurice Richard's St. Patrick's Day game in 1955—the night of the Richard Riot. It didn't play out as a nation watched. It was seen only by those in the Forum and became known through newspaper accounts, accompanied by grainy photos taken in the arena, and black-and-white newsreel footage. Contrast that with Crosby's gold-medal goal at the Vancouver Olympics. Four out of five Canadians watched at least some part of the game. In the US, more than 26 million tuned in, the largest home audience since the Americans upset the Soviets at the 1980 Winter Games in Lake Placid—a bigger number than those generated by World Series games and the final of the NCAA basketball championship that year. When Crosby skated towards Ryan Miller in the US goal and shouted, "Hey Iggy," he was heard around the world. And it lives on: YouTube hosts various video clips of the goal with more than a million views per.

However we feel about those greatest players from the 20th century, however much we respect their talent and character, we have experienced Sidney Crosby's career more fully than any of them, and probably more than all of them combined. The entire world has been along for his ride.

———

While he has been thrust into this public role, Crosby remains one of the more private figures in the game. He's a contrast to some of the other faces of their leagues. Derek Jeter made his peace with landing on the front page of the tabloids, and then seemed to revel in it. LeBron James presents a serious side, decrying police shootings of innocent young black men in America, but also seems comfortable taking on a guest turn that amounts to much more than a cameo in *Trainwreck*. Peyton Manning would have been happy with a spot in *Saturday Night Live*'s repertory cast if he could have wrapped it around the NFL schedule. Crosby will lend his name and presence to a good cause but is too cautious by nature to either enjoy the spotlight much or use his celebrity to leverage some sort of greater celebrity. Gretzky did try his hand at *SNL* and appeared on a soap opera, but it's impossible to imagine Crosby agreeing to do either—his audiences with reporters around his stall after practices and games more than suffice, representing all the time in front of microphones and cameras that he cares for.

If you looked to the list of hockey greats for a similar ambivalence about celebrity, you'd likely land on Lemieux. When Lemieux was in recovery from lymphoma and from his back injuries, he retreated from the public eye and his privacy was respected. But even all these years later, he has never really fully emerged. When he became the proprietor of the franchise that he once starred for, Lemieux went farther down into his bunker. These days he looks down on Crosby from the owner's box at the arena, but otherwise is little seen and never heard about. He golfs, collects wine and seeks refuge with his family, making him very unlike Gretzky on that count.

Crosby has never had anything like Lemieux's ambivalence about the sweat and toil that life in the NHL entails. True, he doesn't enjoy losing, and he has had a falling-out with a coach or two—okay, definitely two—but he has never looked at the arena as the house of his ordeals. He still glories in the game. The greatest thing that his wealth can afford him is a near-escape from fame. With a day off around the holidays, he'll grab a flight out of Pittsburgh and get back to Halifax and spend time shooting pool with friends from his teen years in the old neighbourhood haunts. He becomes a tourist of sorts to a place he might not have left, where he can envision a life that he might have led. Those in his circle think this connection with his home and his past either keeps him grounded or demonstrates that he has stayed grounded. Maybe it gives him a perspective on how far he has already gone. Regardless, it remains, as ever, his comfort zone.

On most counts, Crosby didn't seek out influence—never positioned himself as a leader of anything but his team. His influence simply spun out of his excellence. And his influence is felt most profoundly within the game, more so the deeper and higher you go in the game. More than anyone on that list of the 10 greatest players, Crosby serves as an aspirational figure—no one at the highest levels of the game looked at Gretzky and said, "If I just do as he did, if I stick to his recipe, I can be a star." There's no willing yourself and working towards Gretzky's vision and creativity.

Crosby has inspired a cult following. That by itself doesn't make him remarkable in sport. All kinds of athletes have a band of fans who dedicate an unusual amount of time and energy to the study of their lives. What does separate the cult of Crosby is that it takes in an unusual number of NHL players—including the league's elite. Because of his success, they've studied him, and the fact is, he did do things differently, from a very early age. Well before he even played in major junior, he was not only training for the NHL but training in a way that none of the historical greats had, in a way that none of the contemporary stars in the NHL were. It was as if the formula for hockey greatness had spun out of a middle-school science fair.

And from his teens, Crosby has been keenly aware of and in command of his image—we know only as much about him as he wants us to know. For all his stardom, his heroics on the ice and his presence in the marketplace, he is well respected and mostly liked, but not too well known.

I had a sense that he was cautious by nature when I first met him when he was 16, but some of his experiences soon thereafter must have made him even more so—it's one thing to be upbraided by a parent, another to have it play out in the national media in your teens. Chris Kunitz, who played on Crosby's three Stanley Cup teams, suggested that the Pittsburgh captain is content to fade into the background when he's not on the ice or being called to represent the Penguins or the league. "I think [the burden on Crosby] gets lost," Kunitz told *Sports Illustrated*. "You know he's a little shy, that he doesn't want to be in the forefront."

I'm not calling Sidney Crosby an enigma; I'm just positing that we know better what he has become and how he got here than who he is. And, yes, by his design, which in itself is telling.

What he is: the best player in a league that now features better players than ever. And the reason why the league features better players than ever is that the best player made them get better. He led them, if never intending to. More importantly, he showed them the way. His life story gave them not only hope but also a blueprint. Maybe he wasn't "another Wayne Gretzky," as those radio commentators suggested back in 2005, but his impact on the game is arguably greater, and his impact on his peers definitely so.

Nobody worked harder than Sidney Crosby. Maybe Crosby's story gives false hope to those who believe that they can get there on work alone—or worse, to those who believe their sons and daughters can get there by dedicating their youth to hard toil. It was, of course, more than a matter of volume. No hours were wasted. He didn't just work long; he worked *smart*. And what others youngsters would consider work or practice, he made into play. After the better part of 16 years of watching Crosby up close, I would draw one lesson from the experience: work is not your means to genius in a chosen field, but rather the path to self-actualization, making the most of the gifts you possess. Sidney Crosby made himself the best Sidney Crosby he could be. That just happened to be the game's best player.

CHAPTER 3

THE LITTLEST TALL POPPY

There's a difference between history and lore, history being matters of documented fact that cannot be denied, lore being somewhat more fluid, stories passed down by word of mouth that, for the sake of tradition and community, must be believed even if difficult to trust. So it is with the lore attached to the Canadian hockey hero—it says as much about the worshippers as the objects of idolatry. There's stuff that is true and stuff that we hold to be true, the latter sometimes just because we wish it to be.

A common thread runs through the hero's lore. We want to feel that they did not just come from here, but that this place made them. They were products of their environment. This assumption allows those who tell the story—and those who receive it—to believe that they play their small part in the hero's success. That the game and the talent that feeds it are organic and ours at the grassroots. With every great player, it seems, there is a necessary sense of place—*this is the place that made him.*

As the nation evolves, so do the stories of its hockey heroes. Those from the middle of the past century reflect a former version of Canada that has ceased to exist. With Maurice Richard, it was a family moving from rural Gaspé to Montreal. The listed birthplace on Gordie Howe's hockey card was Floral, Saskatchewan, a hamlet on the rail line that long ago ceased to exist. Bobby Hull grew up in Point Anne, which sprung up around a cement plant on the Bay of Quinte but withered when the company left town and can now be found only on old maps and an online catalogue of ghost towns.

The narratives give us comfort: Bobby Orr playing on frozen ponds around Parry Sound; Wayne Gretzky skating deep into the night on the backyard rink flooded by his father, Walter; and Mario Lemieux being inspired in his teens by his hometown Canadiens, the most dominant team of their and perhaps any era.

For Sidney Crosby, it's Cole Harbour, Nova Scotia, which over the course of his career has become Canada's best-known suburb of 21,000 by virtue of every hockey card, every Chyron on broadcasts, by umpteen visits from hockey writers and television crews. Prior to Crosby's arrival in the NHL, the best-known products of Cole Harbour were likely two of the Trailer Park Boys, actors Robb Wells and John Paul Tremblay; safe to say, they have dropped to a distant third behind Crosby and Nathan MacKinnon.

The name Cole Harbour is not as haunting as Floral or Point Anne. It is, however, plainly Canadian—early in his career, you were ever on the lookout for American publications to drop the U from any reference. Cole Harbour is located in central Halifax County, the mouth of its harbour located northeast of Halifax's main harbour. It was settled 200 years ago by what historical documents describe as "Foreign Protestants"—settlers who had been enticed by the government to settle the area to farm and supply food for the city. You'd have to look hard, past the strip malls, big-box stores and other touchstones of 21st-century commerce, to find ties to pre-Confederation history, with the exception of the Cole Harbour Rural Heritage Society's Heritage Farm Museum. Otherwise it looks like suburbs that have swallowed quaint villages whole across the country. You'd have no idea at all what region in Canada you were looking at if you were handed a snapshot of the four-lane main thoroughfare, lined with fast-food chain outlets, that runs through Cole Harbour. It's Anywhere, Canada—on the face of it, seemingly as likely as anyplace else to turn out a hockey star.

And yet, in calling Cole Harbour his hometown, Sidney Crosby is a very separate and distinct case from other great players. Not the community per se, but the region. Great hockey talent has come from a lot of places—just never the Maritimes.

It's instructive to compare Crosby's home province of Nova Scotia with Saskatchewan, which has turned out more NHL players per capita than any other province. In terms of population, they're almost a wash—when Crosby was born in 1987, Nova Scotia's population was 893,000, Saskatchewan's 1.03 million.

According to quanthockey.com, the most comprehensive website for the game's history, 60 players from Nova Scotia had played in the NHL before Crosby's rookie season. Of those, six played a single NHL game, and seven more played fewer than 10. Five were born in the 19th century and skated with teams back in the 1920s. Fourteen of the players are listed as being born in Halifax, but how much of a claim the city could lay to them is an open question—for instance, Bobby Smith, the first-overall draft pick in 1978, was born in Halifax but his family moved to Ottawa when he was young. Before Crosby, the best-known hockey player out of the Halifax area was Glen Murray, a journeyman who logged more than 1,000 NHL games, most with the Boston Bruins. Only one player in the Hockey Hall of Fame hailed from Nova Scotia: defenceman Al MacInnis, who was born and raised on Cape Breton Island.

Saskatchewan can boast that 32 of its native sons played at least 900 NHL games, and to date, 508 have played at least a game in the league. Fourteen, including Howe and Eddie Shore, are in the Hockey Hall of Fame.

There are myriad reasons why Nova Scotia has lagged behind Saskatchewan and other provinces when it comes to turning out NHL talent. For one, there's the very basic matter of ice and its relative scarcity in the Maritimes. In Saskatchewan and other regions, outdoor pads, artificial or natural, community or backyard, were available throughout the winter to anyone ready to play until numb with the cold. In Nova Scotia, and Halifax in particular, climate was the enemy. Cold you can play in, sleet not so much, and thus even when temperatures dropped, a lot of days were write-offs. Then there was the matter of booking time at arenas. Darren Cossar was the director of Hockey Nova Scotia in 2005 when he told me about the challenges that faced teams when Crosby was playing minor hockey in Cole Harbour. "We're squeezed [for ice time] by a bunch of sports, whether it's figure skating or short-track speedskating or ringette, and more recently by the growth of recreational men's hockey," Cossar said. "Ice time is getting so scarce in Halifax that some teams are actually booking practices at rinks a half hour out of the city at all hours of the morning."

Of course, the challenges Crosby and his minor-hockey team-mates faced were lost on them. They didn't know anything different, at least until they talked to players from other regions.

Said Tim Spidel, a teammate of Crosby on Cole Harbour teams starting in novice, "When we would go out of town for tournaments, we'd talk to players from other cities at our hotel, and we were always amazed to hear how much ice time and practice time these other teams were getting. We were really lucky to get a third practice in a week every once and a while. Usually it was just two. These other kids had practices or games every day. Sometimes, they said, they were practising in the morning and having a game later. Plus, they were skating through the summer. We were playing baseball or doing something else. You know, we didn't even really think about [skating during the summer]. And the thing was that it was like that not just when we were seven, eight and nine years old. Right into bantam and midget, that was the usual thing —two practices a week."

At least Crosby and Spidel and their teammates did travel to some out-of-province events, like the Quebec peewee tournament. Historically, though, players in the Maritimes, even talented ones, were effectively sequestered Down Home. While the western provinces had their major junior leagues, and likewise Ontario and Quebec, the Maritimes were shut out. Only in the '90s did the Quebec Major Junior Hockey League establish a footprint in New Brunswick, Nova Scotia and Prince Edward Island. To that point, the region hadn't been intensely scouted, and any players who wanted to take their shot had to leave home for a chance to get seen—hard to do at any age, harder still at 14 or 15 years old. And really, at that stage, the window is very narrow. Crosby's uncle Rob Forbes was a case in point. Forbes was considered by many to be the best all-around athlete in Halifax—he excelled at any game he picked up. "The game was good enough at home, but we didn't play out of our region," Forbes says. "Before I headed off to play major junior in Quebec, I had never played a game that was farther than New Brunswick. We were isolated. Nobody knew who was playing out here, and not even the most talented guys left."

At 19, Forbes landed a tryout with Laval of the Quebec league, made the cut and put up pretty good numbers: 17 points in 19 games (on a team that featured 15-year-old Mario Lemieux). But there could be no doubt that the development window for Forbes was closing. "I was an exception just getting out and taking a shot at all," he says. "Lots never leave home."

And at home, minor hockey in the Halifax in the '90s felt like, well, minor hockey, at least in contrast to the programs in the big cities. This wasn't the Greater Toronto Hockey League (GTHL), where player dues run into five figures before expenses and former NHLers are fixtures behind the bench. Nor the Detroit market, where Compuware and Little Caesars have had NHL owners bankrolling their programs, which cross the country for tournaments on a weekly basis. Nor the Burnaby Winter Club, nor any other western Canadian hubs that annually send half their roster to major junior or NCAA. Nothing at all like the hothouse programs in Europe, such as the hockey "gymnasium" in Ornskoldsvik, a town of 30,000 in northern Sweden, that produced Peter Forsberg, Henrik and Daniel Sedin, Anders Hedberg and Victor Hedman.

Though intense year-round private skills and skating programs were gaining traction in other cities, Halifax had traditional summer hockey schools, a week or two of off-season practice. But although minor hockey in Cole Harbour and Halifax was starved for places to play, it didn't lack for expertise. It was more than just a glorified house league. For instance, Crosby's first coach in novice hockey, Paul Gallagher, was then the eastern Canada and Quebec league scout for the Florida Panthers. "[Coaching] was all driven by volunteers and it felt like a real community," says Gallagher, who now scouts for the Vancouver Canucks. "Everyone knew each other away from the rink, which was probably different [than the big-city programs]. There probably wasn't the same sort of pressure on coaches or the kids that there might be other places."

Back in the spring of 1995, the Halifax *Daily News* assigned a writer from its news side to write a feature about the local scene and the long odds of a kid making it all the way to the NHL. On page 42 of the April 10, 1995, edition, Sidney Crosby stared out from the page, a seven-year-old as serious as a Game 7 participant, looking remarkably like he does on his first hockey card, except that his hair is buzzed down to a crewcut. His first quote in print: "They say you have to do your best and work hard and things will happen."

Young Sidney's words weren't just a recitation of a bromide overheard; they represented a system of belief. Without a doubt, "hard work" would be a common thread among the all-time greats. Carl Fleming, then the editor of the *Daily News*, used to coach his sons' team in Cole Harbour, and when they arrived at the arena at 6 a.m. Sidney, then nine or ten years old, would be wrapping up workouts with his father, Troy, running the show. "Getting up that early tested the soul of a lot of our players, some good kids, some who went on to play in the Quebec league," Fleming told me. "I've come to know Sidney and Troy over the years. [Troy] had played at a high level and knew the game. Still, I'm convinced that this wasn't a case of Troy forcing his son to do something—to practise before dawn. I don't think that there was some sort of plan that Troy had for Sidney—nothing like that. I don't think that you could make a kid do something like getting up at dawn to practise if he didn't truly want to. Likewise, I don't think that a father would put himself through something like that unless he was sure that his son was benefiting from it and enjoying it. And if it was a case of a father dragging his son out in the morning and forcing him to do something he didn't want to, well, I think it would cause a lot of resentment later on, and I can't see any evidence of that with Troy and Sidney. They really are very close. The only sense that I have is that Troy was prepared to go to practically any lengths for his son."

Inevitably a phenom has to run the opponents' gauntlet on the ice, and so it was with Sidney Crosby. Paul Gallagher watched it play out every game. Sometimes opponents were just desperately trying to keep up. Sometimes they tried to goad him into taking a retaliatory penalty to get him off the ice. And sometimes they were trying to bang and bruise him and put him on the sidelines. Gallagher saw it all and tried to head it off before the puck was dropped. "I would talk to the officials before the games," he says. "I told them that I understand that they can't call everything—if they did, we would have been on the power play all game. I just told them, 'Look, if you can get the cheap and dangerous stuff, when they go after him with the slashes on the gloves [or] up the arms.' [The refs] were actually really good about it. They understood that this was a special player. Not like he needed special treatment or protection or anything. Just that other teams shouldn't be able to get away with things to drag him down to their level."

You'd imagine a tight-knit community would rally behind any exceptional kid as a point of pride, and for the most part Cole Harbour did, but it wasn't always the case. As unlikely as it sounds, a kid about five feet tall was the object of the tall poppy syndrome, resented and criticized for towering over the competition in talent even though he was a head shorter. The stuff that Crosby would face in his junior and professional years, right up to the shot by Niskanen in that playoff game, has always been there and was toxic by the time he moved up to AAA in bantam and midget.

You can read between the lines of old news stories about a phenom scoring hundreds—yes, hundreds—of goals in minor hockey. One *Daily News* column suggested that people at the arena had made "a target of Crosby off the ice" and that some believed his performance was "meaningless because the calibre of the Nova Scotia league is weak this season." Even more telling was this line: "Some of the criticism directed at Crosby might be misplaced anger from those who object to Troy's behaviour in the stands. But seriously, folks, how you feel about Troy Crosby should have no bearing on your opinion of [his son]." All of this more than faintly echoes the account of Walter Gretzky's experiences in Brantford back in the early '70s: "It placed a great deal of pressure on him because he just couldn't play the game and have fun. He was cheered, booed and criticized by other players and parents. Some said he was ruining the leagues because he scored so many goals. It upset his life and his schoolwork suffered. He's a quiet sort of kid who keeps things bottled up inside. At one time, we thought he was going to explode."

The antagonism wasn't limited to sniping around the arena and veiled mentions in the newspapers. In fact, a battle between the Crosbys and officials in Nova Scotia's minor-hockey association wound up in court. Sidney playing up against players two or even three years older hadn't been an issue back in the years when he skated rings around tyke and atom leaguers. Officials weren't worried about any perceived risk of injury. Big-impact collisions at that level were more likely to involve teammates losing their compasses and skating into each other rather than a real bodycheck. The stakes, however, changed in the bantam and midget ranks.

In bantam Crosby had to watch the Irving Oil Challenge Cup, Atlantic Canada's AAA championship—which should have been a personal showcase played in his home arena in Cole Harbour— from the stands. Officials in the Cole Harbour hockey association blocked the 12-year-old Crosby from playing in the championship and suspended bantam coach Harry O'Donnell for a game for putting the phenom into an earlier tournament. O'Donnell was exasperated. "What would have happened to Wayne Gretzky if they did that to him?" he said. "I knew that I would get spanked for it, but I didn't expect this. I just wanted to put the best players on the ice . . . that's the bottom line. They didn't agree with that." Officials from the Cole Harbour Hockey Association didn't explain the decision. The CHHA president said only that it was an "internal" matter, rebuffed the press and hung up on those who called to plead the youngster's case. Making matters worse was that a few peewee-aged players from other associations in the Maritimes were allowed to play in the bantam tournament, including a player in the Halifax association. A disappointed but precociously worldly Crosby said, "It's pretty cheap . . . I wanted to finish my season this weekend playing in the bantam Atlantics, but now I can't. It's just politics, I guess."

The fight over the bantam tournament turned out to be only a prelude for a more heated battle against the provincial body. The situation boiled over when Crosby wanted to play for the Cole Harbour midget team at 13. "He actually made our team as a 13-year-old, but Hockey Nova Scotia wouldn't let him play," Brad Crossley said. His parents wound up going to a Halifax civil court to try to get a court order allowing him to play. "A bunch of us went to bat for him to make the case that he wasn't just good enough to play," Gallagher said, "but he was going to be a dominant player at that level."

And again, Crosby's story echoed Gretzky's.

Gretzky in fact had landed in the Ontario court system back in 1975, when he was looking to join the Toronto Young Nationals of what was then the Metropolitan Toronto Hockey League (now the Greater Toronto Hockey League). Gretzky had previously played with a team in Brantford in the Ontario Minor Hockey Association but had outgrown the level of competition in that league. The Young Nats were considered a significant step up. Gretzky had moved into a billet home that, on its face, seemed to satisfy the residency requirements of the MTHL and of the Canadian Amateur Hockey Association. Nonetheless the OMHA considered it an end run, if not a complete sham—in retrospect, a cobbled-together legal guardianship that didn't pass the smell test. The OMHA refused to approve Gretzky's transfer to the MTHL. Gretzky and family went to the Supreme Court of Ontario seeking an injunction to allow him to play for the Nats, and the court decided to butt out. The presiding judge wrote, "In my view, the Court in this case ought not to become involved in a minute legalistic analysis and interpretation of the rules of the (CAHA)." In the end, things worked out—and maybe for the better for Gretzky. While minor hockey had residency requirements, junior hockey was wide open; instead of playing for the Young Nats, Gretzky joined the Toronto Nationals (later, the Seneca Nats), a Junior B team. At 14 he was playing in a league with 19- and 20-year-olds.

The lesson to draw from Gretzky's experience: judges aren't inclined to insinuate themselves in the affairs of the arena. And that turned out to be true again in Halifax. The Crosbys' case didn't get a sympathetic reading, and the Cole Harbour association was left to manage its affairs as its officials pleased. "[The Crosbys] lost but the one who seemed to take it best was Sidney," Paul Gallagher says. "When he showed up for practice [with the bantam team] after the court decision, I took him aside. I wanted to make sure that he was in a good place about it. It would have been tough to handle anything like that, and especially if you're 13. But what I loved about Sidney, he just looked at me and said, 'It's okay. Let's just go win the championship.' And that's what we did that season. We ended up winning the Atlantic Canada title with him that year, and I'll never forget the goal in overtime. He set up the goal with a pass between a defenceman's legs to get the winner. Andrew Newton scored it. Did [the court decision] bother him? I'm sure it did. Did it affect his play? Not for a second."

There was no doubt about 14-year-old Sidney Crosby's readiness for the 2001–02 Midget AAA season. More physically mature at five foot eight and 165 pounds, he signed on to play for the Dartmouth Subways Midget AAA team. The numbers told only a part of the story: a year after being told he wasn't ready to play midget, still two and almost three years younger than the rest, he rang up 106 goals and 217 points with a plus-103 rating. Though the team had only a couple of players who would be considered even fringe major junior prospects, Dartmouth went 61–17–5, sweeping to provincial and regional championships. As Gretzky had done when he lost his court case at 14, Crosby also skated against 19- and 20-year-olds when he moved up for a few games with the Truro Bearcats of the Maritime Junior A Hockey League. But it was his performance in the national midget championship that turned heads.

Brad Crossley, then a high school teacher, knew the game. He had been with the Dartmouth program for nine years, four as a head coach, before Sidney came along. He also had known the Crosbys for years. He had played junior hockey with Troy and gone to high school with Sidney's mom, Trina. "You know that you're lucky to get a chance to work with one player like that in your life-time as a coach," Crossley says. "And it was a lot easier for everyone involved because [of the history]. [Sidney] set the standard for work and intensity. He didn't need to be loud. But other guys could see how he went about things in the dressing room and on the ice. He never did things halfway. His commitment was total. It's a cliché to talk about a star making everyone on the ice a better player—usu-ally it just means that a star creates scoring chances and some guys bank in some rebounds, or he opens up the ice for others with all the attention that other teams give him. But with Sidney it really was true. He made his teammates want to be better. He made them believe that they could be better. They saw what he was able to do —what he had done with himself with practice and work and imagination—and they wanted to get there too."

Crosby went from a local sensation to national news when the Subways went to the Air Canada Cup, the national midget cham-pionship—as Crossley describes it, "Sidney's coming-out party." The tournament was broadcast by TSN and received notice in newspapers across the country. The Subways weren't playing at home, but with New Brunswick hosting, it was the nearest thing. Atlantic teams had rarely made much of an impact in the first 24 years of the tournament, and none had ever made the final. Crosby and the Subways were the crowd favourites and an evolving story across the country by the time they reached the championship game against Saskatchewan's Tisdale Trojans.

The Subways came up one game short. Against Tisdale they started out nervously, made a few errors in their defensive zone and soon trailed 3–0 in the first period. Fact is, they looked gassed. Crosby did have one breathtaking highlight-reel moment. Midway through the second period, with Dartmouth down 4–0, Jeff Kielbratowski hit a streaking Crosby at centre ice with a tape-to-tape pass and he finished the play with a flourish. It was the high point in the game for the Subways, who had to settle for a silver medal after the 6–2 loss.

"They definitely caught us by surprise," Crosby told reporters after the game. "We were a little nervous at the start and we didn't get our feet moving. We might have been a little bit tentative playing in front of a national television audience, but we can't use that as an excuse. They beat us and they're a great team."

The champions weren't reluctant about heaping praise on Crosby. Tisdale captain Michael Olson told Crosby during the post-game ceremonial handshake, "You're a hell of hockey player and I'll probably be watching you someday on TV." Myles Zimmer, who scored three goals for Tisdale, said the Trojans had a basic game plan. "We knew all about this kid, the youngest kid in the tournament, 14 playing against some really big 17-year-olds," Zimmer said. "We just matched Tyson Strachan against him— Tyson was the one guy from our team who made the NHL and he had at least eight inches on Sid. Now, it's cool to think that there have been thousands of guys who've played against him and been beaten. I just had one chance to be on the ice with him and had my career game." Added Trojans coach Darrell Mann, "For a 14-year-old, I can't believe his mental toughness and his physical toughness. Every team here keyed on him all week long, and for him to put up the numbers that he did is incredible."

The final line of numbers were just as Mann described them: incredible. He led the tournament in scoring with 11 goals and 13 assists in seven games against players two and three years older than him. Though the Subways would go home with silver medals, Crosby could add the tournament's most valuable player award to his trophy case. Hockey Nova Scotia officials called the Dartmouth team a shining example of the game's growth in the province and claimed that the team wasn't Crosby and a bunch of kids named Joe—though that didn't pass the laugh test. "We rode on his shoulders for the last seven days and he's pulled us along greatly with a lot of poise," Crossley said.

After the medal ceremonies, after the television lights were turned off, after the fans left the building, several Dartmouth players spared the arena crew a bit of cleanup work—they grabbed the signs and banners decorating the rink. This wasn't just their last midget game. This was as far as they would go in hockey. And they were going to be able to say, like Tisdale's Michael Olson, that they were on the ice with Sidney Crosby—they even had the banners to prove it.

In an era when the game has been priced beyond the reach of so many families, when it's in danger of becoming something like a country-club sport, when academies are springing up every year to churn out young talent as if on so many production lines, a kid whose background was very modest, a kid facing all kinds of obstacles, made himself the best player of his time and one of the best of all time.

Do we draw the lesson that talent will always find a way no matter what the challenges are? That would be a reach and a

49

cliché, right up there with a seven-year-old's expressed belief in hard work. There's no calculating how many gifted kids were denied a chance along the way. Another rosy spin: talent can blossom when the challenges and resistance only forge resolve.

Seventeen years later, it's hard to play what-if. Could Crosby have become the world's best player if he had stayed in his lane—if, against his and his father's better judgment, he had opted for a less ambitious course? Or would his progress have stalled, exacting a toll? It's hard to imagine that he would have lost interest or enthusiasm. Just look at how he regrouped after losing the court case to play in the midget league at 13.

What is maybe most telling about Sidney Crosby is that he always came home. Orr has lived his life away from Parry Sound, Gretzky from Brantford and Lemieux from Montreal; in fact, they abandoned Canada entirely, settling in Boston, Los Angeles and Pittsburgh, respectively. It's too early to say whether Crosby will follow suit someday, but for now he goes back to Halifax in the off-season, and during the season if time allows.

What really informs the character study of Sidney Crosby is the fact that he has moved past any of the hard times he had while growing up and playing the game. Though his father was, as he described himself, no angel, Sidney Crosby is clearly the guardian angel, white knight and most famous benefactor of the grassroots game in Cole Harbour.

Near the front door of Cole Harbour Place, the sports complex a few blocks from the house Crosby grew up in, there's a showcase full of *objets d'etoiles*, his personal hall of fame. It's stuff he could have held on to for his personal collection, stuff the

Hockey Hall of Fame would love to display, but instead Crosby donated it to the arena where he played his first game at age six. Behind the glass there are sweaters—from teams he played on at this arena; from Rimouski, where he played in junior; from the Penguins; from Canadian national teams. There's an autographed stick and puck, photographs from every stop along the way. All of it would fetch about six figures on eBay in the first 15 minutes, but just so nobody gets any ideas there's a sign in big letters: SHOWCASE ALARMED.

There's that newspaper clipping under the glass too, with Crosby in a crewcut saying, "They say you have to do your best and work hard and things will happen." It's the message that is received by the kids who come out to Cole Harbour Place for the Sidney Crosby Hockey School every summer, not the least of the alumni Nathan MacKinnon.

Beyond the memorabilia and the sponsorship, Crosby has given back to local minor hockey. He has made well-publicized contributions—when he played at the worlds and won gold in 2015, he and MacKinnon donated their winnings to the Cole Harbour Hockey Association. Crosby's charity isn't always advertised, and in this he has proven himself bigger than those on the local scene who didn't recognize young genius or, if they did, didn't know how best to support it. He has looked past the animus of those who bristled at Troy's protective attitude and forced them to reassess. As an intimate of Crosby says, "If you're a kid there with some talent and ambition and your family doesn't have the money to let you play, *someone* will find it for you. No one is going to slip through the cracks."

Crosby has also remembered those who volunteered their time to help him out along the way.

Over the years, NHLers, including Toronto's John Tavares and Ottawa's Matt Duchene, have come to work out with Crosby in Halifax during the summer, going to school on the regimen that made him the best player in the game. Their gym time has been overseen by Andy O'Brien, Crosby's longtime trainer. In the on-ice sessions, it's Brad Crossley who's blowing the whistle and running the drills. Crosby spent his youth trying to get from his hometown to the NHL, but now the flow has reversed.

Still, it's at the grassroots in the community and the city he grew up in that Crosby has had the greatest impact. Says Paul Gallagher, "Players see what Sidney has done and it's made them believe that they can get there too, maybe in a way that, 20 or 30 years ago, kids just didn't think about. They can see a way of getting to another level, whether it's junior or college or the pros. Just since Sid made it to the NHL, a bunch of hockey academies—private schools with hockey programs for boys and girls—have sprung up and some of them have put some real money into it. It's like that way across the country, in Toronto or Calgary or wherever. But there's no doubt Sidney opened people's eyes to the opportunity."

Says Brad Crossley, "Sidney was the catalyst for all the players who are coming out of the area. Since he broke through, there's more ice time out there for kids, more sheets with year-round availability. And there's more coaching and support. Sidney always wanted to be better, and that how kids and even coaches think around here now."

The point is seconded by Darren Sutherland, Hockey Nova Scotia's director of high performance. "Sid playing for Team Nova Scotia in the Canada Winter Game and playing the way he did in that tournament, and all he'd done in minor hockey on a national stage before he got to major junior, were a huge influence in attitudes here, both of the players and the support around them," Sutherland says. "There was a perception out there that the players in our region were a bit behind other parts of the country . . . that it was tough to even compete. That's gone by the wayside. He set the stage for Nathan [MacKinnon] to play for Nova Scotia in the Winter Games in 2011 and for a kid like Shane Bowers from Halifax to go in the first round in 2017 [to Ottawa, later traded to Colorado]. We had four kids go in the NHL draft in 2018 and we're sending more kids to major junior or like Shane to the NCAAs, more kids getting invitations to the under-18 and under-20 camps. We had the Cape Breton West Islanders that won the Telus Cup [the Canadian national midget championships] in 2017 and that's the first time a team from Atlantic Canada won that tournament. Maybe it's not a direct influence that Sid had on that team, but there is something there about his proving it can be done. Whatever the mindsets were before, he changed that. We've closed the gap on the rest of Canada. [Nova Scotia] finished fifth at the last Canada Winter Games, which numbers-wise put us ahead of provinces that had a big advantage in registrations and populations. We were maybe a little unlucky to lose to [eventual silver-medalist] Alberta by a goal. The one thing about being smaller is that we're not likely to miss a kid with talent—our attitude is to support the players we have and not think about the players we don't have or that we'd want. We can focus on players early and help them as much as possible. It has taken a lot of people to get where we are today, but it would look very different if he hadn't come along when he did."

The course of Sidney Crosby's career has left many wondering exactly how he did it. *What was his formula? What was the secret sauce?* Many supremely talented youngsters had the benefit of support that was unavailable to Sidney as a youth-league player, yet none of them really came close to matching him.

Crosby's former teammate going back to grade school, Tim Spidel, asked another less likely question: What if? Strange as it may seem when we're talking about one of the greatest players the game has ever seen, Spidel wondered whether Sidney Crosby might have been an even better player with a different sort of start —if he had grown up not in another time, but in another place. "[Coming from Halifax] makes it all the more amazing that Sidney became as good as he did," Spidel told me. "Everyone talks about how some kids don't have a chance to develop into players, but I always wonder how much better Sidney might have been if he had been growing up somewhere with a great hockey program, lots of practice time and all that other stuff."

To which I can only say *maybe*. Would he have been challenged by playing with and against better players? Possibly. A little while ago, I spoke to John Tavares about playing in the GTHL with the Toronto Marlboros, playing with and against kids who would go on to be first-round NHL draft picks, working on a daily basis with a coach, Dave Gagner, who had played more than 900 NHL games. "I learned what it takes to become a professional [in the GTHL]," Tavares told me. "When I was 12 coming to the Marlboros, I was in awe of Dave and Rick Vaive [whose son Justin played for the team]. To be around two very successful NHL players just made [the NHL] seem accessible."

It's easy—and tempting—to speculate about the potential upside of facing stiffer challenges in youth hockey, akin to, say, enriched courses of study in school. But in talking to Tavares and his teammates who came up through the GTHL, it became clear that greater opportunities for some pose risks for others. If Crosby had played for the Marlies, Little Caesars or the Burnaby Winter Club, would a more intense atmosphere have translated into greater pressure? Would the fishbowl have been a distraction and taken some fun out of the game? It did happen with more than a few talented kids Tavares played with and against, and inevitably, their best years turned out to be their time in youth hockey.

Minor hockey in Cole Harbour and Halifax seemed more "minor" than the quasi-professional youth organizations to be found elsewhere, and based on the long-run results, you could claim that it was close to perfect for Sidney Crosby. But with MVP honours at the Air Canada Cup behind him and with no shot of being granted an exemption to play for the major junior Halifax Mooseheads as a 15-year-old, Crosby had gone as far as he could at home. Troy Crosby had said as much. Sidney's only option was to light out for a place that could keep up with his talent and ambition.

CHAPTER 4

THERE'S SOMETHING ABOUT SHATTUCK-ST MARY'S

The Air Canada Cup had put Crosby on the radar of the hockey world. Agents wanted to land him as a client. Junior teams coveted him. Scouts imagined him in their lineups—and not just those working for teams in the junior ranks, but also those employed by US colleges and Hockey Canada, the latter projecting him into their rosters in international tournaments a few years down the line.

On its face, it looked like he was in a world-is-his-oyster situation. The hard truth, however, is that at 15, he had reached an end, and quite possibly a dead end. Obvious options on the ice were exhausted. There was recent precedent for someone his age playing in major junior hockey: Jason Spezza had played a season for the Brampton Battalion of the Ontario Hockey League at age 15 and had even taken some shifts with Hockey Canada's national men's team before entering the OHL's midget draft. Out of consideration for Spezza's age, the Ontario league allowed him to play for a team in his backyard and live at home. The Quebec Major Junior Hockey League wasn't about to grant Crosby early entrance along the lines of Spezza's; owners of QMJHL franchises based in the province of Quebec weren't inclined to give the Halifax Mooseheads any advantages, regardless of the best interests of the young player—or, for that matter, the profile of the league.

The teams with the worst records in the league in 2001–02, the Sherbrooke Castors and Moncton Wildcats, owned the first and second picks in that year's QMJHL draft, and the latter seemed like a possible destination if the league's board of governors could be coaxed into granting Crosby early entry. The matter didn't get that far. The board was willing to walk away from what was sure to be a boon to marketing and attendance revenues.

As for a return to the Dartmouth Subways, well, it would have made for a nice storyline—the attempt to win one more game and a national championship. Fact is, however, there were a lot of players in their last year of eligibility on that Subways team. No matter how much Crosby might improve, the surrounding talent really wasn't there for another deep run. And besides, he was just too good for the league. Skating with the Truro Bearcats in Junior A, as he had done on occasion the season before, wouldn't have offered much of a benefit either. Given Crosby's drive and ambition, most would think he would run little risk of stagnating, but Sidney and Troy would have dissented—he had grown as a player by constantly playing up and facing bigger, more skilled players. He was at a critical juncture in the arc of his development; thus, it would seem an inopportune time to spend the season running in place.

Crosby had been able to focus on his game in relative peace, if not in a complete vacuum. Young phenoms in the big cities had grown up in the spotlight, reading profiles of themselves in newspapers while they were in junior high school. Not that it was ever really to their advantage; it was frequently to their detriment. Heads can get turned, but heads can swell. And people will talk. For better or worse, the Air Canada Cup had made Sidney Crosby a public figure. To whatever degree he had been known in Cole Harbour and Halifax, it was celebrity in a minor key: a bit of coverage in the media, his name being known around the rinks, not much more than that. After the national tournament, though, Sidney and Troy had a sense that life was never going to be the same on that count.

In covering hockey for more than 30 years, I have talked to a lot of players who were anointed in their teens as future stars. Some struggle with the attention, but I'd say most have a sense of their place in the game and the life that awaits them. I've also talked to these young stars' parents, and in many ways their lot is tougher to manage. Again, most hope for something close to a "normal" childhood for kids whose lives might be closer to those of professional athletes than their own peers in school. I have also seen parents who might claim to have their kids' best interest at heart but look for special consideration at every turn. There's no doubt that Troy and Trina Crosby hoped that Sidney could have a normal youth. That, however, was not possible in the fall of 2002.

You only needed to talk to Troy Crosby for a few minutes to come away with a sense of his fierce protectiveness for his son. I had met other parents like that, though I had never met any who surpassed his intensity. In this case, the son had a sense of where he could take his game, while his father had a sense of where the game could take his son. He was in this way hypersensitive, a man who would mistake a shadow for a threat. He had expressed his anger with a turn in the environment in once-friendly rinks in Halifax. He told the *Daily News* after the Air Canada Cup, "The last couple of years have been pretty hard on him, on the ice as well as off the ice. As a parent, you try to protect him from the verbal comments, but it's hard to. He gets more support when he goes away than he does here at home. He doesn't say much about the crap that goes on around him, but I know he hears it. There's a lot of good people here, but there's also a lot of animosity and resentment."

Troy made it clear that Sidney's leaving home to play elsewhere was going to be for the better. He'd say that it was going to be "only one or two years." This suggested that Sidney would be open to coming back and playing for the Mooseheads. Really, though, given just how angry Troy was with the sniping and the court case and all the rest, it was hard to see Sidney returning once he was gone.

It was just a question of where he would go. Troy made it clear that he and his wife wanted to ensure that Sidney would not have to compromise his education and a quality living environment for the sake of playing at a higher level. A couple of Canadian school programs soon emerged as front-runners.

Many NHLers from western Canada, including Wendel Clark and Rod Brind'Amour, had spent years with the Notre Dame Hounds, a Junior A and midget program affiliated with the Athol Murray College of Notre Dame, a private Catholic boarding school in Wilcox, Saskatchewan—population 300. More recently, Notre Dame had attracted elite players from the east, including Vincent Lecavalier from Montreal and Brad Richards from Prince Edward Island. Notre Dame's Junior A team was a significant step up from the Truro Bearcats and the league back in Nova Scotia. The college also covered off the Crosbys' interest in a solid scholastic environment. Truth be told, though, Notre Dame wasn't then—and has never been—for the faint of heart. I remember Richards, a future Stanley Cup winner with Tampa Bay, telling me that when they first arrived in Wilcox, he and Lecavalier lay in their bunks and cried at night. "I was so homesick and it was so cold out [that] I wondered what I had signed up for," he said.

There was talk about Upper Canada College in downtown Toronto, a private school founded in 1829. UCC played a full schedule against other city and regional high school teams as well as exhibitions and tournaments against prep schools in the northeastern US. Tuition at the school and expenses at UCC would have run over $40,000 but the school would have surely found a scholarship or patron for a young phenom. And UCC had started to ambitiously recruit talent. But although the school had won five provincial high school championships in the previous 10 seasons and had almost limitless resources, including its own arena on campus, the quality of hockey would have been a step down from what Notre Dame had to offer.

Outside of a scholastic environment, the Crosbys also gave some thought to the Georgetown Raiders, a Junior A club in Ontario. The level of hockey would likely be highest there; a good number of Junior A players could step directly into the OHL, but opt instead to go the NCAA route. And the program had attracted elite prospects from even farther away: Stanislav Chistov, the fifth-overall pick in the 2001 NHL draft and arguably the best player on the Russian team that won the World Junior tournament in January 2002, had put in a season with the Raiders.

Georgetown would have been a significant step up, and maybe two, from the calibre of junior hockey available in Nova Scotia. What it might have lacked, though, was a level of protection, any sort of academic integration—Sidney would have had a group of friends at school and another, much older, group on the team. What it certainly lacked was any sense of enrichment—hockey would have been the only real takeaway with the Raiders; academics, no matter what the team would have been able to come up with, would have seemed to be taking a back seat.

It's a common theme that runs through hockey at many levels. Talent doesn't necessarily open doors. Talent doesn't necessarily yield special consideration. Just look at Wayne Gretzky's history— sometimes, organized hockey doesn't know how to best foster transcendent talent. Sometimes talent limits options or, at least, forces tough decisions. The most talented players are often done no favours by the development streams in place. So it was with Crosby. The closer to home the options were, the worse they became. The Canadian hockey establishment really didn't offer him a place to land for the coming season. In the meantime, though, he would get inside looks at what awaited him in the junior and NHL ranks.

Whenever a phenom happens onto the scene, his arrival only registers with the media and hockey fans in their NHL draft year, maybe a season before. But by that time, young players are already deep into relationships with agents certified by the NHL Players' Association.

First contacts with players' families might begin at bantam, maybe even earlier. (For those looking to remain eligible for college hockey, the agents are designated as "family advisors" and they operate on a handshake basis.) Thus, an agent who's representing an NHL star in negotiations with a team for a contract worth $60 million or $70 million in the afternoon might be found in a community rink watching 13- and 14-year-olds and talking with parents that night. And all the major agencies retain stringers—regulars at arenas who scout tournaments, spot talent and make preliminary contact with parents.

For Crosby in 2002, there had been something akin to a feeding frenzy—the smaller boutique agencies that keep a short list of clients knew they had little shot at him, no matter how persuasive they were, no matter how much personal attention they could offer. The right to represent Crosby was going to come down to the big dogs in the industry: Newport Sports, the Bobby Orr Hockey Group, Octagon and the International Management Group (IMG). The four didn't quite have a monopoly on NHL all-star talent at the time, but it was close.

It was no big surprise that IMG would win the day. It was the original sports representation agency, founded by Mark McCormack in the early '60s, with Arnold Palmer as its foundational client. For more than a decade, IMG focused on golfers and tennis players, but it branched out into other sports in the '80s, establishing its large and enduring footprint in the NHL when it landed Wayne Gretzky. IMG Hockey focused on the league's elite and was happy enough to let others handle the rank and file. Crosby would turn out to be the last major client IMG Hockey locked up —McCormack died of cardiac arrest a year later, and in 2005 his survivors sold off the agency's hockey, baseball and football divisions, among other assets, to CAA.

The point men on the signing of Crosby were Pat Brisson, a former teammate of Pat LaFontaine with Verdun in the Quebec league, and J. P. Barry, a New Brunswick–born lawyer. Both would stay on at CAA, with Brisson taking the lead on Crosby's file. And getting a commitment from Crosby would turn out to be a huge win, for reasons that went far beyond the commissions on his contract. He would at once be a trophy, a source of bragging rights for the agency, and a magnet—the likes of Patrick Kane, John Tavares and Nathan MacKinnon all followed Crosby's lead and signed with Brisson.

But you have to presume that the stakes couldn't really have been foreseen back in the early summer of 2002. It would have been seemingly impossible to connect the hundreds of millions in play throughout Brisson and Barry's client list today to a kid more than a year away from his first major junior game. But in what have become the most famous summer workouts of all time, Wayne Gretzky saw the future, and its name was Sidney Crosby.

IMG had arranged for off-season workouts in Los Angeles for its younger player-clients, something for them to take home over the summer and build on when they started to skate again in August. The players were going to be put through their paces by Stan Butler, the head coach of the Canadian team at the two previous World Junior tournaments. The agency invited the 14-year-old Crosby not just to meet the pros, but to skate with them. He happened to be on the ice with the likes of Henrik and Daniel Sedin when Gretzky walked into the rink. Since his retirement three years before, Gretzky had not laced on skates even once, but watching Crosby triggered something in him that had been dormant—in one early piece I wrote about Crosby, I compared Gretzky standing on the other side of the plexiglass that day to "Einstein spying a kid running through complicated equations on a blackboard in a lecture hall." Gretzky asked around at the rink for a pair of skates, gloves and a stick and stepped onto the ice to throw the puck around with the phenom. If you were cynical, you'd presume that this was a piece of work—that the agency somehow wanted to impress Crosby. It was, in fact, entirely unscripted, and this single brief session prompted Gretzky to offer up a seemingly hyperbolic scouting report, in which he predicted that his scoring records were threatened by the kid he had just skated with. The assessment echoed around the hockey world and was met with, well, skepticism in the media. As Gretzky later explained, "Sidney saw everything on the ice. He saw the game the same way I did when I was 14. He just had these incredible skills and a real love of the game—an incredible desire to do whatever it takes to be better. He's the best talent to come along since Mario, and what makes him different [from the stars who came along before] is the attention to conditioning and work in the gym."

In midsummer, Stan Butler made a call to Marc Habscheid, who had been named as coach of the Canadian team at the World Juniors. With the tournament to be played over the winter holidays in Nova Scotia, Hockey Canada was going to stage its summer evaluation camp in Halifax, and Butler asked Habscheid if Crosby could embed with the team, go behind the curtain with 40 of the nation's best teenage players. It was, to be sure, an unusual, if not an entirely unprecedented request and it took Habscheid aback. Butler assured him that Crosby would be playing for the Canadian juniors down the line and would stand to benefit from early orientation.

In retrospect, it's safe to say that the best player in the Halifax Metro Centre in those sessions would prove to be the stick boy. The stakes were high for the players in camp—they aimed to land on the coaching staff's radar, if not be selected to the team—so Crosby didn't skate in practice or scrimmages. Still, he went to school on the experience. "I'm just trying to absorb a lot," he told the Halifax *Daily News*. "You can tell they're focused and they want to go somewhere, and they really want to represent their country."

The best-known player in the summer camp was Jason Spezza, the second-overall pick in the 2001 NHL Entry Draft. Even though Crosby was on the periphery, Spezza couldn't help but notice him. "We heard all about how good he was going to be," Spezza told me. "He didn't skate with us, but sometimes when we'd be coming back for our afternoon practice, he would have gone on the ice during our lunch break. You could tell that he had something special happening. He wasn't a great big guy, and he had a baby face, I guess. But when we saw him just skating, playing around, well, we all know what it's like. It was easy to tell that he had some real amazing skill. And then when he came off the ice, you could tell he was in amazing condition, just for a 14- or 15-year-old, he was in shape like a pro."

Spezza had himself been regarded as a phenom, playing major junior in the Ontario league at 15 and even taking shifts with the Canadian men's national team while in 10th grade. He had also been put through the wringer by the management of his NHL team, the Ottawa Senators, having been knocked, if not outright ridiculed by the coach, Jacques Martin, as not being ready "for the men's league." At 19, Spezza might not have seemed like anyone's idea of a mentor, but he did offer some hard-won advice to Crosby. "I told him that there are going to be a lot of things said and written about you and you're going to get pulled in a whole bunch of directions," Spezza recalled. "And I told him that no matter what goes on, have fun. Don't forget that it's supposed to be fun."

And Crosby left a lasting impression on the players at the camp, Spezza says. "He just wasn't like most other kids his age. He got along with everybody, you know, having a laugh. That much you'd expect. But you could tell that he was really watching every little thing that was going on. He was a few years younger but we treated him like he was one of us."

He would catch up with this bunch of World Junior players at the Christmas break, although not Spezza, who would split time between the Senators and their AHL affiliate in Binghamton. But a couple of weeks after the summer camp wrapped up, Crosby was packing to head off to school. He eschewed Notre Dame, Upper Canada College, the Georgetown Raiders and other options that were only on the table briefly. He defied convention, going off the board—at least for an elite Canadian teenager prospect—and decided to go the US prep route, to Shattuck-St. Mary's. Before Sidney Crosby enrolled there, only one alumnus had played in the NHL: Peter Ratchuk, a defenceman who had played 32 games for the Florida Panthers a couple of years previous.

In the US northeast, prep-school hockey programs are as old as the game itself. Some private schools, including Groton, Hotchkiss and Choate, have Ivy League auras about them and have long been pipelines to the hockey programs at prestigious colleges. While you wouldn't characterize any New England prep school as a production line for major-league talent, a few NHL players have emerged from the scene, most notably Hockey Hall of Famer Brian Leetch, who was drafted out of Avon Old Farms in Connecticut, and Brian Lawton, drafted first overall out of Mount St. Charles in Rhode Island.

The site of today's Shattuck-St. Mary's was originally the home of Bishop Seabury University Primary School, an institute founded in 1858 by Episcopal priests to educate the children of Faribault, Minnesota, a bustling fur-trade outpost. "A school is the fashioner of childhood for the work of manhood," said Bishop Whipple, one of the founders. Early on, the school expanded its focus from God to country, training young men for the military, and Bishop Seabury became the Shattuck Military Academy, merging in the 1970s with a girls' school, St. Mary's Hall, and a school for young boys, St. James, into Shattuck-St. Mary's.

Sports also became a component of school life: back in the 1900s, Shattuck's football team debuted, and in the '20s the varsity hockey team hit the natural ice pads for the first time. The school thrived through the middle of the 20th century, and its alumni included not just decorated officers and generals, but also Marlon Brando, Hall of Fame football coach Bud Wilkinson and broadcaster Brent Musburger. Military academies lost their cachet during the Vietnam War, and enrollment at Shattuck plunged below 200 students, not enough to parade in formation or field a football team. Dropping military training, going coed—it seemed as though nothing could slow the school's decline. By the '90s, Shattuck-St. Mary's was careening towards obsolescence and insolvency.

Hockey proved to be Shattuck's salvation. Craig Norwich, a native of Minnesota who played 104 NHL games over the course of a 10-year pro career, came in to coach the school's team in 1990 and recruited talented players who were looking to earn college scholarships. When Norwich left the school in 1996, he handed the program off to J. P. Parise, who had become something of a folk hero with the expansion-era Minnesota North Stars in the late '60s and early '70s. Other than his name value, Parise might have seemed like an unlikely choice for a position with a prep school. As he told me back in 2008, he had dropped out of high school to focus on hockey when he played Junior A in Niagara Falls the late '50s. "The coach, Hap Emms, said, 'You're going to have to make a decision,'" Parise told me. "'School's starting to interfere with your hockey.' So I quit."

After his playing days ended in 1979, Parise decided to get a proper education. He took a course at a local college in Minneapolis, but got discouraged—he was pushing 40, in a class of 18-year-olds—and did not complete it. Parise regretted that he had sacrificed his youthful school days to his prowess with the puck, and he hoped that returning to school might prepare him for future opportunities.

"I thought if I ever had a chance to be in a hockey program, I'd want to get it right. Back in '96 I was living in Bloomington, and Craig Norwich asked me if I wanted to coach Shattuck's bantams," Parise told me. "He had maybe 10 grand to pay me with. I told him I'd do it so long as my older son, Jordan, could enroll there. [When Norwich left,] I go from something like a volunteer to the head of the program. We started with two teams my first year. Four years later we had four boys' teams, two girls' teams, 140 students playing. Tuition was 10 grand. Four years later it doubled."

Across five seasons Parise's teams had sent a couple dozen players to NCAA Division I schools. A few had been picked in the NHL draft. One alum, Ryan Malone, son of former Pittsburgh Penguins centre Greg Malone, had been drafted by his father's old team.

By 2002, Shattuck-St. Mary's was still off the media's radar, but was emerging as a phenomenon in hockey circles. The USA Hockey development program had launched a few years before, rounding up the top 16- and 17-year-old players in the nation to train winterlong in Ann Arbor, Michigan, for international tournaments. Shattuck had sent an underclassman, Patrick Eaves, to Ann Arbor, where he played for his father, Mike, a former NHLer.

Eaves's linemate at Shattuck, Zach Parise (J. P.'s younger son), had won MVP and all-star honours at age-group tournaments and was also coveted by USA Hockey, but he chose to stay back in Faribault and play for his father. When USA Hockey sent its team to the world under-18 tournament in the spring of 2002, the staff added Zach to the roster. He wound up leading the team to the championship, the first gold medal for the USA Hockey program, which was under significant threat of having its budget slashed unless it started to yield results internationally. It's not an overstatement to suggest that Shattuck alums saved the program.

J. P. Parise had gone with a Shattuck team to the prestigious Mac's Midget AAA tournament in Calgary in December 2001 and, like a lot of college recruiters and junior scouts, got an eyeful of Crosby. By the spring of 2002 he had real results to pitch to the Crosbys and Pat Brisson.

The school was known in Halifax. Brent MacLellan, a defenceman whose family had just moved from Toronto, was considered a very good major junior prospect. Instead of playing locally, though, MacLellan opted to go to Shattuck for what would have been his minor-midget season, and he gave it a glowing recommendation. "It was really an option that my agent, Todd Reynolds, had put out there," says MacLellan, who is now Dr. MacLellan, an anaesthesiologist at McMaster University Medical Centre. "I hadn't heard of it. The school was really just starting to get a national profile [in the US]. I had considered college, but really I was thinking more of major junior at that point. It was an amazing experience. The coach that season was Andy Murray, who had coached the [Canadian] national team and was an NHL-quality coach."

———

I remember visiting the Shattuck campus for the first time on assignment for ESPN in 2007. Crosby had left in 2003 and Jonathan Toews had graduated in 2005 and moved on to the University of North Dakota, following the lead of Zach Parise. I had a preconceived idea of what I'd find. I knew about the tuition, which was more than US$30,000 a year. I knew the psychic pull of the hockey program, how the success of Parise and especially Crosby had built the Shattuck brand. Parents on both sides of the border wanted to send their sons and daughters there in the hope of landing college scholarships and maybe a shot at the pros. It wasn't just NCAA recruiters who visited; NHL scouts made it a priority destination on their rounds because many of the players finishing their senior year were eligible for that summer's entry draft.

I was expecting a hockey hothouse, something along the lines of the tennis academy founded by Nick Bollettieri in Bradenton, Florida, a boarding school that churned out the likes of Andre Agassi and Monica Seles in the '80s and forever changed the course of age-group tennis. I thought Shattuck would be the Bollettieri Academy without the palms, and that campus life revolved around the game that had drawn the famous alumni there. I fully expected to find an environment where hockey was No. 1 and everything else was tied for a very distant second place.

Suffice it to say, what I found was nothing like that.

While I didn't imagine Faribault as Bradenton-by-the-Frozen-River, the hardscrabble town of 20,000 an hour from the Twin Cities struck me as a) isolated and b) desolate. I'm sure Faribault bustled a fair bit more back in its heyday as a fur-trading centre. The main drag was lined with century-old brick buildings that had more than a few empty storefronts. A few small businesses, like Jim & Joe's Clothiers, dated back to the 1800s, and those that were a going concern posted signs in the windows advising customers that they would be closed during the Faribault High hockey game. A kid looking to get into trouble can find it anywhere, but he would have to work a lot harder in downtown Faribault, I supposed, and Shattuck was shut off from even that, being on the other side of the Straight River.

The 35 acres that make up the main school grounds, along with the limestone school buildings and rectory dating back to the late 1800s, have been designated a national historic district. Inside, dozens of oil paintings of the founders and later school figures lined the walls, as did photos of school teams, battalions and graduating classes. You could see some evidence of enduring traditions, such as the school uniforms and mandatory chapel attendance. It seemed like the farthest thing from a youth-hockey factory. If the Bollettieri Academy offered country-club comfort, Shattuck-St. Mary's evoked the historical hardship of settlers, the making do without. Shattuck's teams had played in a decidedly humble arena with a low ceiling and not enough seats to accommodate parents and scouts taking in games. The varsity team's dressing room was immaculate but claustrophobic. The weight room in the main building was spartan — most public high schools would have more to offer their athletes.

I've covered hockey played by teenagers for a quarter century or so and followed it going back to the '60s. I've watched the business and politics and psychodynamics of the game evolve. The easy take: professionalism has crept into the amateur game, and not so slowly and maybe even absolutely, rendering it almost indistinguishable from the NHL. I've been around parents who knew precisely how much favour and privilege they could squeeze out of the system. Teams have enabled it: I've known junior players who cooked up deals under which they were gifted with cars—courtesy rides—by their teams. The teenagers have also made their own independent end runs: I knew one player with the Canadian World Junior team who, unbeknownst to the coaches and in violation of their policy, had a deal to call a radio station in his hometown every morning, for which he got hundreds of dollars a throw. Teams have been broken by it: the London Knights, the franchise with the deepest pockets in junior hockey, flew its star players home on a long playoff road trip while the rest of the team took the bus, effectively creating a toxic culture of privilege that turned teammates against each other.

I say this to explain why I wasn't quite prepared for what I saw when I first landed on the Shattuck-St. Mary's campus. The culture of the pampered youth sports star was nowhere to be found. Once the cheque for your tuition cleared and you checked in, any sense of entitlement would have been ground into dust. Students had to fall into line, and players on the varsity team particularly so —it was at once an egalitarian and disciplinarian environment. For everything, there was a rule and it was to be followed with absolute rigour. A bunch of exceptional kids congregated in a setting offering no exceptions. That impression formed when I arrived at dawn and the varsity hockey team was waiting outside the dining hall—no one could go in until every team member was present. The team moved as a pack. Even though no faculty member or coach was on the scene to enforce the rule, the players stood around, waiting for the one who was running two minutes late. When the tardy teammate arrived, he was razzed good-naturedly for sleeping in, even though some of the others had been up since 5 a.m. and managed to sneak in a skate at the arena before the scheduled Shattuck day began.

That didn't necessarily surprise me, though. I put it down to a cultural remnant of Shattuck's time as a military academy, as well as to the game they played. Teams in junior and at the pro level run on "hockey time"—if you're not 10 minutes early for a designated time, you're effectively late. Woe be to the last to arrive and miss the bus. Timeliness is something more than next to godliness. No, what surprised me was the emotional barometric pressure at that point and over the course of days. In this structured and regulated environment you couldn't find a loner or rebel or any kid who pushed back. The players—and the rest of the student body—weren't simply compliant with the Shattuck program. It seemed like they embraced it. In retrospect, I suppose that you'd grow weary and eventually break if you simply got along to get along. And I suppose that Shattuck, while not for everybody, served a certain type of kid particularly well in a way that had nothing much to do with the game of hockey: the Type A personality. Those who drive themselves didn't seem to mind being driven at all. Shattuck didn't feature the rank pulling that is built into West Point—and, I suppose, the sort of military prep that Shattuck was back in the day. Instead, there was a team aspect, everyone balancing their personal striving with the collective greater good. In this way the attitude on campus evoked The Right Stuff.

I've talked to hundreds of teenagers, and I would bet that even some of the most disciplined would struggle at Shattuck—or worse. Crosby, though, had nothing but warm memories about a cold place.

"It was my first experience away from Nova Scotia, and I had to catch up academically," Crosby told me. "I struggled with it at first. But I loved the atmosphere. You can have friendships wherever you play, but at Shattuck, it was different than other teams.

You can have teams that are close and you can have friendships wherever you play, but at Shattuck you lived together, went to class together, travelled and played together. You get to know each other —everyone—a lot faster and a lot better."

This wasn't just Crosby revising history. It was just as everybody remembered it. "At Shattuck, Sid was just Sid. Not Sidney Crosby the hockey star," coach Tom Ward told me. "Just Sid. He was a kid, just a boy, on a lot of counts and really he didn't get any special attention. He just blended in and he liked that a lot, I know. His spot on the team wasn't guaranteed when he came here. He had to try out like everyone else—and I think that he liked that. And even at 15, at some level he knew that this was the last time it was going to be like that. He was also an old soul. He knew what kind of talent he had and he knew better than all of us exactly how far he could go with it—and not that we were underestimating him. People asked how good Sid was and J. P. told them he could play in the NHL *right now*."

Crosby made the Shattuck prep team as a sophomore. On its face it may not seem to be a remarkable achievement. When the postscripts for his career are written, this wouldn't make it as a footnote. But consider: neither Jonathan Toews and Nathan MacKinnon nor a bunch of NHLers who followed were able to land a spot on the prep roster in their sophomore year—that is, playing up two years. Further, it wasn't as though he was playing up with a bunch of kids from his hometown; rather, these were elite prospects, and he would lead them to a national championship.

His teammate Drew Stafford, a future NHLer, told the Minneapolis *Star-Tribune*, "He was just heads and shoulders better than everybody. For a 15-year-old, he already had the body type, the same kind of style he plays now—that power skating, where it's power moves. His legs were enormous. He was built to be a hockey player, and it was pretty cool to see just how skilled he was."

Crosby's best friend at Shattuck-St. Mary's was Jack Johnson, a brash defenceman from Michigan. If you look at the long history of great players, you'll see that many have a penchant for befriending antic and edgier wingmen (for example, Gretzky with Eddie Mio, Orr with Derek Sanderson, Beliveau with John Ferguson). So it was with Crosby and Johnson. The story of Johnson getting kicked off the baseball team has become part of Shattuck lore, with an opposing pitcher throwing a beanball at Johnson, who in turn charged the mound. In Johnson's wake, it fell to Crosby to hold back the catcher. They saw their friendship carrying on up to the NHL ranks—by the accounts of many around the team, they talked how they would one day sign as free agents with the Montreal Canadiens, Crosby's favourite team growing up.

Johnson was a great all-around athlete and an immense talent, and his presence in the lineup only starts to give you an idea of the depth of talent around Crosby on the Shattuck prep team. When Crosby was selected first overall in the NHL draft in 2005, Johnson was selected two picks after. Stafford was the 13th-overall pick in the 2004 draft, and a couple of lesser lights wound up being drafted in the late rounds. Ryan Duncan wasn't drafted but later won the Hobey Baker Award as the top NCAA player of the year.

The team steamrolled everything in its path and really had trouble getting a good game against other prep schools. Crosby wore out the competition and set school records as a 15-year-old: 72 goals and 162 points in 57 games. The numbers are all the more impressive when you consider that Crosby wasn't always a first-liner with the team; Ward didn't want to shortchange his upperclassmen to give the phenom extra shifts. In fact, Shattuck's dominance doubtlessly factored into Crosby's decision not to come back for what would have been a junior year and a certain second national championship. Leaving was, Crosby told me, "the hardest decision I had to make." Perhaps, but it was also one made with clear eyes and one that Shattuck staff and teammates didn't begrudge. "Sid didn't go to Shattuck just to stay one year," Ryan Duncan told me. "He liked it there and he was looking hard at NCAA instead of junior." Crosby looked for a way to combine his junior and senior years to get to college ahead of his class, but it was just too big of an ask. And two more years with the prep team would have presented the same issue he had faced at home after the Air Canada Cup— just as the Canadian hockey establishment had run out of ready challenges for him after the Subways' great run, so had Shattuck and US prep hockey before his 16th birthday. His only real option was to head off to the Quebec Major Junior Hockey League—in retrospect, that door opened to him a year later than necessary, but he didn't look at anything in his rear-view mirror.

Ryan Duncan says that the Shattuck experience influenced Crosby more deeply than you might imagine a single season would, that his time in Faribault shaped a lot of his values. "Sid wants to bring the Shattuck way of doing things into every dressing room he hangs his skates in," Duncan says. "We all want it that way. We all go into Shattuck different and all come out the same." It sounds extreme, but Duncan's claims have crossed my mind when I've talked to Jonathan Toews. I couldn't help thinking that he sounds and carries himself exactly like Crosby. In terms of personality, it's not necessarily true that all 23 NHLers who have passed through the gates at Shattuck are out of the same mould as Crosby—Nathan

MacKinnon is wise-cracking, self-deprecating and fun-loving and Jack Johnson is a loose cannon. Still, whether it's Zach Parise or Drew Stafford or most others, there's a certain seriousness and sense of purpose that sets the majority of alums apart and places them well above the NHL median by measures of drive and focus.

Crosby's actions also suggest that his year at Shattuck meant more to him than you might suspect. When his sister, Taylor, reached high school age, she enrolled there with her brother picking up her tuition. In fact, Taylor Crosby stayed a full four years, eventually winning a spot in goal for Shattuck's nationally ranked girls' hockey team. All students in the senior year have to get up at an assembly and give a brief speech about their time at Shattuck and their lives going forward, and Taylor Crosby spoke about her brother, though she never mentioned his name or hinted unnecessarily about his athletic celebrity. In just a few lines, Taylor laid out a telling description of the bond with her brother and what life was like in the Crosby home. "When I was six years old, my brother left home," she said. "I felt devastated. Our weekday breakfasts of toast and strawberry yogurt would end. So would the summer nights we spent waiting for the other to fall asleep so that we could steal the only fan. We were born eight and a half years apart, so we never really fought. He was always busy with hockey while I was busy playing with Barbies. He has worked hard to reach his goals. He taught me to be competitive by racing me to the car and then pulling my arm so I couldn't reach it before him. He taught me that you don't stop, you just keep running until you reach the car. He has taught me the qualities of an athlete, but also a person. All people need someone to look up to. My role model is my brother." With no limit of school options available to Sidney Crosby for his sister, they settled on Shattuck, which must stand as the ultimate endorsement. And while the Crosby family received financial assistance to send Sidney to school for his sophomore year, he not only paid Taylor's full tuition but also generously donated to the school. Said one school official, "Whatever Sidney received, he paid back many times over through the years."

Many other former Shattuck students have maintained an even closer relationship with the school than did Crosby. Zach Parise, for instance, has long kept a summer home on a lake near the school, and in the summer he works out and skates at Shattuck with other former players. Drew Stafford's father taught and coached at the school for years. Nonetheless, in the media, Crosby is the one first and most often associated with the school. When he arrived there, a rebuilding of the hockey program was already in progress and it was soon feeding talent to USA Hockey's under-17 and under-18 programs. Nonetheless it was Crosby who truly boosted Shattuck's profile—even before he made it to the NHL, the school was mentioned in every profile of the junior sensation and prospective first-overall draft pick. By the time he became the cornerstone of the Pittsburgh Penguins, Crosby was already the face of an entirely different franchise: Shattuck-St. Mary's.

The hockey team's success gave Shattuck's administration confidence to expand its intensive, specialized approach. The trustees poured resources into the girls' hockey program and wound up sending five alumnae to the US Olympic team, including Amanda Kessel. Likewise, the school stepped up its soccer and golf programs. It even went beyond sports and now offers a music conservatory and enriched streams in biomedicine and engineering.

Hockey is still first and foremost at Shattuck, and the school's influence is felt far beyond Faribault. Dozens of institutions have tried to recreate its model. Some long-established schools have placed greater emphasis on their hockey programs. A good example is St. Andrew's College in Aurora, north of Toronto, which heralds itself as "the best private boys boarding school in Canada." Founded in 1899, St. Andrew's iced varsity hockey teams that played on the regional private-school circuit for its first century or so, but over the last 10 years the program has stepped up its commitment to coaching, support resources and scheduling—alumnus Warren Foegele is a regular in the Carolina Hurricanes lineup, and NHL teams selected two players directly from the St. Andrew's roster in the 2017 entry draft while a third alumnus, Robert Thomas of the London Knights, was selected 20th overall by St. Louis. St. Andrew's, or other schools in the Ontario-based Conference of Independent Schools Athletic Association, would almost certainly be a more viable option today than CISAA member Upper Canada College was for Sidney Crosby in 2002. So too would several other private schools in Canada—Stanstead College in Quebec's Eastern Townships can brag on Mark Jankowski, a regular in the Calgary Flames lineup who was drafted directly from the school in the first round of the 2012 NHL draft.

Likewise, institutions that weren't even around back in '02 would be on any young phenom's radar. Founded in north Toronto in 2006, the Hill Academy, a private coed school, can already claim an emerging NHL star as an alumnus—Mitch Marner of the Toronto Maple Leafs—but virtually any kid of either gender on the varsity hockey or lacrosse teams has a far better than even shot at landing a scholarship if he or she is looking to go the NCAA route. The Hill Academy evokes Shattuck less than it does the Bollettieri academy—in the academy's pitch to parents, the emphasis falls more on athletic enrichment than the whole-student experience. Founded in the same year in Dartmouth, Nova Scotia, the

Newbridge Academy offers up a program similar to that of the Hill Academy—Newbridge did a slow build, effectively starting as a private middle school and adding upper grades as they went, moving up from bantam teams to midget, all with Hockey Canada's seal of approval and a commercial relationship with Gatorade, one of the brands Sidney Crosby has long endorsed.

Other schools are more explicit about their selling hockey up front and their celebrity educators. For example, the Rolston Academy in suburban Detroit is headed up by former NHLer Brian Rolston, a veteran of over 1,200 NHL games and a three-time U.S. Olympian. Although his career dates back to the mid-'90s, before Shattuck grads had landed in the NHL, Rolston retired in 2012, so he spent several seasons playing against Crosby. There's little mistaking what's being sold up front—the Rolston Academy's website offers "Detailed Hockey Training by NHL Professionals and Accredited Academics by Certified Teachers."

Nowhere has Shattuck's "academy" model had a greater impact than in western Canada. The Canadian Sport School Hockey League (CSSHL) launched in 2009 with three schools icing prep teams and two more joining in the bantam ranks. Within eight years the CSSHL has expanded to seven leagues for boys and girls, with 70 teams from 18 academies across the four western provinces, plus one in Coeur d'Alene, Idaho. In that time, the CSSHL has turned out seven first-round NHL draft picks and 18 more in later rounds, along with the dozens of players the league has sent to the Western Hockey League and the NCAA. Virtually any major event, from the world juniors to the NCAA women's Frozen Four, is bound to have connections to the most important feeder league in the game in North America. Some of the schools predate Crosby's arrival at Shattuck—the Edge School in Calgary, for instance, was founded in 1999. Others are not as old as the CSSHL itself—the Delta Hockey Academy, for example, launched in 2013. The CSSHL hasn't bucked the establishment so much as it has become the establishment—Notre Dame, the historic program in Wilcox, Saskatchewan, that Crosby passed up, has joined the league. Likewise the Burnaby Winter Club, the history-rich minor-hockey program in the Vancouver region for decades, has adopted the academy model for its teams.

When Sidney Crosby was 14, it seemed like he had no options to play close to home—or in Canada at all. Shattuck was a stand-alone, an outlier. His successes at Shattuck not only prompted existing prep schools to boost their hockey programs, but also spurred an entire new industry in minor hockey. Had Crosby come along in 2019, he'd have no end of destinations.

CHAPTER 5

THE HONOUR STUDENT OF '87 ENROLLS WITH THE CLASS OF '86

Summer 2003

I had heard about Crosby back when he took Dartmouth to the finals—I had even talked to an editor at the paper I was working for about doing a feature on him. The idea wound up getting shot down. There were NHL games to cover and other more obvious, more pressing concerns, however pissed I might have been. The editor couldn't get his mind around the fact that this was a 14-year-old worth the time and expense; there was no way of knowing whether he was going to turn into a star—or even an NHL player at all—no matter how many testimonials rolled in.

My confidence was rooted not just in expert testimony, but also a bit of personal history. My friend from high school, Stan Butler, had been the coach on the ice with IMG's prospects when the paths of Sidney Crosby and Wayne Gretzky crossed for the first time. Butler assured me that Gretzky's words were exactly as reported and that he had legitimate cause to be so enthusiastic. Some coaches are "salesmen" who push a bill of goods on you about the players in their fold. Stan has always trended in the other direction—not a critic as much as a sober skeptic. "Really good" was always bookended by "but." He had coached Jason Spezza as a 15-year-old in major junior. He had coached Rick Nash, the first-overall pick in 2002, with the Canadian team at the World Juniors that season. He had seen talent but hadn't worked on the ice with anyone in Crosby's category. "Everyone in the game knows how good he can be," Stan told me.

Maybe everyone inside the game did, and maybe some who had played with and against him in his time with the Subways or at Shattuck-St Mary's. Beyond that, he was unknown and would be for as long as he remained unseen.

About six months after hearing about Crosby lighting up the Canada Winter Games, I saw that Hockey Canada had added him to the list of players being invited to its selection camp in Calgary ahead of the Under-18 Junior World Cup, to be played in the Czech Republic and Slovakia in August 2003. I also noticed that Crosby's first hockey card—issued ahead of his first year of junior hockey—had gone up for auction on eBay for US$11. As of this writing, one of these cards can be purchased on eBay for US$5,800. The commoditization of Sidney Crosby had commenced before his 16th birthday.

These developments prompted me to take another stab at selling a feature on Crosby, and this time I managed to convince a magazine of the merits of doing a story—I suspected the editor was more impressed by the fact that a 15-year-old's hockey card was being traded on eBay than Hockey Canada's endorsement of the phenom. The editor asked if Crosby was going to play in the NHL someday, and I convinced him that it was a given. I took a pretty bold swing, telling him the best way of building the story was to follow Crosby at the under-18 tournament. He gave me the green light as long as Hockey Canada would guarantee that he would make the team. That point worried me. I explained that Hockey Canada executives would never tell you a player was a lock to make a team, just as a point of etiquette. I imagined that this was particularly true, given that every other player in camp had experience in major junior hockey, a far more demanding level than the prep-school game Crosby had played in Minnesota.

I tried to lower the bar, telling the editor that the organization had a history of extreme caution with young players—Hockey Canada officials had allowed the hype to build up around Eric Lindros at that age, and the perceived favouritism wound up having a negative effect on teams he played on. Thereafter, talented players could count on being knocked down a step rather than being given any preferential rides. Jason Spezza, for instance, barely played for the Canadian world junior team at 16. As I spun it, it was likely going to be a matter of baby steps for Crosby at this tournament; the coaches were probably planning to give him a taste of the international game for seasons ahead. No matter; the editor asked me to get as much of an assurance as I could before he'd budget the story.

I wasn't optimistic when I called Brad Pascall, who was then Hockey Canada's vice-president of operations. I laid out for him the awkward position I was in—only because of my editor was I obliged to ask him whether there was any way Crosby might not make the roster. I wasn't ready for Pascall's answer: "He'll be on the team and I'll be shocked if he isn't the centre on the first line." I had never heard that sort of enthusiasm in the better part of 15 years of dealing with the organization, and in that time several first-overall NHL picks and future Hockey Hall of Famers had come down the pike.

Over the years, Hockey Canada had rotated scouts in and out —if a longtime NHL scout found himself between contracts, a job scouting for the world junior team provided a soft landing until another position with an NHL franchise opened up. And a few of the scouts who had worked for Hockey Canada were slaves to conventional wisdom and old-school hockey. That is, players were expected to wait their turns until their birth years came up in rotation for the respective teams—i.e., all the 16-year-olds going to the under-17s, all the 17-year-olds to the under-18s, and the world juniors, the under-20s, being a 19-year-old tournament. Per the selection, priority was given to size and to "character kids"; players from certain teams were regarded as having the advantage of pedigree. Those outside the box needed not apply. The program had had no idea what to make of Mario Lemieux when he was coming up— he became the only junior star to pass up a chance to play for the program back in his draft year and the coach of the team, Brian Kilrea of the Ottawa 67's, basically said good riddance. Hockey Canada's scout back in 2003 was Blair Mackasey, and to his credit he wasn't beholden to the same-old-same-old. I have no doubt that a few of the scouts who preceded him would have come up with reasons to make Crosby wait his turn.

In the late '90s the Czechs and Slovaks hosted a small summer tournament with Hockey Canada sending a team. It was a make-do situation. Hockey Canada had initially taken part in the tournament because it did not send a team to the International Ice Hockey Federation's under-18 world championship in April, which directly conflicted with the Canadian Hockey League playoffs, leaving most of the top Canadian players in that age group unavailable. Hockey Canada's fear was that other nations were using the world under-18s to identify their best players, and then having them play and practise together in the seasons that followed, giving them an advantage in the most prestigious age-group tournament, the world juniors.

In 2002 Canada finally sent a team to the world under-18s in the spring, an improvised squad made up of players whose teams had missed out on the CHL playoffs or had been eliminated in the first round. And other national programs had started to send teams to the Under-18 World Cup—by 2003 it featured an eight-team field. Still, the summer tournament was more meaningful to Hockey Canada than to the other nations—it was the one time that Canada had a chance to field its best players in that particular birth year.

As it turned out, there wasn't a Canadian player in the 1986 birth year who, with a year of major junior hockey experience, could really keep up with a kid born in '87 who had been playing at the high-school level the season before.

I was on a flight to Prague with more than a dozen NHL scouts in early August of 2003. The Under-18 World Cup was regarded as the opening of their business year. As much as they took a professional interest in the world juniors over Christmas and New Year's, their work focused on players who were going to be available for the coming NHL Entry Draft—by the time the vast majority of players made it to the world juniors, they had already been drafted. So the 2003 Under-18 World Cup was the first chance the scouts would have to evaluate the 2004 NHL draft class and, moreover, a chance to see them compete head to head. And scouts are reluctant to put off seeing the elite players until a later date—a prospect might get hurt early in the season and, playing through injury or sidelined entirely, never offer scouts a chance to get a clear reading of his skills.

While they were enthusiastic about a pair of Russian forwards at the top of the list of players eligible for the 2004 draft, the scouts regarded the class overall as a soft one, especially in the wake of one of the deepest and richest drafts in history, held just a couple of months before. Draft classes don't quite sync up to calendar years. The 2003 under-18 tournament featured players born in 1986, but NHL draft eligiblity begins on September 15 rather than January 1. So it was that the best players eligible for the 2004 entry draft weren't on hand at the 2003 Under-18 World Cup. Chief among them was Alexander Ovechkin, born in September 1985. I had seen Ovechkin play as an underager at the 2002 under-18s, in which he was regarded as the tournament's best player. Another Russian, Evgeni Malkin, was the best of the '86-born prospects playing at the 2003 Under-18 Junior World Cup, and he would wind up ranked behind only Ovechkin on the NHL Central Scouting Bureau's list of top Europeans. Central Scouting put another '85-born player, Canadian forward Andrew Ladd, at the top of the list of North American skaters, just ahead of a defenceman, Cam Barker, who anchored the blue line for the Canadian team at the World Cup. Suffice it to say, NHL scouts saw a big drop-off after the first two picks in the draft.

I gleaned all this and more from a passenger sitting behind me on the flight to the Czech Republic: Tim Burke, who headed the San Jose Sharks' scouting department. A native of Massachusetts and a former NCAA and minor-pro defenceman, Burke had 15 years of experience as a scout, starting out with New Jersey before signing on with the Sharks. I had known him for several years, and he'd always been a clinical sort, not easily excited by prospects, so that made the transatlantic flight all the more interesting—Burke bent my ear talking about Crosby for a couple thousand miles. He told me that he regretted missing Canada's opening game in the tournament, a narrow win over Finland in which Crosby scored the tying goal late in regulation and registered the winner in the shootout.

"I'd pay to see this kid play," Burke told me. "I think it's true of anybody in our business. Yeah, we're supposed to be skeptical about the players we evaluate, but I think we love the game more than anybody else. What's more, we respect the game and want the best for it. It's not just that this kid can be good in the NHL. He will be—that's something that you can only say about a handful of players over the years. Thing is, he can be good for the NHL."

That seemed to me like a stretch at the time—to talk about a kid being an *asset* to one of the big four professional sports leagues before he'd even entered the feeder system. In retrospect, though, maybe it wasn't so far out of the box. Just weeks earlier, the Cleveland Cavaliers had selected a teenager out of a high school in Akron, Ohio, with the first-overall pick in the NBA draft—and no one in basketball circles doubted that LeBron James would become a major NBA star. Maybe the higher up the scale of talent you go, the earlier and more obviously athletes present themselves.

Burke didn't stop there. I asked him what type of game Crosby played. I presumed that, given his stature—somewhat less than the NHL average—Crosby might have been a player in the mould of Pavel Bure, whose blinding speed forced bigger opponents to play catch-up. Burke said that Crosby was a very good skater, but didn't have Bure's horsepower going north and south. "What's really great [about Crosby] is the fact that the kid looks after himself on the ice," Burke said. "He fights his own battles. He doesn't just take it. He dishes it out. He's fearless out there."

That Burke emphasized Crosby's toughness struck me as odd. Sure, "dishing it out" was a quality you'd see in selected elite players; you'd cite it when putting together a thumbnail profile of, say, Gordie Howe or Eric Lindros or, as it would play out, Alexander Ovechkin—stars who brought a certain physical dimension to their game. But no one would have marked Wayne Gretzky as a tough or fearless player—"elusive" was more apt. He didn't have to play through big hits, managing across his career to elude them. Likewise, Mario Lemieux didn't have to take hits to make a play —he was just imperiously above it all, opponents too concerned about getting undressed by his puck skills to think about running him. Neither had to "fight his own battles." That would have been akin to Tiger Woods carrying his own bag. And yet, here was a 16-year-old who stood not quite five foot ten, smaller than the aforementioned, who according to Burke seemed not just willing to weather a physical game, but eager to embrace it. I couldn't quite conjure up Crosby's game in my mind's eye—Burke hadn't given me a "comparable." Then again, the more common the talent, the easier it is to name similar players, while you'd struggle to come up with comparables to the stars name-dropped here.

———

NHL scouting was once seasonal work, but these days, with national team evaluation camps and the like, scouts' assignments can land in any month of the year. To anyone who doesn't draw an NHL paycheque, watching international hockey in August might feel out of sync, sort of like surfing in an Arctic winter. This was never more true than at the 2003 Under-18 Junior World Cup, as Europe was in the throes of the worst heat wave in almost 500 years, with temperatures reaching the mid-40s Celsius. Ice making in warm weather is a test at the best of times—NHL players have always voiced complaints about ice quality in the US South, and when one of those teams has made it to the Stanley Cup final in June, air-conditioning units the size of big-box stores have been parked by the sides of arenas in a vain effort to give players a passable playing surface. The organizers in Breclav, Czech Republic, and Piestany, Slovakia, didn't have the wherewithal to do much more than turn their refrigeration units up high and pray.

Even if conditions were more forgiving, the summer under-18s —and really, any summer tournament—do no favours for the talent on the ice. The supposed showcases present challenges that prospects don't face in season. Lineups are cobbled together with players who can barely keep their teammates' names straight, let alone develop any on-ice chemistry. And players haven't skated in game situations for two months at the very least. The rule of thumb for scouts holds that a player might make a good impression at a summer session, but you'd never hold an indifferent one against him. So it was that I was prepared to adjust the bar for Crosby. When I heard the reports of Canada's win over Finland, I thought I had likely missed the best game he'd play at the summer under-18s. A bit of a gut shot, but not as bad as the one at the first game I did take in, which I feared would be the last one he'd play at the tournament.

Anyone who has reported on sports long enough knows that the odds will catch up to you—when you parachute in to write about an athlete, there's always a risk that, with no notice, your subject will be sick and not even make it to the arena. There's every chance that a shot off a skate on the first shift will put him in a cast and on the sidelines for a month. Go to an arena a hundred times and this will happen. Go to an arena a *thousand* times and you can start to collect horror stories. And so it was that I thought I had crossed the ocean to see Sidney Crosby skate only a handful of shifts.

In the first period against the Swiss, Crosby was exactly as billed. Skating on a line with two players from the Ontario Hockey League, Evan McGrath of the Kitchener Rangers and Wojtek Wolski of the Brampton Battalion, Crosby seemed to do something creative every time he touched the puck. The Swiss were the bigger team and skated well enough to give the Canadians trouble, even taking a 1–0 lead in the first period. If you subtracted Crosby from the mix, Switzerland might have had a chance to upset the Canadian '86s, and that was exactly what they attempted to do: subtract Crosby. In a scrum after a whistle, a Swiss forward named Mathias Joggi delivered a stiff and well-aimed cross-check to the side of Crosby's helmet, just above the temple, and Crosby dropped. That set off hostilities, of course, and Joggi was sent to the penalty box while Crosby staggered to his skates and made his way woozily to the Canadian bench. I spotted Crosby's parents, Troy and Trina, in the crowd—only four sets of Canadian parents had made the trip —and Trina in particular looked stricken. The sinking feeling that I had—that the phenom touted by Burke might be done for the tournament—lasted not much more than a shift. Within a minute, Crosby was over the boards on the power play and the first Swiss player who dared to breathe the same air as him was Ginsu-ed for his troubles. Just as Burke said, Crosby was fearless and didn't mind meting out justice on his own.

Canada prevailed over the Swiss by a score of 6–3, and that was fairly indicative of the play. Off that game, though, it was clear that Crosby was almost certainly the only Canadian player you'd mark as a certain or even likely first-line player at the NHL level. Looking back at the lineup now, the only other Canadian who had a truly noteworthy NHL career was goaltender Devan Dubnyk, the team's ostensible backup. The Edmonton Oilers would go on to draft him in the first round in 2004 and eventually write him off as a bust; only after a couple of other teams gave up on him, the better part of 10 years after he was drafted, did Dubnyk break through and establish himself as an all-star with the Minnesota Wild. A few would make the league and stick out—none longer than forward Blake Comeau, who has logged more than 800 career games but scored more than 20 goals in a season only once, making him far more of a journeyman and replacement-level player than a star. Defenceman Cam Barker would be selected third overall in the 2003 draft and make a couple of Canadian teams at the world juniors, but his run in the NHL was unremarkable and, considering his draft position, relatively brief. What Brad Pascall of Hockey Canada had told me about Crosby being slotted as a first-line player on the team was at once a testament to his ability and an indictment of the balance of available talent.

Crosby imposed himself on the game in the third period—with the game tied two-all, he scored two goals and set up another in furious flurry. His first goal—a solo effort that gave Canada a 3–2 lead, undressing two Swiss defencemen and fighting through a hook by a backchecking forward—would be the best goal you might see if you watched an entire season of major junior hockey.

"When he needs to, he can get it done," Tim Burke had told me, and that scouting report seemed to be dead on the mark. Wojtek Wolski put an even finer point on it: "I've never played with someone who does the things that he does. He forces you not to take your attention off the puck for a second. It could be coming anytime."

The next morning I sat at the coaches' table with Crosby in the hotel dining room and took a calculated risk, ordering eggs that were laminated with grease. What passed for orange juice started out as powder and had a metallic aftertaste. The rest of the menu was no more promising. Crosby seemed as leery about the fare as I did, and when I asked him what his usual pregame meal was, he demurred. "I don't want to get into any superstitions that I can't control," he said. "I like my routines. I'm superstitious about a bunch of things. I dress right before left. After I finish working on my stick before a game I never let it out of my sight. I don't just put it in the rack. But a pregame meal, that's something I can't control."

I made small talk with Crosby about his decision to go to Shattuck, about the QMJHL deciding not to allow him to play for Halifax—considering how he had shone so much more brightly than all the other Canadian '86s, there should have been no doubt about his ability to compete. He wasn't going to second-guess the league's ruling against him. "I don't think about what's fair," he said. "I just make the most of whatever situation it is."

A few hours later I watched the Canadian team's practice and studied Crosby. He was, as he would be whenever I scoped him in the junior ranks, the first player on the ice and the last one off. He was also, conspicuously, the one who seemed most engaged

—when the coaches were drawing up a power-play set-up on an erasable board, Crosby was at the very front of the crowd, on one knee, eyes never wandering from the Xs and Os. Which is to say that Crosby had both a Type A personality and an A student's work ethic.

Away from the arena, Crosby seemed a bit of a kid apart from the rest of the team. Most players knew at least one or two of their teammates, some more than that—they might have played on the same teams in rep hockey or on regional teams that had played at Hockey Canada's under-17 tournament the previous season. Crosby, though, was the only kid from the Maritimes, and he spent long stretches talking about his game with his father—when the team made a bus trip to Brno on a down day, Sidney sat with his father and mostly listened as he talked about opponents trying to get him off his game. He did connect with his teammates, but nonetheless spent more time with Troy and Trina than did the other players whose parents made the trip. While he was just making acquaintances with his teammates, they were up to speed on him, having heard about him when he was playing with the Subways—some had played against him at events going back to the Quebec peewee tournament or the one sponsored by the Brick furniture-store chain in Calgary. But it also dug deeper than that. There was the matter of style: Crosby looked like he was observing Shattuck's dress code, while a few other teammates walked around in T-shirts with sleeves cut off to reveal shoulder-to-wrist tattoos. Crosby was listening to country music, to Toby Keith and Shania Twain, while most of his teammates divided their listening between metal or hip-hop.

According to scouts who had done the work-up on players in the Canadian lineup, a few of the teenagers came from very well-to-do families, and for them money was no object when it came to individual coaching, extra ice time and top-of-the-line equipment.

Perhaps unfairly, the scouts wondered about a degree of entitlement, not something an NHL team would want to take on. On this count, though, Crosby was spared any of the broad-stroke criticism about privilege, simply because his family circumstances were modest by comparison, his time in an expensive prep school notwithstanding. The scouts knew that this hadn't been the family footing the bill.

In their final game of the opening round, the Canadian team faced the host Czechs in front of 6,000 fans, the largest crowd of the tournament to that point, probably a few only looking for a place where they could beat the heat. The Czechs followed the same sort of game plan that the Swiss had against Crosby, and the home team was getting away with hooks, slashes and elbows with impunity and without penalty. Even stuff that played out right in front of a ref was allowed to pass. Worse were the calls that went against Canada and put the visitors on the penalty kill for long stretches in the first two periods; still, the Czechs only led 1–0 going into the third. Just as he had against the Swiss, Crosby again raised his game with every shift in the late going and twice had glorious chances to tie the game. The Canadians ran into a hot goaltender, and against the run of play the Czechs picked up an insurance goal and another into an empty net. "We outplayed them and lost," Crosby told me, which looks far more matter-of-fact on the page than it sounded in real time. It wasn't ideal but it wasn't a full-blown disaster either—the loss made Canada the second seed in the group and meant they would have to travel across the border to Slovakia and play the US team in the semifinals in Piestany.

——

I wound up spending an hour or so talking with Crosby in his hotel room the day before the semifinal. When I arrived he was on the phone to a radio station in Halifax—though I could only hear his half of the conversation, he fielded questions like a seasoned pro, without a pause or stutter. "We outplayed the Czechs . . . I was surprised by Wayne's comments . . . it's really early for any talk like that," he said. So it went for five minutes. Outside the room his teammates were noisily playing with their purchases from the trip into Brno—mock Uzis that shot plastic bullets—but Crosby seemed deaf to it and not particularly amused.

Malcolm Gladwell's *The Tipping Point* was a few years from being published, but when I asked Crosby about learning the game, his answer captured Gladwell's theory that it takes 10,000 hours of practice to achieve genius. His young life was saturated in sports in general, and hockey in particular. "I played as much as possible," he said, "whether it was organized games in a league or shinny at our local rink. I grew up in Cole Harbour. We were in a row of town-houses and there was a bunch of us who always played together. I'd knock on doors after school and on weekends, trying to get guys to come out to play. And we had a really good bunch of players. We called it 'our dynasty.' We won a lot of championships."

And while I had a sense that he wasn't an entitled kid, I was caught a bit off guard by some hard-earned perspective he had on his life to the age of 16 years and one week. "My parents were real young when they had me," he said. "They lived at my grandparents' house when I was little. I used to take shots on my grandmother in the basement when I was two or three. She wasn't easy to beat. My parents had to struggle sometimes, I guess. After games on week-ends sometimes, my parents and I would go out and deliver fliers. That was to get enough money to pay my league fees. We made it something like a family outing. No matter what, my parents made sure that I had good equipment, never second-hand."

I asked him if he had ever envied those players whose families didn't have to deliver fliers, if he had ever felt cheated when he'd see a teammate throw his equipment bag in the back of a BMW.

"Honestly, I never did."

At this point, I had a sense that he thought I was beating the hardship angle to death and he tried to lighten the conversation with an obvious point.

"Of course, it gets easier from here," he said. "My parents always told me, 'Remember where you came from, work hard and good things will happen.' I just try to be the same as I was as a six-year-old kid going to the rink."

Looking at these words on the page as I type them, that may seem like an empty bromide and yet, watching Crosby at 16 for a week or so, I was able to tap into that inner first-grader. After we wrapped the conversation, we wound up in the hotel's games room —really, just a Ping Pong table with ancient, cracked racquets. I wound up with match points against Crosby in Ping Pong but he roared back to take four straight rallies and win. That, though, wasn't *the* moment. Crosby stayed on the table and took on Devan Dubnyk, the backup goaltender, who turned out to be a complete shark on the Ping Pong table. Dubnyk won game after game against Crosby, who, despite one-sided loss after loss, insisted on taking another shot, as if he was going to find a way to win. He seemed sure that he was going to beat Dubnyk if he just tried harder, a self-belief that was childlike—perhaps not always ideal in the material world, but a virtue in the arena.

———

When the Canadian team arrived at the arena in Piestany before the semifinal against the US, officials were worried that the game would have to be cancelled. The heat wave was unrelenting and water was pooling in some areas on the ice—even where it was solid, it was as soft as soap. Instead of producing snow, skaters were building up slush. Players wondered if the shadows they could see on the ice were the refrigeration pipes showing through. The heat in the arena meant the game was going to be an endurance test, although in fairness, the conditions didn't favour one team over the other.

It would have seemed that the Canadians should have had a significant advantage going into the game. The teams USA Hockey had always sent to the summer under-18s were made up of players who don't enter the US National Team Development Program (NTDP), which attracts most of the elite American prospects. Instead the organization sends what is essentially the second string: teenagers who are going to play for high school teams, for prep schools and in the junior United States Hockey League. USA Hockey takes this approach to get a read on players who might be called up to play in the IIHF world under-18s the following spring. If this wasn't much of a year for the Canadian team other than Crosby, it seemed to be an even more mediocre group at the other end of the ice. As of this printing, the forwards in the US lineup have combined to play a career total of 10 NHL games, most of them having gone undrafted by NHL teams and maxing out at a season or two split between the American Hockey League and ECHL. The defence did feature a pair of players who have each played more than 800 games in the NHL: Keith Yandle, who played for a Massachusetts prep school, and Matt Niskanen, a high school player from Minnesota. And ultimately the difference maker in the game was the US goalie: Cory Schneider, another prep schooler from Massachusetts who would become a first-round pick in the 2004 draft and go on to a long, distinguished NHL career.

Meanwhile, the Canadian team was banged up. Wojtek Wolski was on crutches after the loss to the Czechs—he was diagnosed with a ligament strain in his knee. And Crosby's other winger, Evan McGrath, was on the limp with a badly bruised ankle, having taken a shot flush in the side of his skate. Both Wolski and McGrath played, but they were far less than 100 percent. By game's end the entire team would be less than 100 percent, though. An annoyance that might have been a portent of issues down the line: the water in the bottles on the Canadians' bench was carbonated, more like club soda than sparkling water. After just a couple of sips, the players were burping. The trainers couldn't rustle up any flat water or energy drinks. Crosby told me later he didn't have a sip of water the entire game—not advisable in normal conditions, but potentially dangerous for a forward who would log more than 25 minutes. And especially not advisable in an arena where one thermometer in a hallway at ice level registered the temperature at 24 degrees Celsius.

The game couldn't have started worse for the Canadians. They were called for penalties on the first two shifts of the game, on what were marginal calls at best. While they managed to kill off a long five-on-three power play, any expectation of a romp was put on hold. Like the Swiss and the Czechs, the Americans didn't let Crosby draw a breath without a slash or an elbow—I even put down "whiplash-inducing elbow" in my notes, which said something about the Americans' intent and something about my note-taking, I guess. Late in the first, though, Crosby set up a pair of power-play goals, the first a slapshot from the point by defence-man Cam Barker, and then an Alex Bourret tap-in of a rebound in a goalmouth scramble. Up 2–0 going into the dressing room for the first intermission, the Canadians could feel pretty confident about their chances of advancing to the final.

Just 20 seconds into the second period, however, the Americans scored on a harmless-looking shot that handcuffed Canadian goaltender Julien Ellis-Plante and the game turned 180 degrees. They threw 15 more shots at Ellis-Plante over the next 19 minutes and scored twice more. By the end of the second period, Ellis-Plante was sopping wet and only half of it was sweat—every time he went down, it was with more of a splash than a thud. Conditions were deteriorating so rapidly that pucks that might have gone for icing got stuck in puddles in the faceoff circles. In between periods, Canadian officials went to the tournament organizers and pressed them about the ice conditions and at what point they might be considered unplayable.

In the third period, Canadian coach Bob Lowes threw Crosby out every other shift, looking for a tying goal, and the Americans dialed up the physical assault on him. A couple of times Luke Lucyk, a defenceman with four inches and more than 30 pounds on Crosby, stretched out Canada's best hope. Once, Lucyk landed on top of Crosby, who was contorted awkwardly as if he were locked into a submission hold. On the bench the Canadian coaches were worried that he might be seriously hurt, at least until they could hear him yelling at the refs, looking for a call. It seemed like Crosby's desperation grew with every passing shift—it evoked his pressing Devan Dubnyk for another game on the Ping Pong table, and I thought it might wind up being no less futile. But then, with less than three minutes left, Crosby set up Mike Blunden for the game-tying goal. Canada and the US were headed for a

10-minute overtime period and a shootout if necessary. As it turned out, things wouldn't get that far.

Five minutes into the overtime period, with everyone in the building seemingly aware of Crosby's location on the ice, he managed to get behind the US defence for a clean breakaway, more than three strides behind the Americans scrambling to get back. Crosby tried to deke Cory Schneider but the American goaltender made a sprawling save. Crosby was so far ahead in the clear that he had time to take the rebound behind the net and try a wraparound. This time Schneider dove across the net, just as his defence arrived on the scene. Just 20 seconds later, Luke Lucyk threw a harmless-looking shot on the Canadian net and Julien Ellis-Plante just waved at it. The US advanced to the final, where they would narrowly beat the Russians to claim an unlikely gold medal. Canada was relegated to the bronze-medal game, where they rolled over and played dead, losing to the Czechs 8–2. But really, Crosby's first tournament wearing the Canadian maple leaf ended with that overtime in Piestany, just seconds after he had all but won the game and then, skating furiously back, watched helplessly as the red light went on behind Ellis-Plante.

What I remember most vividly about that tournament wasn't any single play on the ice, but the scene after that loss to the Americans. Parched and downcast, Crosby and his teammates left the rink, boarded the bus in a terrible silence and headed into downtown Piestany for a postgame meal in a smoke-filled restaurant that doubled as a jazz club. Billie Holliday, Miles Davis and Duke Ellington gazed out at them from posters lining the walls. At the end of a cover of John Coltrane's "Nocturne," the bandleader, a saxophone player, switched from Slovak to English. "We would like to welcome the Canadian team," he said. "We know you do not feel good tonight but you will be champions someday."

They were the most encouraging words they'd hear all night. Crosby hung his head and didn't look up when a chicken-and-rice dinner was dropped in front of him. He hated losing more than anyone—that was a point of pride bordering on pathology for him. And thus this exquisite pain: in the biggest game of his life up to this point, he had come up an inch short.

The bus ride and border crossing took a couple of hours. Before the players disembarked, Scott Salmond, the team's manager, stood in the aisle at the front of the bus and announced the schedule for the tournament's last day. "I'm not going to bullshit you. Tomorrow's game will be the last chance a bunch of you have to wear a Team Canada sweater. It's up to you whether you want to play or not."

Sidney Crosby had to believe and really know in his heart that he was going to wear a maple leaf again, and yet the words seemed to sting him no less than anyone on the bus. He might have mistaken himself for the goat in the loss when he had in fact been the best and maybe only hope. He'd tell me later, "This was an embarrassment. I'll always remember this. Next time you can write that we get the gold."

CHAPTER 6

IT HAD WHAT HE NEEDED

2004

I went out to see Sidney Crosby towards the end of his first season with the Rimouski Oceanic, the team he played for the QMJHL after leaving Shattuck-St Mary's. This wasn't the first time that I had gone to the town on the south shore of the St. Lawrence with expectations of seeing a transcendent talent. Seven years before, I had driven out there to see Vincent Lecavalier. His coach, Roger Dejoie, unhesitatingly described the 17-year-old from Montreal as "the best player out of the Quebec Major Junior League since Mario Lemieux." Others said that he could be the heir to Jean Beliveau's mantle as the greatest player the province had ever produced. Even just watching him work out, it was easy to see how those names came into the mix—Lecavalier was a centre in their mould, six foot two, maybe a bit taller, rangy but athletic. He also had a great hockey sense—in his NHL draft year he took full command of QMJHL games. He didn't just *hope* to make the NHL; he fully understood that he was just a year away from being the No. 1 pick in the entry draft. And he didn't mind in the least the comparisons to Beliveau; he even chose to wear the Hall of Famer's number—No. 4—on his sweater.

Lecavalier's pre-Rimouski story had read somewhat like Crosby's: playing up, excelling against older kids, running out of places to play, looking for a hockey challenge that also offered quality academics, keeping his options open to play NCAA hockey. In Lecavalier's case, going to a US college would mean following the lead of his older brother Philippe, who had played four seasons at Clarkson in upstate New York. Vincent wound up choosing one of the options the Crosby family had considered: Notre Dame in Wilcox, Saskatchewan. He put in a season there along with another 15-year-old who would wind up in Rimouski, Brad Richards. Rimouski had been a choice for the Lecavaliers—the Oceanic owned the fourth pick in the 1996 QMJHL midget draft and the family could tell the teams with the top three picks that Vincent wouldn't report if they selected him.

"I was able to attend a private school close to the Colisée, so school was okay," Lecavalier told me. "I didn't care how many people there were in Rimouski—there were more than at Wilcox." Lecavalier struck me as a 17-year-old going on 30—he had a courtesy car (yes, a Chevy Cavalier) that was on loan from a local dealership and a strong sense of where he fit in the hockey universe, very forthright in his expectation to go first overall in the 1998 NHL draft.

So by 2003 I knew not only how to get to Rimouski, but, having seen Lecavalier at the same stage, I had an idea of what to expect from a phenom when I got there. But even more than Lecavalier, Crosby had not only made it into the public eye but also built up a bit of a legend by the time I made it down to see him.

In his first exhibition game with the Oceanic he racked up eight points and earned the nickname "Darryl"—the identity of the teammate who coined it is a matter of dispute, with some pointing to Mark Tobin, a forward from Newfoundland, and others to Eric Neilson, a tough guy from Moncton who would be Crosby's billeting roommate. The name alluded to Darryl Sittler, the Toronto Maple Leafs Hall of Famer who set an NHL record with 10 points in a game in 1976. The moniker was not the first hung on him after that game—"Gretz" was the original tag, but Crosby wasn't altogether comfortable with it, especially given that Gretzky's anointment of him at age 14 had proven to be more of a curse than a blessing. "Darryl" also evoked the dim-witted brothers who shared the same name on the 1980s sitcom *Newhart*—highly ironic because almost no one in any dressing room Crosby had ever walked into was more dialed in than he was.

As impressive as that exhibition game had been, Crosby had been lights out in his first regular-season game with the Oceanic. In Rouyn-Noranda, the Huskies had a 3–0 lead over Rimouski at the end of two periods, but then Crosby took the game over with a hat trick, including the winning goal, in one seven-minute stretch. Within a couple of weeks he was the talk of the QMJHL, but as such he was a parochial interest—the league's media reach didn't extend very far west of the Quebec–Ontario border and didn't even include Montreal, whose franchise had relocated to Charlottetown, PEI, for the start of the 2003–04 season. I was in regular contact with NHL scouts whose territories included the Q and I'd regularly hear reports back—mostly that he had seamlessly picked up

where he had left off at the summer under-18s. At this early juncture he was already the odds-on favourite to be the first pick in the
2005 NHL draft.

By all accounts, the atmosphere in the arena for Crosby's first
games was more electric than it had been back in 1999–2000, when
Brad Richards led the team to championships in the Quebec
league and the Memorial Cup. Fact was, Crosby had made
Rimouski the centre of the junior hockey universe. He had made
a small buzz in the media when he led the Dartmouth Subways to
the national final, but that was 18 months before, and during his
year at Shattuck he had been almost entirely off the media's radar
—there had been occasional updates in the Halifax newspapers,
and a short video had shown up on the CBC, but even that had
presented Crosby more as a fish out of water, not a phenom so
much as a kid who had to leave the Maritimes to pursue a hockey
dream. But in Crosby's first couple of months with the Oceanic,
the world was coming to Rimouski.

Although the Oceanic had basically stayed close to home,
Crosby was already a story in the national and even international
media. Two months into his junior career, Crosby was already the
subject of a short feature in *Sports Illustrated*: the magazine's
Montreal-based correspondent, Michael Farber, had come down
the St. Lawrence to interview Crosby. In describing his hockey
genius, Farber dropped a reference to Mozart into the lead. If
Crosby had been uncomfortable with "Gretz" as a nickname, he'd
have to have been happy that "Amadeus" never stuck. Canadian
media outlets followed *SI*'s lead, although somehow the reporter
for the *Globe and Mail* referred to Taylor Crosby as Sidney's
brother. The *Hockey News* even named him as one of the 100 most
powerful people in the sport, slotting the 16-year-old in at No. 98.

On the eve of the selection of the Canadian roster for the world junior championship, by which time he had barely played three months of major junior hockey, Crosby managed to unwittingly kick hockey's most famous hornet's nest, becoming a target of *Hockey Night in Canada* commentator Don Cherry's scorn. In what was a routine game against the Quebec Remparts at the Colisée in Rimouski, the Oceanic had a 4–0 lead in the third period when Crosby found himself behind the visitors' net. With defenders cautiously choosing not to chase him, preferring to mark his linemates in front of the net, Crosby scooped the puck up on his stick and did a wraparound move, straight out of box lacrosse, to make the score 5–0. The Oceanic won 7–1 and Crosby wound up with two goals, four assists and a brutal lesson about the media industry. In the video of the play, the home crowd exploded. And on his nationally syndicated radio show, Don Cherry did the same. "This is a hot dog move, and the Quebec Remparts are going to remember that the next time they play," said Cherry, the self-styled conscience of old-school hockey values who had made a fortune selling videos of hockey fights. "He's gonna get hurt. They're gonna grab the mustard and put it all over him."

The tempest stretched over the course of a week—Cherry himself was criticized by many for beating up on a 16-year-old, but true to form, the commentator refused to walk it back. "People reacted like I said something about the pope," he said. "I want to warn the kid [about] what can happen." Cherry then lobbed a couple of bombs at the QMJHL, calling the league soft and suggesting the players were "floaters" who might let Crosby get away without deserved retribution. Sidney wasn't about to give the hornet's nest another hoof, but Troy Crosby called Cherry's comments "ignorant," and agent Pat Brisson also mounted a spirited defence.

Still, as always, the message that is heard most is that of the guy who holds the megaphone.

Hockey Canada did select Crosby to be the youngest member of the under-20 team that went to the world juniors in Helsinki; although he became the youngest Canadian player to score a goal in the tournament, Crosby only played a supporting role on a team that, after a dominating performance in the preliminary round and semifinals, squandered a two-goal lead in the third period of the gold-medal game, losing to Team USA. As it had done with the likes of Jay Bouwmeester and Jason Spezza, the coaches selected Crosby with the idea of prepping him for world junior championships down the line; thus, the hyped Crosby, while his name was becoming increasingly better known, remained a bit of a hockey mystery. Hockey fans could track Crosby's numbers and Rimouski's results, but because the Oceanic's games were neither broadcast nor streamed online, his games were seen only by those in Rimouski or in Quebec league outposts like Baie-Comeau and Victoriaville.

I finally made it down to Rimouski for the playoffs that season, seven months after I had watched Crosby at the summer under-18s in Breclav and Piestany. Crosby had run away with the league scoring race, with 135 points in 59 games, and his winger Dany Roussin was the only other player in the league to record more than 100 points. Crosby had also swept all the major trophies, but still his team's season was a bit of a mixed bag—despite winning their division, they finished just six games over .500. Earning a bye into the quarter-finals, the Oceanic were matched up against the Shawinigan Cataractes, who had finished 12 points ahead of them in the regular-season standings. Because of their division title,

Crosby's team had home-ice advantage in the series, but that wasn't much of a plus because the Cataractes had won the last two games they played in Rimouski.

Game 1 wasn't anything resembling a personal showcase for Crosby—there'd be no lacrosse-style wraparound goals. And it would be easy to collect evidence from this game that the QMJHL's style of play was, despite Don Cherry's claims, anything but soft. Crosby was consistently chased, jabbed, slashed and, when the opportunity presented itself, run and pounded. Crosby picked up an assist on a power-play goal in the second period and the Oceanic held a 3–1 lead until late in the third, but the Cataractes got a late goal to close within one, and then pulled their goalie to press for the tie. Crosby stepped in front of a slapshot from the point and collected the puck for a 160-foot empty-net goal, after which he celebrated, although muted by a limp.

I had arranged with the team to meet with Crosby after practice the next day and arrived at the Colisée early. The scene was a Canadian pastoral, a suitably bucolic setting within a hockey context. The Zamboni had just finished flooding the ice and when the gate was shut behind it, the arena fell silent. A couple dozen people, mostly retirees, wandered in through the main entrance and took places along the glass behind the net with their coffees and waited for the team to come onto the ice for practice. They could hear some chatter in the hallways, players and arena staff talking. Finally, Crosby opened the gate, stepped onto the ice and dumped out a bucket of pucks. His teammates and the coaches were still getting dressed and laced up, so Crosby was on the ice alone for a good 10 minutes. He went through a stickhandling drill, his hands a blur, the sound of his stick on the ice echoing around the arena. He was at once laser-focused on the geometry of the puck's track and lost in the exercise—how many thousands of times had he done this, hard-wiring his hand-eye coordination? Those on the other side of the glass talked among themselves and only occasionally glanced at Crosby—it evoked those occasions when a master classical musician busks in the subway and the passers-by are unaware of the genius in their midst.

The players and coaches came onto the ice in an uneven procession and the dull routine of practice—warm-ups, stretches and line rushes—followed for an hour. As the time passed, the work became a little more specialized—the power-play unit breaking away to work at one end of the ice, the goalies getting a little extra attention at the other. The head coach, Donald Dufresne, left first, followed one by one by his assistants and the players, until Crosby was again alone on the ice. It wasn't quite 10 minutes this time before the arena workers opened the end gate and put the key in the ignition of the Zamboni, getting ready to flood the ice for the figure-skating practice that was scheduled next. At that point, Crosby got the bucket, took off one glove, stooped and gathered the pucks, the housekeeping chore that falls to rookies—a rule from which Darryl was not exempted and which he even seemed to embrace. First on, last off.

I waited for Crosby in the players' lounge, a room that had been converted into a makeshift bar for season-ticket holders during games. Labelling it a lounge probably doesn't fully capture how humble the surroundings were—dominated by a Ping Pong table and beat-up couches. Maybe "common room" is a better fit. There was certainly nothing to suggest that something along the lines of hockey history was unfolding here—beyond a nod here and there to the Memorial Cup championship of '99, the walls were most prominently lined with black-and-white photos of local teams from the first couple of decades of the past century, a surprising number of the players and local sponsors being Anglo and Irish in a district that had been represented in Parliament for a decade by a member of the Bloc Québécois. Crosby seemed to be immune to the politics of party or language. "English-speaking guys have excelled in the league," Crosby told me. "Pat LaFontaine is one. My dad played against him. He said [LaFontaine] was really liked. My father told me it doesn't matter what language you speak. The way you handle yourself and the way you play is the way you get respect."

For this reason the criticisms from Don Cherry had to bother him more than he could say at the time. "I know the unwritten rules," he said. "My father taught me all about respect in the game. I didn't try to embarrass anybody. A reporter in Quebec even went to the Remparts goalie and asked him if the goal [embarrassed him]. He said it didn't—that I was just trying to put the puck in the net."

Crosby struck me as being as self-possessed as Vincent Lecavalier had been, equally aware that this was a stopover on his way to the NHL; in contrast to Lecavalier, however, the game wasn't just business to Crosby. He wouldn't just get the work done in Rimouski, but would make the best of it. Brad Richards had suggested to me that an Anglo player could feel a little stranded in the early going in Rimouski, but Crosby had no complaint—he said the town was "perfect . . . not huge, but it's got what you need." He admitted that he sometimes felt a bit "stuck" at his billet home. He killed time watching movies with Neilson—they had seen just about every action movie stocked by the local video store. They watched vintage VHS tapes of hockey from the '80s. "Watching classic games, it's unbelievable how much fun was in the game," he says. "It's down and back, end to end. Basically they were letting players play. There weren't a lot of systems. The odd team might trap, but the only reason a team did that was that it was less skilled. Now Detroit, with so much talent, plays the trap. You wonder what would happen if one team stepped up and said, 'Let's play hockey.' But you'd really need 20 teams to do it."

Unlike Lecavalier, Crosby didn't have a courtesy car. Without a driver's licence or a car, Crosby depended on his 19-year-old roommate Neilson for protection on the ice and safe delivery around town. The 98th most powerful person in the game was being chauffeured around in a rusted Mazda as old as he was.

Culture and language aside, Crosby had landed in a pretty reasonable facsimile of his situation at Shattuck. He was able to work on his game with minimal distraction and was able to build friendships with kids who, if they were on very different career paths, at least understood his. He wasn't living the life of an average kid by any means, but I imagine it was a lot closer to average than, say, that of the young Eric Lindros or a tennis prodigy. He wasn't sheltered so much as isolated, but nonethless was fairly well protected from adverse influences.

Crosby's performance in Game 2 against Shawinigan was much more indicative of a phenom and perhaps evoked the style of game he screened in those videos from the high-scoring '80s, the highlights provided by Gretzky and associates. Whether it was nerves or the Cataractes getting tired of chasing him, Crosby shone. Every time he stepped on the ice he did something that made you sit up and take notice. One shift, it was owning defenders on the cycle. The next found him showing a preternatural awareness of a teammate on the ice. The breaking moment for Shawinigan came late in the second period, with Rimouski up 4–0, Crosby having scored two goals. It looked like the Cataractes might rally when an Oceanic penalty killer was whistled for slashing, setting up a five-on-three Shawinigan power play. Dufresne sent Crosby out to take the draw in the Rimouski end.

The Cataractes controlled the puck on the faceoff and Crosby kept his position at the top of the triangle, going side to side as the shooters back on the point tried to strand him and open up a clear lane for a shot from the blue line. But when one Shawinigan defenceman got too cute with a pass, Crosby pounced on the puck and had a clean breakaway. Five thousand fans rose to their feet and Crosby deked the goaltender for the rarest goal in hockey: short-handed, five on three. Crosby spun and glided into the corner with his stick and hands raised, ready to accept congratulations from his teammates . . . only to realize that the nearest one was more than 100 feet away. Crosby would later tell me that of all the hundreds of goals he had scored going back to childhood, he couldn't remember ever scoring one on a five-on-three penalty kill.

I looked for Troy Crosby to gauge his reaction. He was in a seat at centre ice. He didn't clap. He didn't smile. This was just the stuff his son could do. "The Quebec league is really a 19-year-old league," Dufresne would say later. "It's not that a 16-year-old shouldn't be scoring while killing a five-on-three. But Sidney brings skills and speed to the game that I've never seen in a 16-year-old."

The Oceanic would wind up sweeping Shawinigan and then losing to a veteran Moncton team in five games in the next round. Crosby's playoff numbers (seven goals and nine assists in nine games) only hinted at what he would do down the line.

———

I've watched a lot of hockey but would never consider myself a professional evaluator of talent. That said, after watching Sidney Crosby at 16 in the playoffs in Rimouski back in the spring of 2004, I would have bet both my kidneys that he would be ready to step directly into the NHL as an 18-year-old. It seemed he had little to prove and nothing to learn by playing with teenagers. When I watched him in that first season in Rimouski, I had to wonder if J. P. Parise had been speaking the literal truth when he suggested that Crosby could have played in the NHL when he was in Grade 10.

Though he played in the QMJHL, the little brother of Canada's three major junior leagues, Crosby owned the Canadian Hockey League awards simply by the weight of his numbers and testimonials. *Gretzky can't be wrong.* Crosby became the first 16-year-old ever to win the CHL rookie of the year and player of the year awards. (When Gretzky as a 16-year-old scored 70 goals and 112 assists in 64 games with the Sault Ste. Marie Greyhounds of the Ontario Hockey League back in '77–78, he won the Ontario league's rookie of the year, but its player of the year trophy went to Bobby Smith of the Ottawa 67's, who set scoring records that still stand.)

What I didn't know, what those on the Oceanic staff couldn't have suspected, and what NHL scouts never saw coming was what Sidney Crosby's next season would look like. Anyone could have made projections about the numbers Crosby could post. Likewise, anyone could have made optimistic predictions about the Oceanic's season or how the Canadian team might fare at the 2005 world junior tournament, with Crosby back for a second try and doubtlessly in a more significant role.

All of this was subtext, however. What awaited him was bigger than that. As clearly as he saw his future unfolding, he could not have foreseen the fact that he was about to become the most famous 17-year-old in hockey history. It was a tribute to his talent and a function of the proliferation of media. It was a by-product of circumstances unique and beyond his control.

As great as Orr, Lafleur, Lemieux or Lindros were as juniors, no matter what glories they and their teams went on to, they had to share the spotlight with the NHL—even those who went on to play for or win the Memorial Cup. In Orr's last junior season, when his Oshawa Generals lost the Memorial Cup final to the Edmonton Oil Kings, the Montreal Canadiens led by Jean Beliveau won the Cup. When Lemieux was taking Laval to the Memorial Cup in '84, Wayne Gretzky was leading the Oilers to their first Stanley Cup. Gretzky was a bit of an outlier, having signed to play in the World Hockey Association at 17, but his games in Indianapolis and later Edmonton were completely off the radar while the Canadiens were winning their fourth consecutive Stanley Cup. When they were teenagers, these future legends always had to compete for the fans' attention with the pros. And in those days, most of their games in junior went unseen—you had to be a deeply invested fan to track their progress in those last seasons before they jumped to the NHL.

In this sense, Crosby was about to become the true outlier: at 17 he would be playing in the brightest spotlight. Heading into the 2004–05 season, the NHL had made major junior hockey the highest level of the game in North America.

Alexander Ovechkin donned a Washington Capitals sweater on the stage at the 2004 NHL Entry Draft in Raleigh, North Carolina, but none of the executives in the arena expected that the Russian sniper would make his NHL debut that October, or even in that calendar year. When the Capitals selected him with the first-overall pick, they knew he'd be playing for Moscow Dynamo in the fall. Likewise, the holders of the No. 2 pick, the Pittsburgh Penguins, expected Evgeni Malkin to skate with Metallurg Magnitogorsk. Every NHL executive was resigned to the fact that his arena would remain dark in October, and for as long as league commissioner Gary Bettman and NHLPA director Bob Goodenow remained at an impasse in negotiations for a collective agreement.

Professional hockey wouldn't be shut down completely. Some of the NHL's biggest names would be on the ice, but they would be among the hundreds who bolted North America for teams in Europe. Younger pros not yet established in the NHL headed to the American Hockey League for an extended apprenticeship. Older NHLers were looking at losing one of the last of their income-earning years, and a bunch of future Hockey Hall of Famers — Mark Messier, Peter Forsberg, Al MacInnis and Brett Hull — missed out on farewell tours. With the NHL shut down indefinitely, major junior hockey was quite definitely as good as hockey got in Canada. And the game that Crosby played would be the best of what was on offer, its beating heart.

Fans despaired as days turned to weeks and then months with no progress towards a collective agreement. In the lockout's darkest hours, experts and fans speculated that the NHL might not even be open for business in the fall of 2006, when you'd have presumed that Crosby would be heading to his first NHL training camp. All but the pathologically pessimistic tried to put thoughts like that out of their minds and focus on what remained in the game — in particular this phenom who swept up all the junior awards in sight. For those who had a crisis of faith in the game, here was a reason to believe.

The professional vacuum gave rise to an extended silly season. Whenever a labour dispute in sports even looms, inevitably there's a spike in crackpot stories. The media actually gave some time to a couple of promoters who talked up their intention to start up a new professional league as a rival and substitute to the dormant NHL: the World Hockey Association—why bother with an original name? They recruited Bobby Hull as a celebrity endorser. And, of course, they said they'd be open to having Sidney Crosby sign on, even offering him $7.5 million for a three-year commitment, with $2 million up front—his to keep whether the league ever got off the ground or not. Wisely, Crosby regarded the WHA as radio-active. "He has made up his mind right now about where he wants to play," Troy Crosby told reporters. "He wants to stick by his plan to play another year in Rimouski. He's 17 and he is not playing for the money right now. He feels playing junior is the best way to continue to develop."

This sideshow mattered not. In the season when he would be the most famous 17-year-old in hockey history, he'd also have one of the greatest seasons at this level of the game.

Crosby attended the world junior camp in Calgary in August, rather than playing in the summer under-18s for a second time as he would have been eligible to do, and he did arrive in Rimouski in late August for training camp. That fall, the pro hockey season launched as if the NHL and the players' association would find a way to save their 2004–05 campaign. Together they staged the

World Cup of Hockey, eight years after the first one, with Canada winning and Vincent Lecavalier adding the tournament's most valuable player honours to the Stanley Cup ring he earned in June. But it was just so much whistling in the dark. On September 16, less than 48 hours after Canada edged Finland 3–2 in the World Cup final, the NHL announced it would lock out the players, as it had done in the fall of 1994.

As in previous rounds of collective bargaining, the owners were pursuing a salary cap. This time, though, Gary Bettman was prepared, even empowered, by the owners to go to the wall, not only to get a cap on payrolls, but to break the players' association —a bit of cold revenge for management's perceived loss to the help 10 years prior. News of the lockout dominated sports pages—and even the front pages—in newspapers' September 17 editions. You would have had to look very hard to find, buried in the agate type, scores from the QMJHL's opening night.

Two nights later, on the first Saturday night of the season, Crosby and the Oceanic won their season opener, after travelling more than 1,100 kilometres to face their farthest-flung opponent. In front of a crowd of 2,302 at the Dave Keon Arena in Rouyn-Noranda, Crosby scored a shorthanded goal and picked up a pair of assists in the 6–3 win, a raucous, bad-tempered affair in which 90 minutes in penalties were handed out. The next afternoon Crosby would add a goal and four assists at the Palais du Sport in Val-d'Or in front of 2,001 paying fans. These were the only games in their respective towns, but with the nearest NHL rinks—in Ottawa and Montreal—dark, they were the only games anywhere, or at least in the area code.

———

Sidney Crosby's second junior season got off to an electric start—
four goals and 18 assists in his first seven games—but in a game
in Rimouski against Halifax, he and the Oceanic had a big scare:
a collision with Frederik Cabana, a teammate at the summer
under-18s the year before. Midway through a fight-filled first
period, Crosby took a knee-on-knee hit, one that he thought was
a blatant attempt to injure. So did the referee, who gave Cabana
a five-minute major for kneeing and a game misconduct. Cabana
skated off the ice, but not before Rimouski defenceman Patrick
Coulombe chased him down and filled him in. Crosby returned
to the game in the second period and played through the pain,
picking up a couple of assists. The knee swelled up after the game,
though. Doctors determined that he hadn't torn a ligament; he had
just suffered a bone bruise. Crosby would be off skates for 10 days
and out of the lineup for two weeks. Rimouski lost the game to
Halifax 4–2, but by fractions of an inch avoided losing a lot more.

Fred Cabana would tell me years later that the collision was
just accidental. "People were so angry that I couldn't leave my billets' house," he said. "The media were out on their lawn, waiting for
me." As if it could get worse, Cabana's billets lived in Cole Harbour.

The QMJHL interviewed Cabana, reviewed the tape and had
him submit a written statement. He pleaded his innocence, but the
league was not convinced and handed him an eight-game suspension. The Halifax media jumped to Cabana's defence and made the
case that Crosby enjoyed special status with the QMJHL officials.

Hockey fans would remember how the Oceanic's season finished, but only those in Rimouski or around the QMJHL would
remember much other than the Cabana incident in the first three
months of what was, to that point, an unremarkable season, at least
from a team standpoint. Crosby was leading the league in scoring

when he shipped out to join the world junior team, but the Oceanic's record stood at .500 and they had a few brutal nights along the way—a 10–2 loss to Lewiston at home in late October was probably the low point. The team looked like it would creep into the playoffs but do little in the postseason. Not exactly the parade to the NHL draft that you'd script for the generational talent—although the draft itself was somewhere between a hypothetical and a chimera at that point.

When Crosby returned from the under-20 tournament, the Oceanic had an entirely different look. In fact, they would lose just one game and tie another through the month of May. Doris Labonte relieved Donald Dufresne of his duties as head coach, and made him the assistant who handled the Oceanic's blueliners. Then Labonte traded for defenceman Mario Scalzo Jr., an overager with Victoriaville. With these two moves, Rimouski took flight.

"I was shocked when the trade was made, but really happy because I was hoping to get seen by scouts," Scalzo says. "It was a little strange coming into the room for the first time because I was always matched up against Sidney and we went at each other pretty hard. We just sort of looked at each other, but then we smiled . . . whatever went on before, no problem. We ended up becoming roommates on the road that season and good friends. And it was amazing how it worked out. Doris never said to me that he wanted me to do this or that. He just put me with the guys and said, 'We'll keep the five of you together.'"

"The guys" Scalzo mentions were four of his new teammates: defenceman Patrick Coulombe and the forward line of Dany Roussin, Marc-Antoine Pouliot and Crosby. They were the minutes-eating first line. They were the first power-play unit, and fairly often they stayed out for all two minutes of a minor penalty. In their first month together the Oceanic cashed in 45 percent of their opportunities with the man advantage. The team went 9–0–1, outscoring opponents 61–21. The team surged in the standings and it should have been all good news for the Oceanic, yet Crosby was getting carved in the media.

In the middle of that run in January, Crosby advised the powers that be that he wasn't going to the CHL's Top Prospects Game in Vancouver. The league had announced its list of invitees before the world junior tournament, and Crosby was at the top of the list, the main attraction and the selling point for the event. When he let the CHL know that he was begging off, he cited a back injury that he had suffered at the world juniors and had played through with the Oceanic.

Even if Crosby had been 100 percent, a trip to the Top Prospects Game seemed like a ridiculous ask. It had already been a long season—he had gone from the summer camp for the under-20 team to training camp and the regular season with Rimouski, and then to Winnipeg for the training camp ahead of the world juniors and on to Grand Forks, North Dakota, for the tournament. When Crosby came back to Rimouski after the tournament, his schedule didn't ease. The Top Prospects Game fell on a Wednesday, and on the weekend before the Oceanic were scheduled to play in Charlottetown on a Friday night, Halifax on Saturday night and Moncton on Sunday afternoon. (Crosby's back was troublesome enough that he ended up sitting out the first game.) The team would have arrived back in Rimouski in the a.m. on Monday and Crosby would have had to fly out that day—a small plane from Rimouski to Quebec or Montreal, and then another six hours to

Vancouver—to make it in time for practice and publicity appearances on Tuesday and the game on Wednesday. On Thursday, he would fly back east and be on the ground not a full 24 hours before an Oceanic game Friday night. No one should have begrudged Crosby bowing out of a game that meant nothing in the standings, that really wouldn't benefit him in anyway.

His teammates appreciated Crosby's decision. "Obviously, he was putting our team ahead of personal stuff by not going [to Vancouver]," Scalzo says. "It meant a lot to us. Sid was 17 but he has always known what's the right thing to do . . . the message that should get sent."

Yet Crosby received anything but a sympathetic reading from many outside the Oceanic's organization. Ron Toigo, the owner of the Vancouver Giants, the hosts of the game, lit into him. "For the guy who wants to be the next Wayne Gretzky . . . the history of Wayne Gretzky is that he would be here with one leg if that's what it took because it's good for the game," Toigo said, seemingly oblivious to the fact that no one tried harder than Crosby to tamp down any comparisons to Gretzky.

Don Cherry, one of the coaches in the Top Prospects Game, spared Crosby criticism in Vancouver, saying that he wanted to focus attention on the players who were in the lineup for the showcase. But when Crosby played for the Oceanic in two games the following weekend, the gloves came off. "Crosby said he was very tired, very fatigued and that he had a bad back," Cherry said on his syndicated radio show. "The thing that really gets me is [that in] the two games just before that, he had eight points in two games. It's beyond me how a guy could have a bad back and do that. I'm giving him the benefit of the doubt. I'm not knocking him, so now, he plays the next game for Rimouski a day and a half after the game, right? I see him knock down a defenceman, get the puck, put it in the top corner, I see him get a breakaway and take the guy and put another puck in. So much for a bad back and fatigue."

Crosby didn't return fire, but his agent did. Pat Brisson called the CHL's association with Cherry "a disgrace" and didn't stop there. "As far as Don Cherry is concerned . . . he's more an entertainer and a clown than someone whose opinion I would respect."

A couple of weeks later I asked Crosby about his back and the fallout from the CHL Top Prospects Game. He and his teammates were checking in at the Colisée Pepsi in Quebec City for a game against the Remparts. Crosby wasn't going to second-guess himself. "Just what we were doing on the ice would have been tough, but when you bring in the travel it just made it that much harder," he told me. "It's only in the last few weeks that I feel comfortable and rested again."

Crosby was standing in the eye of a media vortex. Hundreds of 12-year-olds in town for the Quebec peewee tournament were lined up to get their sweaters and hockey sticks autographed. That night more than 13,000 would fill the stands at the Colisée, the former home of the Nordiques before that franchise relocated to Denver in 1995. A decade later, this Oceanic game approximated the excitement of the former NHL team's glory days. RDS, the French-language sports television network, broadcast the game. Reporters from Montreal and beyond had made the trip. Doris Labonte didn't try to isolate Crosby or have him sneak into the arena undercover. "He is our star, our Mick Jagger," Labonte said. "This is just how it is and how it's going to be."

The game was also a window into what the future would hold for Crosby. The Remparts did their best to hook and hold Crosby, to rough him up at every turn, and their best was close but not enough for two points. Despite the adolescent shrieking that erupted every time Crosby stepped on the ice, he registered only a single assist, on an opening goal by Pouliot, in Rimouski's 2–1 win. He did draw five minor penalties and put his team on the power play, but Maxime Joyal turned aside 30 of the Oceanic's 32 shots.

The Remparts were trying to find a goal to tie up the game, but within a couple of minutes the action on the ice was thrown into eclipse. A buzz went down press row late in the game: RDS reporters were trying to confirm a rumour that the NHL and the players' association had reached a tentative agreement that included the implementation of a salary cap. The preliminary sense was that the only remaining stumbling block was a dollar figure for the cap. Print reporters were off to the races as well, chasing down sources around the NHL. The rumour turned out to be nothing more than speculation, but after the horn sounded the assembled media had to break the "news" to the one person most likely to be affected by the NHL rebooting: namely, the presumptive No. 1 pick in the draft.

The media descended on the Oceanic dressing room after the game. Crosby handled interviews in English and French—in the 18 months since he arrived in Rimouski, he had acquired enough of the latter to soldier on through interviews, and his status as a player was such that no one was about to question his pronunciation. Reporters didn't ask him about the game, which by now was old news. "Relieved," Crosby said when asked how he'd feel about a settlement in the NHL talks if—*if*—true. Reporters also quizzed him about the possibility of the talks falling through and, in the worst-case scenario, the lockout carrying on into the start of next season. "I'm not thinking about [the NHL] at all right now," he said. "I'm honestly not. I'm concentrating on playing for this team and playing for a championship."

The rumour turned out to be nothing more than a death gasp. Hours later, Gary Bettman announced the cancellation of the NHL season.

February 16, 2005, was a day of mourning in hockey, and maybe something more than that in Canada. Coverage of the cancellation of the NHL season was elegiac in tone. The *Globe and Mail*'s Roy MacGregor wrote, "The NHL game may have been killed yesterday, but the national game is as alive as ever, perhaps even more so this winter as fans have turned to the games at hand rather than the games at the end of the remote control." MacGregor went on to talk about pond hockey and road hockey and the game in the community arenas. The loss of an NHL season, he reckoned, didn't matter a whit to the game you found there. It did, however, push junior hockey into the news cycle like never been before.

Halifax, May 2005

Back in 2002, the QMJHL had denied Crosby an opportunity to play with the Halifax Mooseheads as an underage player before he went to Shattuck, a decision that denied him the chance to play on a regular basis in front of friends and family. Across two seasons, he had single-handedly drawn unprecedented attention to the league, so it seemed he deserved some sort of send-off, a make-good. In the NHL, that might have taken the form of a farewell tour—a player announcing his intention to retire a few months down the line at the end of the season, and then a long goodbye. In junior, though, there's an inevitability that comes with the clock ticking down to the end of a player's eligibility. In Crosby's case, he had two years of junior eligibility remaining, but it was fairly clear he would not be back in the fall of 2005 to play in the league as an 18-year-old (assuming the NHL went back to work). For once, the fates and the schedule accommodated: in his last games in the Quebec league he was going to skate close to home and hear cheers from familiar voices. At 14 he'd had to go away to pursue his hockey dreams. At 17 he was going to get to play Games 3 and 4 of the QMJHL final against the Mooseheads. It couldn't have been better scripted. As his coach with the Dartmouth Subways, Brad Crossley, told me, "Halifax had to get one last look at Sidney before he went off to bigger things. But I'm pretty sure that it's our last look at him as a player, not his last look at this city. He'll always come back."

Because of Rimouski's slow start in the fall, the Oceanic had been chasing the Mooseheads in the QMJHL standings for most of the winter, finally catching—and overtaking—them as the regular season wound down. Both teams had smoked their opponents in the playoffs, each losing just one game in advancing to the final. Though they had split their four head-to-head games during the regular season, Rimouski had to stand as the heavy favourite to win the series. For Crosby, any hard feelings about the Cabana incident had been put to rest—so too the run-ins and trip to court with the Cole Harbour Hockey Association. Crosby had played a leading role in Canada's first under-20 title since 1997 and he was on his way to repeating as the CHL's player of the year. Halifax could bask in the glow that reflected off the brightest star in a game gone dark, and the fact that the city had hockey when none of the NHL markets did.

As much as he had excelled at stages along the way, from lighting it up at Shattuck to carrying Canada's best '86s on his back at the summer under-18s, he played his best hockey yet in the QMJHL playoffs, as if seeking closure befitting his time. Tom Ward talked about Crosby sensing that life was going to be different after Shattuck-St. Mary's; it was also like that as his time wound down with Rimouski. After the Oceanic lost Game 4 of the semifinal series against Chicoutimi—given his time at the world junior tournament, Crosby's first loss since the first week of December—he came back to score four goals in a 5–1 series clincher. One veteran scout, probably the least inclined to hyperbole of those I know, told me, "I haven't seen anyone in junior play at this level." At home for the first two games of the QMJHL final, Rimouski coasted past the Mooseheads—after Game 2, Crosby was named second star with the *premier étoile* being given to defenceman Patrick Coulombe, who grew up in nearby Saint-Fabien.

I made it out to Halifax for Games 3 and 4, and if the volume of the booing was to be trusted, the majority of the fans in the arena regarded him not as a local hero so much as the opponents' captain. They hadn't forgotten the incident with Fred Cabana and it went beyond the standard booing when the teams came out for the warm-up or when the lineups were announced. One fan brought out a giant inflatable baby pacifier.

At the games I wound up sitting with Rick Bowness, a former head coach of four NHL teams and these days an assistant in Tampa Bay. He raved about Crosby and, as a Moncton native, took some measure of pride in Crosby as a product of the Maritimes. "It's the mistake that people make about Sidney," Bowness said. "They think that he's small. He's not. He was shorter, but now he's around five foot eleven, big enough. But when you see him during the summer, walking around in shorts, his legs are huge. He has glutes like Ray Bourque had. People who don't know about him would wonder if he'd be able to stand up to the punishment. But he'll be dealing out punishment, not taking it. If he were any taller, he'd be the most [physically] dangerous player in hockey."

Crosby was dangerous in these games, though mostly with the puck and a threat to break ankles only with his change of direction on the cycle. The Mooseheads put up some resistance and did what they could to neutralize Crosby and the rest of the five-man unit. He did score the opening goal but didn't show up in the scoring summary thereafter—the goal was his 31st point in 13 playoff games, putting him 11 points ahead of the field in the scoring race and good enough to secure the QMJHL's playoff MVP award. Just as Crosby had picked up his teammates so often during the regular season, in this game they came to the fore—Mark Tobin, who had been a second-round pick of Tampa Bay, wound up scoring the winning goal in Game 4, the one that sent the Oceanic to the Memorial Cup tournament. At game's end, Troy, Trina and Taylor Crosby came down onto the ice and posed for photos with Sidney. By then the boos had faded and the applause was appreciative and not grudging.

Crosby would stay on with his parents in Cole Harbour when his teammates boarded the bus after the game. The first game at the Memorial Cup was 10 days away and the team wasn't going to be on the ice for two days. Said Mario Scalzo, "You're young. You don't know just how special it is at the time. I think Sidney did more than most of us, just because he's so aware of things. There was so much that he had already done . . . and he'd have a chance to do a lot more.

"You knew that. But he understood that it was a special time. . . . This team was only going to get one shot at it and we'd never play together again. We had so much fun. We had to make the most of it. And he led the way. We knew that it meant something special for him being able to play those games in Halifax."

London, Ontario, May 2005

The Memorial Cup is by definition a national competition, one that annually attracts a media contingent that represents the whole country, albeit a small one—somewhere around a dozen scribes in an average year, a reporter or two from each of three out-of-town teams, a few based in the host city and maybe a couple more from national outlets. The interest in the 2005 tournament was on an unprecedented scale: the CHL fielded more than 300 requests for media credentials. That's effectively twice as many as turn out for the Stanley Cup final these days.

It was a perfect storm in the sports media. The usual schedule was completely disrupted—no Stanley Cup playoffs, no NHL awards, no entry draft and, too often, no news about negotiations between Gary Bettman and the players' association. With the world championships having played out in Austria and the NCAA tournament long in the rear-view mirror, the Memorial Cup had the undivided attention of the hockey media—and, effectively in Canada, the national sports media.

It was a four-team tournament, but half the field amounted to the supporting cast. No one in London was coming out to see the Western Hockey League's Kelowna Rockets, even though they were the defending champions and had a hard-hitting defence-man, Shea Weber, who had been Crosby's teammate on the Canadian under-20 team. And the Ontario league's runners-up, the Ottawa 67's, were even a less interesting attraction, a sixth seed in the OHL's Eastern Conference, barely a .500 team during the regular season. Kelowna and Ottawa would have been intriguing stories in other years, but in London they were just placeholders. This Memorial Cup was going to boil down to Crosby's Oceanic versus the host London Knights.

Ten teenagers in the Knights lineup would play in the NHL down the line. Their roster featured two first-rounders, including future Hart Trophy winner Corey Perry, Crosby's linemate from Team Canada; two second-rounders; and two more taken in the third round. London steamrolled the OHL, going 59–7–2–0 during the regular season and 16–2 during the playoffs. The Knights had been guaranteed a spot in the tournament when they were named hosts the previous year, and the showdown with Crosby seemed like a sure thing at some point in late winter when the Oceanic began to tear through the Quebec league.

In the run-up to the Memorial Cup, I wrote that the buzz around the rink reminded me of Wayne Gretzky's very brief farewell tour. In 1999 there was only one story in the game, an exercise in nostalgia, and the rest of the hockey world ceased to exist, hard-hearted cynics on press row rendered soft and wistful. In geography and in spirit, there was something about the Memorial Cup that said *hockey*. London is just down the road from the backyard where No. 99 learned the game. The 18- and 19-year-olds at the event who had already skated in NHL training camps weren't so very far removed from their peewee and bantam teams, not above playing road hockey. Crosby against this powerhouse team with a national title on the line: this was what was needed at a time when the business of hockey had thrown the game itself into eclipse. It also provided a telling glimpse of the future, even if we didn't fully appreciate it at the time.

Though Crosby had skated on the national stage a couple of

times at the world junior tournament, skepticism was the default attitude in the media. On a nationally syndicated sports talk radio show, *Globe and Mail* sportswriters Stephen Brunt and David Shoalts concurred on the point that Crosby wasn't "another Wayne Gretzky," a pronouncement they made without the benefit of seeing him perform other than at the world junior tournament. My friend Damien Cox of the *Toronto Star* wrote of Crosby's supposed generational talent, "I don't see it."

They wouldn't have to wait long to see it. Only as long as the ceremonial puck drop and national anthem.

The Memorial Cup tournament begins with a four-team round-robin. The team with the best record advances directly to a winner-take-all final on a Sunday afternoon. The two nearest runners-up face off in a semifinal game on Saturday night. The set-up provides a huge advantage to the team that emerges on top in the round-robin.

The two teams atop the CHL rankings for most of the 2004–05 season met in the tournament's first game, played on a fairly glorious Saturday afternoon. The 11,000 fans and media who crowded into the John Labatt Centre, along with hockey fans everywhere, had reason to suspect that the question of the bye into the final would be sorted out in this first game of the tournament. The Memorial Cup is nothing if not unforgiving in its urgency. No team can afford to warm up for the event—if it takes you a few shifts to find your game, your tournament could be done.

As the player with the highest sweater number on the visiting squad, Crosby was the last player to be introduced. He nervously shifted from side to side on the blue line as the mix of cheers and boos welled up.

Doubts among members of the media about Crosby started to fade away, and shock among the Knights set in within the game's first 10 seconds. On his first touch, he picked up the puck in the neutral zone and bolted down the ice on the right wing. The London defencemen thought they had a comfortable cushion, but all the video, all the coaches' caution and the word of mouth hadn't readied them—despite backpedalling furiously, they couldn't so much as put a stick on him. Crosby threw a pass on his backhand to Pouliot, who wired a shot just wide of the Knights net. It was a near miss, but still a collective gasp went up in the arena—in that one sequence he looked like a pro out for a skate with a Junior B team.

London defenceman Mike Methot opened the scoring three minutes in, but then Crosby took over the play for the rest of the first period. He tied the game at the six-minute mark with a power-play goal that rattled in off a Knight's skate. A couple of shifts later he threw a pass through five sets of skates that found Pouliot, who roofed a one-timer past London goaltender Adam Dennis for a go-ahead goal. With about five minutes left, Crosby drew a penalty and Dany Roussin scored on another power play. Rimouski needed only six shots on Dennis to run out to a 3–1 lead, with Crosby in on each of the goals. The crowd, almost entirely Knights partisans, fell silent but for nervous murmuring. London had no answer for the speed Crosby was bringing to the game. They had lost seven games all year, and now they were having their helmets handed to them. Their one consolation was that it could have been worse. In the dying seconds of the first period, it almost was.

On consecutive shifts late in the first period, the Knights were whistled for minors and the Oceanic had a five-on-three advantage for more than a minute before the intermission. "I've thought a lot about that [power play] because it was our real chance to put the game away," Mario Scalzo says 14 years after the fact. "We had the fast start that we wanted right up until then. Doris [Labonte] kept sending us out there—which was fine. We had been going towards this all year. We were used to playing a ton of minutes. It's a five-on-three—we're playing hard but we also can breathe a bit. We had to score in that situation. If it's 4–1 or 5–1, we would be in complete control of that game."

But the first unit looked a little weary from all the shifts they had logged. A couple of sloppy passes back to the blue line, a couple of saves by Dennis: London killed the penalty and skated into the dressing room able to take some solace in being down only 3–1. "When we went to the dressing room, we weren't going to break down what happened on [the five-on-three]," Scalzo says, "but we knew that a chance had got away from us."

Given second life, the Knights rallied, and if fatigue hadn't caught up to the Oceanic's lead five-man unit on the power play late in the first period, it surely played a huge role in London's comeback. So too did the hosts' huge advantage in team size, strength and depth. The game took on an entirely different feel three minutes into the second period when Dan Fritsche, a Columbus second-round draft pick who had played 19 games with the Blue Jackets the previous season, beat Cedrick Desjardins to pull the Knights within a goal.

Over the last 37 minutes of regulation time, the home team leaned on Rimouski's first line, and Crosby of course received the most attention. London coach Dale Hunter understood the challenge of shadowing a star player—in his playing days he had filled that role at the NHL level, first with the Washington Capitals and later with the Quebec Nordiques and Colorado Avalanche. He achieved a level of infamy for knocking Pierre Turgeon out of a playoff series with a vicious cheap shot while the New York Islanders star was celebrating a goal. Hunter matched his son Dylan, a centre, against Crosby on every even-strength shift, but the dirty work fell to Brandon Prust, a late-round Calgary draft pick who roughed up the Rimouski star away from the puck at every opportunity. Not one of the shots was like Dale Hunter's on Turgeon, but Prust wore Crosby down—death by a thousand elbows and slashes. Labonte lit into the ref and Crosby looked for relief, but none was coming.

Corey Perry tied the game in the third period, and by the overtime the Oceanic looked spent. Marc Methot scored his second goal of the game just before the 10-minute mark of the extra period. Given the structure of the tournament, Rimouski's chances of winning the championship took a major blow. "We knew London is going straight to the final," Mario Scalzo says. "We weren't going to get help from the other teams—they'd both have to beat London in [the Knights'] own building and that wasn't going to happen. We had to win our games, but to turn around and play this team 14 hours after the semifinals . . . we knew how good they were. It wasn't impossible but it was so much harder. Sid got up and spoke to the team after—I was a veteran, an overager, but I looked up to him. And he said we had to get back and play these guys again. He knew what had to be said. We had to get to the final and then take our chances. And we had Sid, so, you know, nothing's impossible."

Swarmed by the media after the game, Crosby did his best to hold it together. "They're everything that everyone said they were," he said of the Knights. "Our goalie really helped us tonight and really kept us in the game," Crosby said. "They had a lot of momentum coming through the second and the third (periods) and we just didn't get a lot going in those two periods."

———

Rimouski's two remaining games in the round-robin were vital, and the Oceanic's wins came by the narrowest of margins, both finishing 4–3. In each game Crosby picked up a goal and assist. Both contests, however, felt anticlimactic, and only in short stretches did the Quebec champions impress. In neither game did they trail—they jumped out to a 3–1 lead against Ottawa and carried a 4–1 advantage into the third against Kelowna, doing just enough in the third period of both games to prevail. The Oceanic certainly didn't look like the same team that had the powerful Knights on the ropes in the early going in the tournament opener; nor did Crosby look like a threat on every shift. Of course, the 67's and the Rockets gave him special attention. First, the 67's took all kinds of physical liberties with Crosby, most of them intended to get under his skin and maybe goad him into taking a retaliatory penalty, though their coach, Brian Kilrea, the only junior coach in the Hockey Hall of Fame, made light of it, claiming his team hadn't been remotely physical enough. "If there were players who hit him, then I'll have to see the replay to see who got him," Kilrea said. Kelowna tried likewise to get Crosby off his game, and the pressure weighed on him, sometimes conspicuously, when he chirped at the Rockets and slammed his stick against the glass after the ref missed a high stick. Still, Crosby managed to avoid Shea Weber's crosshairs and claimed to feel no worse for wear—the Oceanic would have Thursday and Friday night off before the Saturday night semifinal.

Kelowna, the defending champions, went back out west without a win to show for their week in London. So it was that Rimouski met Ottawa for a chance to play for the national championship and

Sidney Crosby gave everyone at the tournament a good look at his skills in full bloom. In what would be the next-to-last game of his junior career Crosby racked up a hat trick and a pair of assists. As he had against London, Crosby created a scoring chance out of nothing much on his first touch of the puck 10 seconds in, and then opened the scoring on his next shift. It was a bravura performance and Brian Kilrea, who had been a bit of a cut-up in the press conference after his team's loss to the Oceanic in the round-robin, could only rave about Crosby's performance in Rimouski's 7–4 win. "You have to give him all the credit," Kilrea said. "His line did all the scoring. There's a reason he's called the next Gretzky."

Crosby maintained that having to play the afternoon after a night game was nothing new, something he'd done a dozen times in his two seasons of junior hockey. Then again, if he had seen it before, it hadn't been against a team like London's, which was lying in wait for the Oceanic. And this take was just for public consumption. Said Mario Scalzo Jr., "It was just too much to ask, I think."

Before the game was three minutes old, the Ontario league ref working the final whistled the Oceanic for two minor penalties for cross-checking on a single shift. The most questionable call he made was to give a roughing minor to Eric Neilson, who knocked down Corey Perry on what seemed like an innocuous bit of jostling. Neilson was tagged not just with the two minutes, but also a 10-minute misconduct. And so it was a reversal of fortunes for Rimouski—instead of having a five-on-three power play to put the game away, as they did in the tournament opener, it was the Knights who had a two-man advantage and the opportunity to jump out to an early lead. Crosby came out to take the faceoff and start the penalty kill, but there was none of the magic there had been in the playoff game against Shawinigan the previous spring—it was one thing to score three on five against the Cataractes, another to hold the five future NHLers on the Knights' main power-play unit at bay. For the better part of a minute, the Knights threw the puck around the perimeter and Crosby went side to side and up and down to preserve the triangle, filling lanes, putting his stick and body in front of shots; but once Crosby was able to get off and Danny Stewart came on his place, London's Dan Fritsche beat Cedrick Desjardins with the only goal the Knights would need. London went up 3–0 early in the second period, and thereafter the Oceanic played out the string—they could mount no pushback whatsoever. The Knights didn't pile on, and didn't need to, winning 4–0 and putting an end to a Rimouski run that had fallen just short.

"We lost the national championship . . . at least our best shot at it . . . when he didn't convert the five-on-three in that opening game," Mario Scalzo says. "We had done it so many times that season. It wasn't that the situation was bigger than us or anything like that. A bounce. Some bad ice. A pass that's just off. Any of that can happen to anyone and it happened with Sid. We were a good team, but not really a great team and we had one of the greatest players ever. As great as Sid is, something so small, like a bouncing puck . . . that can change everything. Yeah, I've thought about that so much over the years—I just had no idea I'd get to play with someone like Sid, not one in a thousand does. It was the biggest moment of my hockey career—if not for the birth of my son, the biggest of my life—and it came up short. But when Sid has won something ever since, it makes a bit of the pain from the Memorial Cup go away."

CHAPTER 7

THE GAME KEEPS CHANGING

Sidney Crosby's third season in Pittsburgh was also the third season after the seismic changes that emerged from the mother of all lockouts. Taken individually, either of the new collective bargaining agreement or the new rules of play would have represented the most immediately disruptive event in NHL history since the first round of expansion in 1967. In fact, there's a strong case to be made that either would have upset the pre-existing power structure even more than the addition of six new teams made up mostly of journeymen back in '67. So shallow was the talent pool available to the new teams that, from one year to the next—and for several seasons thereafter—the best of the so-called Original Six remained the best in the league. Nor did the '67 expansion change the game for the players on the ice; rather than ending players' careers, it extended their careers and opened doors to many who had previously fallen just short of making the cut. But when NHL players prepared to go back to work in the fall of 2005, many found that the market for their services was diminished or had vanished; some struggled to adapt to a game where hooking, holding and obstruction, tactics that had been their bread and butter, now landed them in the penalty box. The league boldly moved to open up the game so that it more resembled the '80s vintage videos that Crosby had watched.

The league's paradigm had shifted in ways that no one could have anticipated, and a period of transition would be required to figure out how to put together competitive rosters within a payroll ceiling. Teams would also have to develop strategies to best exploit the speed that had been injected into the game as well as defend against it. Not to diminish out of hand the Carolina Hurricanes' seven-game victory over Edmonton in the Stanley Cup final in 2006 and the Anaheim Ducks' championship the following spring—these series didn't lack for drama, just star quality. Fans had to wait until 2008 for the first great Stanley Cup showcase of the NHL's new order. The Detroit Red Wings' victory over the Pittsburgh Penguins in six games was sublime stuff, but was out-stripped by Crosby and the Penguins gaining a full measure of re-venge the following spring, with a heart-stopping victory in Game 7 whose outcome remained in doubt down to the final seconds, providing as thrilling a finish as there had been in a generation.

Defending champions go into the next season as the perceived fa-vourites, or at least one of the front-line contenders, while the team that had watched them raise the Cup is usually seen as the top challenger. In reality, for a team to reach the final in back-to-back years is out of the ordinary—prior to 2009, the last to do it was the New Jersey Devils in 2000 and 2001. And for the same *two* teams to meet in the final in consecutive seasons is rarer still: in 2008 and '09, Detroit and Pittsburgh became the first pair of teams to pull this off since the New York Islanders and Edmonton Oilers faced off in 1983 and '84 with rosters loaded down with future Hockey Hall of Famers: Mike Bossy, Bryan Trottier, Denis Potvin, Billy Smith and Clark Gillies for the Islanders; Wayne Gretzky, Mark Messier, Paul Coffey, Jari Kurri, Glenn Anderson and Grant Fuhr for the Oilers.

Those Islanders–Oilers series were marked by a stark contrast in styles, the Islanders favouring the hard-hitting, old-school style while the Oilers relied on their laser show of skill and speed. They also represented one era giving away to another: the Islanders came into the 1983 final looking for their fourth consecutive Stanley Cup, but they had finished fourth in the Prince of Wales Conference with 96 points, 22 fewer than the previous season, when they won the Presidents' Trophy for placing first overall. The Oilers had the league's second-best record in 1982–83 but had won only one playoff series in the three seasons since the merger, and in 1982 their powerhouse team had been upset in the first round by the Los Angeles Kings, who finished 48 points behind them in the regular season. Game 3 of that series, in which Edmonton took a 5–0 lead into the third period, only to lose 6–5 in overtime, came to be known as the Miracle on Manchester after the street on which the Los Angeles Forum was located. The Islanders stymied the Oilers in '83, limiting them to just six goals in a four-game sweep; New York's fourth Cup would be the last of the run, however; in '84 the Oilers blew by them, marking the full ascension of Gretzky, Messier et al.

The splitting of the Islanders–Oilers series along generational lines is one of the only clear parallels to be drawn between the two finals between the Red Wings and Penguins a quarter century later. The Islanders had represented the establishment and the Oilers the insurgents; this was even truer of Detroit and Pittsburgh, respectively. Back in the '90s, the Red Wings had been the team that many of the Penguins watched raise the Cup, even if they had to stay up past their bedtimes—for instance, when Nick Lidstrom won his first Cup, Sidney Crosby was just nine years old.

In the pre-lockout NHL environment, the Wings and Penguins had occupied very different worlds—polar opposites not only financially, but in terms of competitive balance as well. Back in the '90s, Detroit became the Tiffany franchise of the league, and not only because of Stanley Cup victories in 1997, 1998 and 2002. Other teams might rise and fall and then go through a rebuilding period, but the Wings were the exception that proved the rule. They were a fixture in hockey's postseason, qualifying in 25 straight seasons. Mike Ilitch, the billionaire founder of the Little Ceasars Pizza chain, bought the team in 1982 for $8 million, and his ownership not only helped to build his company's brand, it gave him control of the Red Wings' home rink, Joe Louis Arena, where every non-hockey event contributed to his cash flow. According to *Forbes*, whose valuations of sports franchises serve as the industry standard, the Wings were worth a quarter billion dollars in 2004, fifth-highest in the league—the New York Rangers were ranked No. 1, at $274 million, and the Dallas Stars, Toronto Maple Leafs and Philadelphia Flyers were just ahead of Ilitch's club. The Wings had seemingly limitless resources and had become the destination of choice for free agents—their $70 million payroll in 2003 was the league's second-highest, behind the spendthrift-but-misguided

Rangers, who shelled out $79 million on a roster that missed the playoffs for the sixth year in a row. Ilitch's munificence carried over to Detroit's front office—Wings executives often spurned opportunities to leave for more senior roles with other organizations. Turnover in Detroit's front office was almost unknown, and jobs only came open through retirement.

By contrast, the Penguins were unsalvageable also-rans back in 2004, before the lockout, and not just because they finished last overall during the regular season. Craig Patrick was Pittsburgh's GM at the time, but any capital he had generated during the team's two Stanley Cups in the early '90s was just about exhausted. The Penguins played out of the Mellon Arena, also known as the Igloo—less fondly than derisively. An arena with a retractable roof that had been opened only rarely since its construction in 1961, the Igloo offered its tenants virtually no luxury-suite revenue—it yielded about as much ancillary income for the Penguins as an actual igloo would. The team had been on the brink for years; Mario Lemieux had rescued the Penguins from bankruptcy in 1999 when he bought them for $99 million, and through 2004 the team had been treading very cold water, valued at just $114 million according to *Forbes*. The Penguins were worth little more than the Calgary, Ottawa and Edmonton, teams that could at least point to excuses like indebtedness, the effect of a soft Canadian dollar on revenue, and unfavourable tax laws. The Penguins' payroll was $32 million, also near the bottom of the league, and their best player was their owner.

It wasn't that have-not teams like the Penguins could never compete with the big dogs like Detroit. They needed a combination of astute management and good drafting to start to bridge the payroll advantage that the establishment franchises enjoyed. Some had succeeded. New Jersey had won Cups and been consistently competitive for a decade with payrolls no higher than the league's middle ground. Anaheim made it to the final in '03, and Tampa Bay beat Calgary the following spring. All three were in the bottom half of the league in payroll, revenue and franchise values. These were great underdog stories, inspiring to their fan bases, but most likely not sustainable against franchises with the Wings' wherewithal.

Commissioner Gary Bettman fought hard and effectively on behalf of the owners for the payroll cap, and though he might claim that competitive balance had been an objective, it was purely a second-ary one—if the league had simply wanted to even out the distri-bution of talent, there could have been any number of remedies. For owners, the lockout boiled down simply to boosting franchise values and gaining cost certainty—the tying of player salaries to revenues. Maybe someone on the management side knew exactly what effect the NHL's new economic model would have on com-petitive balance; maybe someone anticipated the challenges posed by the need to fit existing contracts under the salary cap; and maybe someone was ahead of the curve in knowing that some veterans weren't going to be able to adapt to a more wide-open game after a year on the sidelines. Maybe. But even those managers considered the sharpest in the league made colossal gaffes in the first couple of seasons in the new-look NHL—New Jersey's Lou Lamoriello at one point had the better part of $8 million wrapped up in three veterans, two just freshly signed, who couldn't play in the league anymore and were demoted to the American Hockey League.

The media's compass was no more reliable—polling its NHL writers across the country, the Canadian Press wire service called

Pittsburgh "a team on the rise," predicting that the Penguins "could make the playoffs for the first time in a few years." The media generally gave GM Craig Patrick favourable reviews for signing veterans Ziggy Palffy and Lyle Odelein. Crosby's arrival in Pittsburgh as protege and understudy to Lemieux was one of the most compelling storylines back in the fall of 2005, though CP's pundits estimated that the rookie's season point total would fall somewhere between 75 points on the high end and 45 on the low end.

It was cascading horrors in Pittsburgh that season, and Craig Patrick had misread the new realities of the business and the game. The Penguins missed the playoffs by 34 points with the worst record in the Eastern Conference and second worst in the league. Palffy had gone home to Slovakia and Odelein had played his last career game, both around midseason, both too banged up to play. Lemieux played his last game in December and had to retire because of a heart arrhythmia. Crosby was the lone bright spot—he racked up 102 points on a team where no other player scored as many as 60. Crosby's rookie season had to have been a weird, not necessarily wonderful time. Much was made of the fact that he had moved in with Lemieux's family—while it's commonplace in the NHL for a kid straight out of junior to move into a veteran's home, it did seem a little unusual for Crosby, the presumptive franchise player, to have a room in the owner's mansion. Crosby was also derided by some of the veterans as a "hockey nerd" when he looked to rent ice for workouts during the All-Star break and whenever coach Ed Olczyk or his replacement, Michel Therrien, gave the team a day off practice. In a league where just about every star thought he wasn't getting enough calls, Crosby quickly developed a reputation for protesting too much, irking not only on-ice officials but also teammates. And, of course, Don Cherry weighed in.

According to one veteran on that Pittsburgh team who asked me not to name him, "It was probably blown up a little too much in the media because he was the centre of attention. So I talked to him and a couple of other guys did as well. He caught on pretty quickly. He wanted to be a good teammate and respectful of the vets. He wasn't wrong about the officials missing stuff . . . he just didn't handle it right. It wasn't his place, not on a team that had Hall of Famers and guys who had been all-stars. It's a mistake a lot of young guys make—it was the rap on Wayne Gretzky when he first came into the league."

The difference between Crosby's first and second seasons could not have been more dramatic. He had finished second to Alexander Ovechkin in the Calder Trophy voting in 2006, but at the end of 2006–07 Crosby picked up the Hart Trophy as the league's regular-season MVP and the Art Ross Trophy as the leading scorer, making him the youngest player ever to win the latter. Moreover, the Penguins improved by 47 points in the standings, finishing second in the Atlantic Division and making the playoffs. Their goal differential went from minus-72 to plus-31. Complaints about Crosby whining to refs or jabs about being Lemieux's tenant were silenced. He was named an alternate captain, which set the stage for him becoming the youngest captain in NHL history at the season's end. (Connor McDavid of Edmonton and Gabriel Landeskog of the Colorado Avalanche have each broken that record by about a month.)

The Penguins' sharp rise in the standings wasn't all Crosby's doing: Evgeni Malkin, the second-overall pick in 2004, burst onto the scene, scoring goals in each of his first six NHL games; Jordan Staal scored 29 goals as an 18-year-old; and 22-year-old Marc-Andre Fleury managed to put a couple of recent horror-show seasons behind him, establishing himself as a No. 1 goaltender. The Penguins were knocked out of the playoffs in the first round in five games by Ottawa. Still, the team was headed in the right direction.

The team's prospects of staying in Pittsburgh had remained in question for most of the season. Jim Balsillie, then the CEO of Research in Motion, had put in a $185 million bid to buy the franchise in October, but by Christmas that fell through. Lemieux continued throughout the season to consider moving the team, but in March the word came down that the team, the state of Pennsylvania and local governments had the pieces in place to build a new arena, one they said would keep the Penguins in the city for 30 years.

The previously troubled franchise was in the midst of a remarkable turnaround and Crosby, still only 19, was a catalyst on and off the ice. Even the most optimistic fans could hardly have foreseen how quickly the Penguins would reach the league's summit.

Although the league had reinvented the game as well as the business of the game, the Detroit Red Wings surprised no one by making the Stanley Cup final in 2008. They had gone into the season as the oddsmakers' second favourite—at 5–1 they were just behind the defending champion Anaheim Ducks. The cap on payrolls had cramped Mike Ilitch's style, and his GM, Ken Holland, couldn't shop as liberally as before the lockout, but the Wings enjoyed success because of the residue of some smart personnel decisions. The scouting department had long been considered the league's best, and the Wings' two forwards, Pavel Datsyuk and Henrik Zetterberg, were sublime talents who had made it onto no other team's radar; each had been selected in the seventh round of his respective draft year. Detroit still had three checking-line forwards who had been with the team through its run to Stanley Cups in 1997, '98 and 2002: Kris Draper, Kirk Maltby and Darren McCarty. And the goaltender, Chris Osgood, had been the No. 1 netminder for the championship team in 1998. The Wings' key player, however, was a nonpareil defenceman, the team captain: Nicklas Lidstrom.

While Ovechkin filled the role of Crosby's rival and foil, it was a matter of frequency—they were in the same conference and their teams would face off four times a year and were more likely to meet in the playoffs through the first three rounds. It was also a matter of history, their paths having crossed repeatedly ever since the world juniors. And it was a matter of timing, Crosby and Ovechkin coming into the league at the same time. That said, coaches for either Washington or Pittsburgh weren't looking to match their respective stars against his opposite number—the coaches behind the Pittsburgh bench would have been looking to assign a checking line against Ovechkin and vice versa with Washington's matchup against Crosby. The head-to-head matchup between stars is more often the stuff of narrative than fact.

In Crosby's first trip to the Stanley Cup final, though, he was matched against the one other active player in the pantheon of the league's all-time 20 greatest. In Detroit's run of Stanley Cups, Lidstrom inevitably logged the most ice time on the Red Wings blue line and was half of the defensive pair Detroit's coaches wanted out there against the opposition's top offensive lines. He was also the first option on the Wings' penalty kill. Back in '97, Scotty Bowman matched Lidstrom and Larry Murphy against Eric Lindros, John LeClair and Mikael Renberg, Philadelphia's Legion of Doom, and in Detroit's upset four-game sweep, the pair neutralized what had been the most dangerous line in hockey that season. The formula remained the same for 15 seasons afterwards: the matchups up front would vary with the Wings' personnel, but Lidstrom and his defensive partner of the moment would roll over the boards to face the opponents' chief scoring threat.

When the Wings faced Crosby and the Penguins in the final in 2008, Lidstrom was 38 years old but he had seemingly lost nothing from his game—scoring 10 goals and 60 assists with a plus-minus of plus-40, logging an average of just under 27 minutes of ice time in 76 games, he earned his sixth Norris Trophy that season. Before Game 1 in Detroit, Mario Lemieux and Steve Yzerman came out to drop the puck for the ceremonial faceoff between the team captains, Crosby and Lidstrom. Lidstrom stayed out on the ice with his partner, Brian Rafalski, and from that opening shift through to the celebration after Game 6, Detroit coach Mike Babcock scrambled to keep that pair matched against Crosby and his linemates, Pascal Dupuis and Marian Hossa.

Says Lidstrom, "I knew some of the other players in Pittsburgh's lineup . . . Hossa and Sykora. I hadn't really played against Crosby. We didn't play the Penguins at all [in the 2007–08 regular season] and we just played them once a year the two seasons before that. [In the 2006–07 season] we played them the first week of the season . . . the only time I played against Malkin. I'd seen the video, though, and I knew that they brought a lot of skill and speed out there. But video can only tell you so much. You don't know until you're actually out there how much of a gap you can give a player. But it only took a few shifts to tell . . . you had to watch [Crosby] every second and be aware of him with or without the puck. I wanted to stay close to him . . . at first. But then I realized that I could be *too* close. If you're too close to Crosby, then there you're in a dangerous place. You can't overcommit because he'll catch you leaning and beat you the other way."

Lidstrom was able to seamlessly adapt to the NHL's post-lockout game because he had always relied on positioning, mobility and reading the play—he was a technician, not an intimidator. His partner on the Detroit blue line, Rafalski, was a perfect complement in the matchup versus Crosby. Rafalski wasn't anyone's idea of an elite NHL prospect when he came out of the University of Wisconsin-Madison—though he had won some collegiate honours in the mid-'90s, he went undrafted and overlooked by NHL clubs because he was only five foot ten at a time when even six-footers were considered undersized. After college, Rafalski played four seasons in Sweden and Finland, where his mobility and puck skills better suited the game on the bigger international sheet. The New Jersey Devils signed Rafalski in what seemed like a bit of a science experiment to many NHL teams that still believed him to be too small. The Devils played him beside Scott Stevens, a defenceman as physically punishing as any in the NHL's first century —it's only half-ironic to suggest that Rafalski's height disadvantage was countered by the fact that opponents shrank at the sight of Stevens. Rafalski's skills contributed to a Devils Stanley Cup before he came over to the Red Wings as a free agent.

"It was a perfect fit for me with Brian," Lidstrom says. "When we were playing other team's top lines, their best players, you have to counter their speed with mobility and positioning . . . that was always true and I think it was really the case after they opened the game up [with the rule changes in 2005]. There were some players who just weren't mobile enough to play after the lockout, but Brian was one of the best in the league that way."

Mike Babcock's matchups against Crosby's line would vary— the coach had an array of top-notch 200-foot players to call on, meaning he enjoyed an embarrassment of riches when it came to options. Over the course of his career Datsyuk would win the Selke Trophy three times, and Kris Draper was selected to the Canadian Olympic team in '06 as a checking-line pivot, a role in which he won three Stanley Cups. Yet in the run-up to the final, Babcock had described Zetterberg as "our top defensive forward," and it might have actually played out that way—the 27-year-old Zetterberg was playing the best hockey of his career, and in Game 1 Babcock sent him out with Datsyuk on his left and Tomas Holmstrom on his right to take on Crosby. Clearly the Swede warmed to the challenge; he dropped shoulders into Crosby in the run of play and a couple of times after.

The easy narrative to impose on the events of the 2008 final was that it came down to experience: the Wings had veterans in their lineup, four skaters who had been with Detroit's Cup-winning teams in '97, '98 and 2002 and a total of eight holdovers from that last championship squad; for their part, the Penguins' leading players—21-year-old Malkin and 20-year-old Crosby—had never before won an NHL postseason series. That said, Pittsburgh had veterans among the surrounding talent—the 29-year-old Hossa up front, 33-year-old Sergei Gonchar and 27-year-old Brooks Orpik on the back end. The Penguins came up short in '08 against Detroit, and while the failure might have been in the stars, blame couldn't have laid at the feet of the star players.

Midway through the first period of Game 1, Wings forward Dan Cleary broke his stick on a penalty kill and was unable to get to the bench, giving Pittsburgh a virtual five-on-three for a long shift. Crosby had the best chance in the sequence in a scramble around the crease, but goaltender Chris Osgood, on his knees, fell back into the net and pulled back a puck that was floating towards the goal line, leaving the Pittsburgh captain looking skyward. On another power play a few minutes later, Crosby set up Hossa on Osgood's doorstep and it looked like the puck might have crossed the line, but the net cam showed it had come to rest under the goaltender on the goal line. Midway through the second period, with the game still scoreless, Crosby sent Dupuis in alone on Osgood, but the goalie fought off the deke. Not that a 1–0 lead at that point would likely have stood up, but it could have changed the flow of the game and 2–0 could have set the Penguins off to the races.

As the game wore on, however, the Red Wings methodically choked out Crosby and company. The Penguins had four consecutive power plays in the first period and were more than trading chances with Detroit, but in the final 40 minutes the Penguins could muster only seven shots on Osgood. The final shot totals told the story: Detroit 36, Pittsburgh 19. Mikael Samuelsson scored twice in the last seven minutes of the second period and the Wings won 4–0, pulling away. It wasn't that the Penguins ran out of gas —they had a full four days off between rounds. Says Nick Lidstrom, "You make adjustments with the coaches between periods. You make adjustments yourself during the game." Clearly, the veterans in the Red Wings lineup were quick studies.

Game 2, a 3–0 Detroit victory, could have passed for the fourth, fifth and sixth periods of Game 1. Matched against Malkin's line, defencemen Niklas Kronwall and Brad Stuart threw their bodies around. Stuart scored the winning goal in the seventh minute and Holmstrom added some insurance a few shifts later. The Detroit defence limited Pittsburgh to 22 shots, and in five-on-five situations the Wings schooled the Penguins.

At this point, the final looked to be history repeating for the Wings—their two Cup victories in the '90s had both been four-game sweeps. The Penguins did push back in Game 3, though it didn't start out that way. Through the first 15 minutes in Pittsburgh, the home team managed to get only a single shot on Osgood. Shots were 9–1 for Detroit with less than three minutes left in the first period, but at that point the Penguins' second shot found the back of the net. Detroit defenceman Brad Stuart's attempt at a breakout pass hit the skates of Zetterberg near the top of the circle and Crosby pounced on the loose puck. He then passed it over to Hossa and bore down on the Wings net. Hossa threaded a puck through traffic to Crosby, who was standing at the edge of the crease and stuffed it past Osgood. On a power play two minutes into the second period, Crosby put the Penguins up 2–0, another goal that travelled the length of a stick. The lead wasn't exactly safe—Johan Franzen's power-play goal made it 2–1 before the second intermission and the Red Wings were chasing hard, outshooting the Penguins 16–4 in the third period, but a goal from fourth-liner Adam Hall provided Pittsburgh necessary insurance in a 3–2 win, the team's ninth in a row at home in the postseason.

Crosby's teammates lined up after the game to give testimonials. "I love the guy," winger Maxime Talbot told the *Pittsburgh Post-Gazette*. "I'm older than him and I look up to him. What a true leader. The rest of us have no choice but to follow."

The Penguins' sputtering power play cost them Game 4 and probably any realistic shot at the series. Hossa scored with the man advantage in the third minute to stake Pittsburgh to the lead, but Lidstrom scored on a screened shot from the point five minutes later. The game remained tense and tied until early in the third period, when the Penguins failed to clear their zone and Wings fourth-liner Jiri Hudler beat Marc-Andre Fleury with a backhand. The heartbreak for the home team came midway through the third when they couldn't tie the game on a five-on-three power play that lasted the better part of 90 seconds. Over that stretch, they managed to get only one harmless shot on Osgood—Zetterberg's work on the penalty kill didn't show up in the scoring summary, but this shift effectively put the Wings a win away from the Cup.

Given the Wings' dominating performances at Joe Louis Arena in the first two games, fans fully expected them to raise the Cup after Game 5, and with the home team carrying a 3–2 lead with a minute to go, officials backstage prepared the Cup for presentation and the champagne was pulled out of the refrigerator. Pittsburgh had taken a 2–0 lead on goals by Hossa and Hall, but Detroit stormed back with goals by rookie Darren Helm, Datsyuk and Rafalski to leave them a few shifts from victory with the Penguins struggling to establish any possession in the Wings' end. But with Marc-Andre Fleury pulled in favour of a sixth skater, Talbot tied the game with 34 seconds left on just the Penguins' fourth shot on net in the period, improbably sending the game to an even more improbable overtime.

During a network TV interview in the intermission, the Penguins' Petr Sykora said he was going to score the winning goal, and he did—midway through the third extra period. The Wings had outshot Pittsburgh 58–32, but the series headed back to Pittsburgh for Game 6.

And there, Crosby and his teammates ran out of miracles. Brian Rafalski scored on a power play in the fifth minute and the Red Wings led the rest of the way. In the first period, Pittsburgh again squandered another long five-on-three advantage, although history almost repeated itself. First, with Fleury pulled in favour of an extra attacker, Hossa scored a power-play goal with 90 seconds left in regulation time to pull the Penguins within a goal at 3–2. Then, in the dying seconds, with Fleury again pulled, Crosby and Hossa had point-blank chances right up until the horn blew.

Crosby tried to find consolation in his team's effort. "That's the way we've played all season," Crosby said. "Guys have been through a lot, and battled through it. It doesn't surprise me that guys never gave up." Coach Michel Therrien made a case that the Penguins were undone by the deep hole they fell into in the opening games in Detroit. "I thought we learned real quick because after Game 3 we started to play our game," he said "They were tight games, could go both ways. Tonight, this game could have gone both ways as well."

Mike Ilitch acknowledged that his team had not only beaten the Penguins, but also a system: a hard cap on team payrolls that was designed to neutralize his franchise's financial advantages.

"This is much more gratifying," Ilitch said. "I'm not saying the [NHL salary cap] is because of us, but everybody wanted a fair shot. People expected us to go down."

One fundamental management strategy became clear soon after the collective agreement was hammered out in 2005: young players on entry-level contracts were premium assets and, really, the prerequisites for assembling a roster. The money saved on their contracts allowed GMs the necessary breathing room to keep their stars locked up. The Wings were still the exception: with an average age of almost 32, they were the oldest team to win a Cup in the post-expansion era, and that wasn't simply a function of little-used veterans holding down spots at the bottom of the roster (such as backup goaltender Dominik Hasek at 43, defenceman Chris Chelios, a healthy scratch during the playoffs, at 46, and fourth-liner Dallas Drake at 39). The Wings' two best forwards, Zetterberg and Datsyuk, were 27 and 29 when they raised the Cup, but core players were well into their 30s—the first pairing on defence, Lidstrom and Rafalski were 38 and 34, respectively. Zetterberg's winger Tomas Holmstrom was 35. The grinding line that had won their fourth Cup—Draper, Maltby and McCarty—had a combined age of 108. In goal, Chris Osgood was 35. Some of them took a financial haircut to stay with a contender where they were comfortable rather than testing the free-agent market. And as corny as it sounds, there was a degree of loyalty to Ilitch—many would stay on and work for him and, after his death, for his family. The players who represented the next generation of Wings, Jiri Hudler and Valteri Filppula, were each 24 years old, already older than the stars who had carried the Penguins to the final—Fleury (23), Malkin (22), Letang (21), Crosby (20) and Staal (only 19).

Making the Stanley Cup final was a small miracle for a team with as many young core players as the Penguins in 2008, but it was no fluke—despite a high-ankle sprain that kept Crosby out of the lineup for 29 games during the regular season, Pittsburgh had finished as the No. 2 seed in the Eastern Conference and ran through the first three rounds of the playoffs with relative ease, never trailing in a series. If general manager Ray Shero could keep his roster together and if the stars were able to stay healthy, they looked like a good bet to be back the next year—the last two losses to the Wings had been by a single goal, after all. Pittsburgh's run to the final had sparked an enthusiasm among the fan base that would have been unimaginable just four years earlier—if *base* is even a term you could use to describe those who followed the Penguins in their darkest days. Not even the Stanley Cups in the early '90s or Mario Lemieux's return from retirement had generated the same level of interest in hockey in the city. During the final, thousands of fans who didn't have tickets congregated outside Mellon Arena and watched the games on big television screens.

Team president David Morehouse put it down not just to the star power of Crosby and Malkin and the others, but also to their youth. What might have been a liability in a matchup on the ice against the veteran Wings was a great selling point in the Pittsburgh sports market. "The youth and the energy that [Crosby and Malkin] have is appealing to young people," he said. "A lot of our players aren't much older than the young fans. The sport lends itself to a younger audience."

Many potential fans hadn't warmed to the team when stars were walking away and rumours of relocation were circulating. That uncertainty had now been set aside. Terms for the new building had been finalized before the season, and just two months after Crosby and his teammates shook the hands of the Red Wings and skated off the ice at the Igloo, a shovel went into the ground just a couple of blocks away, at the site of a new home, the Consol Energy Center. It might be an overstatement to call the venue the House that Crosby Built, but the fact is, it was hard to imagine Lemieux and his management team being able to muster the civic faith needed to invest in the arena if they didn't have Crosby and a collection of emerging stars. Certainly, city hall and the state house wouldn't have given the Penguins' ownership the time of day before the lockout cancelled the 2004–05 season.

The Penguins needed some help to return to the final in the spring of 2009. They seemed to have more of a hangover from the previous season's deep run than did the Wings, who racked up 112 points and the second seed in the Western Conference. Pittsburgh had won only 27 of 57 games and was tied for 10th place in the Eastern Conference when GM Ray Shero fired Michel Therrien and brought in Dan Bylsma as an interim replacement in February. The team instantly responded to Bylsma, who had been coach of the Penguins' AHL affiliate in Wilkes-Barre/Scranton. The Penguins adopted a more freewheeling style and Malkin surged into the league lead in point scoring, with Crosby just behind him. They lost only three of the remaining 25 regular-season games and moved all the way up to fourth place in the conference with 99 points. The Penguins' toughest test in getting to the final came in the second round against the Capitals—Pittsburgh had a chance to clinch the series at home in Game 6 but lost 5–4 in overtime on a goal by fourth-liner David Steckel. People expected Game 7 to be the ultimate showdown between Crosby and Ovechkin, but it never materialized—the Penguins ran out to a 5–0 lead in the second period and cruised to a 6–2 victory to secure a berth in the conference final. Meanwhile, Carolina, a sixth seed, knocked off Boston, who had led the conference with 116 points during the regular season. The Penguins swept the Hurricanes to set up the rematch in the final, and by then Ray Shero had stroked out "interim" from Bylsma's job title.

The rosters had only been tweaked in minor ways from one season to the next, with one exception: Marian Hossa left the Penguins and signed on with Detroit. The snub was unambiguous, given that Pittsburgh management had offered Hossa a salary in the range of $7 million over a five-year term while the Wings offered him little more than that on a one-year contract. "It was a really tough decision for me to make," Hossa said after the deal was announced. "When I compared the two teams, I felt like I would have a little better of a chance to win the Cup in Detroit." This quote remains to this day the NHL's most instructive example of the dangers of tempting fate.

Through the first two games of the final, it looked as though Hossa had in fact chosen wisely, with the Wings winning a pair of home dates to open the final for the second year in a row. It might have seemed like Detroit was poised to win its fifth Cup in 12 seasons. But although both games ended with 3–1 scores, the run of play was nowhere near as one-sided the second time around. In 2008, Crosby and his teammates had struggled to get the puck to the net in the first two games in Detroit, but this year they outshot the Wings. Losing the opening two games of a best-of-seven is a deep hole, and observers on the outside would lay long odds against a challenger winning four out of the next five games against a defending champion. Yet the Wings had a sense that they were up against it.

"What they say is true about Father Time being undefeated," Dan Cleary says. "It went right through the lineup. Nik [Lidstrom] and Raf [Rafalski] were a year older, and Nik had that awful injury when [Chicago's] Patrick Sharp speared him in the conference final. [Lidstrom had to have testicle surgery.] Pavel [Datsyuk] was banged up—he took a shot off his foot against Chicago and couldn't put a skate on, so he only came back for Game 5 and he was a long way from 100 percent. A lot of guys were banged up. [Defenceman] Jonathan Ericsson had an appendectomy and was trying to play two days after surgery. Those first two games we won in Detroit [in 2009,] we owed a lot to Chris Osgood—they say that you look to your goaltender to steal a game in a series, and he might have stolen us two to start with."

"The game after the lockout was changed, but it kept changing every season. It kept getting faster," Lidstrom says. "It did right to the end of my career [in 2012] and still does to this day. We were probably as fast as the Penguins in that first final—we probably did a better job with the puck on the cycle in their end than they did in ours. The next season, though, they did a better job—it wasn't lineup changes, so much as their best young players were that much stronger and that much faster. Because Crosby and Malkin and some of the others were so young that first time we played them, people talked about experience, but maybe they didn't focus on that fact that they were developing players, still growing. They were going to get faster and stronger, just like the rest of the league. In 2009 they caught us at just the right time for them. Malkin was incredible in that final, a pretty unique guy, but Sid was the guy a lot of players looked to and said, 'That's the way I can play. I've got to bring more pace.'

"There have been some guys who played on our Cup-winning teams [in the '90s] who would have trouble with the speed of the game after the new rules opened it up. I think bringing more speed into the league has been a change for the better. It's a better game for fans to watch . . . there's no doubt about that. In a lot of ways it's a better game for players. The only thing is the game is maybe more dangerous now.

"The difference in speed and strength in the young players like Crosby and Malkin from one season to the next was pretty dramatic," Lidstrom says. "They learned a lot from that first series against us. Until you go to a final, you really don't know about the physical price you have to pay and the fatigue. It's physical, but also emotional and psychological. It's a long season even if you don't make the playoffs or go out in the first or second round. But the idea of playing 20 more games, maybe 28, at the end of the season . . . it's something that you know about only from experience.

"Really, the difference between our teams wasn't even that much [in 2008]. We had a couple of good games at home to start, but after that there were some real close games—that they were able to come back and win that Game 5 in overtime [in 2008]. I think they learned a lot from that game about digging down. Really, when we clinched the Cup in Game 6 that year, it came right down to the last play. We knew that they were going to be competitive [in 2009]. I thought we had a better team [in 2009] than we had the year before . . . but Pittsburgh was a *much* better team from one year to the next and of course, Crosby was a key to that."

Some of the corrections were obvious. "The Pens were poor in the [faceoff] circle that first time we played them in the final, but Sid worked on it," Dan Cleary says. "You know that was a big takeaway for him—people talked about that. The next season, Sid's 58 percent on faceoffs, and what was a weakness for him became a strength."

Still, it was going to take four wins in five games against a team that was all too accustomed to playing in the spring.

The series took on an entirely different look after the second intermission of Game 3. The score was tied at two-all, but the action in the second period had been trending Detroit's way, with the defending champions denying the home team a single chance. Crosby's line, with late-season pickups Bill Guerin and Chris Kunitz on his wings, had failed to get so much as a good look at Chris Osgood. It looked like the same chokehold the Wings had applied the season before. But then Lidstrom and his teammates seemed to age with every shift. Bylsma put the captain on a line with Malkin and Ruslan Fedotenko early in the third, and they had two great chances within a minute. That set the stage for Sergei Gonchar's winning goal on a power play, with Malkin and Crosby drawing assists. An empty-net goal made the final score 4–2 and the Wings, trying to rally in the third, managed only three shots on Fleury.

For the next three games, the Wings and the Penguins traded wins on home ice. In Game 4, Crosby's first goal of the series came midway through the second period on a two-on-one with Malkin and it served as the game winner in a 4–2 Pittsburgh victory. Datsyuk made it into the lineup for the first time in the final in Game 5, and Detroit coasted to a 5–0 win. Facing elimination in Game 6 of the final for the second time in two seasons, the Penguins white-knuckled their way to a 2–0 lead on goals by Jordan Staal and Tyler Kennedy. Kris Draper got one back with 12 minutes left in regulation time, but the Wings could get no closer despite two late power plays. Fleury turned aside 14 shots in the third to send the series back to Detroit.

The odds were stacked against the Penguins—of the last 14 times the Stanley Cup final had gone to a seventh game, the home team had won 12. And the Wings had won five of their six home games against the Penguins across the two finals, Pittsburgh's lone win coming on Petr Sykora's triple-overtime winner in what, the score aside, had been perhaps the most one-sided game the previous year. Yet the Penguins had the better of the play in a scoreless first period—both teams played with predictable caution, but it might have been the visitors' best period at Joe Louis Arena in the two finals. Crosby, Guerin and Kunitz skated Datsyuk, Zetterberg and Cleary to a saw-off through the first 20 minutes, and it looked like it would be left to the supporting players to decide the game among themselves.

Pittsburgh took the lead early in the second period when Detroit defenceman Brad Stuart turned the puck over in his own end with Malkin forechecking. Malkin in turn found Maxime Talbot in the slot, and his one-timer beat Osgood high on the stick side. Crosby's final ended a few shifts after that. He was battling for a puck with Johan Franzen along the boards in the neutral zone. Crosby probably put himself in harm's way when he left his skates and tried to hurtle past the big winger's hip check—his knee wound up taking the brunt of the impact as Franzen slammed him into the boards. It was a legal hit but it was clear that Crosby was done for the game, even though Bylsma told Versus broadcaster Pierre Maguire during a break in play that his captain's injury was to his "midsection" and he would return. Skating in Crosby's place midway through the second period, Talbot made it 2–0. Brad Stuart made a risky pinch at the Penguins blue line and Kunitz sent Talbot away on a two-on-one with Tyler Kennedy. Talbot never looked to pass, and he wired a shot past Osgood.

The third period had the visitors playing shutdown—the Penguins only managed one shot on Osgood in the final 20 minutes, while limiting the Red Wings to eight on Fleury. Crosby did come out for one shift in the third period, but it was obvious he couldn't contribute—he took a faceoff and then looked to return to the bench the first chance he got. Ericsson pulled Detroit to within a goal, but the home team couldn't tie it up, Fleury turning aside Zetterberg in the last seconds, just as Osgood had done to Crosby in the last game of the '08 final. Malkin was named the winner of the Conn Smythe Trophy as the MVP of the finals, and he was full value for it.

"I don't recommend anyone trying to watch a Game 7 of a Stanley Cup final sitting on the bench," said Crosby.

CHAPTER 8

ALL THE WORLD'S HIS STAGE

Toronto, September 2016

The 2016 World Cup of Hockey was an event that will not feature all that prominently in the history of the game. When the first World Cup was played in 1996, the tournament represented a non-proprietary rebranding of sorts for the Canada Cup, the series of international tournaments staged in the autumns of 1976, '81, '84, '87 and '91. Along the way, the World Cup became an afterthought—prior to 2016, it was last staged in 2004, on the eve of the lockout that would lead to the cancellation of the NHL season. That 2004 tournament soon faded from memory, and so, too, did the World Cup as a going concern. In fact, over the next decade it seemed a pretty safe bet that it would never be played again. The decision to revive it wasn't motivated by public demand as much as the search for a cash cow for the league and the players' association as well as a bone to throw to sponsors and licensees. In fact, the 2016 tournament felt more like an upgrade on an NHL All-Star Game than an Olympics—never has an international event, an ostensible world championship, seemed so contrived and gimmicky, albeit for the sake of trying to balance the field, get a slate of competitive games and promote the league's young stars.

Depth and balance in a field of tournament teams has ever been an issue. Yes, the game of hockey has expanded to new markets and interest has spiked in places far removed from its traditional homes. Still, at the elite international level, the field is top-heavy, to say the least: two nations from North America (Canada and the US) and four from Europe (Sweden, Finland, Russia and the Czech Republic) won all 15 medals in play at the Olympics between 1998 and 2014; in a best-on-best tournament, only these nations have a realistic shot at reaching the final. As a result, every 10-team (or even eight-team) tournament feels diluted by countries from the next tier: too many outmanned rosters; at least a couple of teams looking for an upset here, valour in defeat there. Organizers of the 2016 World Cup tried to raise the quality of the field and balance off the talent pool with a couple of confections: Team North America, featuring young stars from Canada and the US under the age of 23, served as something like a trailer for the game we'll see in the next decade; and Team Europe, effectively a one-off contingent cobbled together from the best of the minnows, which opened the door to a few players who'd otherwise be left out, like Slovenia's Anze Kopitar, captain of a pair of Stanley Cup champions in Los Angeles.

Sparing no expense, tournament organizers commissioned the renowned architect Frank Gehry to design a trophy to present to the winning team. You'd have thought that, as a Canadian, Gehry would have appreciated that any trophy designed was going to pale by comparison to the Stanley Cup, which is universally recognized as the best in category. He can put the Guggenheim Bilbao or his addition to the Art Gallery of Ontario next to any building and come away with a *prix d'or,* but the NHL's array of silverware is very hard to match and impossible to beat. What Gehry wound up producing for the World Cup—27 inches of stainless steel encased in hard, clear acrylic—might win a design prize from his peers, but to hockey fans it looked like a promotion-sized can of Sapporo beer.

With any late-summer tournament, it's a safe bet that the majority of talents aren't yet in their best form, that those who've been working out aren't looking to peak in September, but rather when the salary is earned and their market value is determined, in midseason. And really, the World Cup was not a complication some looked forward to. While a number were sidelined with injuries, I'd heard through back channels about a couple who begged off, citing ailments they would have played through in the Stanley Cup playoffs.

It was a fairly decorous affair through the opening round. Those who did report to their teams played a "polite" game, a "gentlemen's" game. It was not as hotly contested as you'd find some preseason games to be, when at least a couple of jobs on every roster are open for competition. Was it simply that the players didn't give a lot of weight to the outcome? That would probably be unfair. More likely it was tied to the composition of the rosters— when you get to the NHL playoffs, the dirty work seems to fall most often to those on the bottom half of a roster; the top teams in a best-on-best tournament like the World Cup are made up almost exclusively of first-liners, those intent on out-speeding and out-skilling you rather than knocking you flat on your ass at the risk of getting hurt trying. And if the degree of contact is low, it's a by-product of the evolving nature of the game—more of a race than a fight. All that and the prospect of putting the very best players in the world on the power play—if you can, you avoid it.

It was a case of the world coming to Toronto, seemingly for a made-for-TV event. Every game was played at the Air Canada Centre, which might have seemed more like a studio than an arena. And you didn't have to be too cynical to regard the World Cup as a series in production rather than history in making.

It really didn't seem like Sidney Crosby needed the World Cup. There wasn't much for him to prove by taking part, not with: his name engraved on the Stanley Cup twice; a couple of Olympic gold medals; a world junior championship and even a world championship back in 2015. The World Cup didn't seem likely to provide an enduring memory. This would prove to be a pity.

For Crosby, it's not likely near the top of the list of his career accomplishments, and clearly not on the leaderboard of international moments, but that's a comment on the stage rather than the actor. In the run-up to the final, Crosby put together what was arguably his most dominant performance against a field of the highest quality (even if not for the highest stakes). He was centring a line with Patrice Bergeron, his old running mate from the world junior tournament in Grand Forks, and Brad Marchand, with whom he had sometimes skated in Halifax in the off-season. Seeing him play with those two, it left you to wonder what he might have done—or would do—if he had ever had a chance to play with even one linemate of true all-star quality, never mind two.

Even before the two-game final against Team Europe, he had clinched the tournament's MVP award. In a way, his excellence had elevated and legitimized the World Cup—if it all seemed so blatantly like a contrivance, didn't anyone tell him? Crosby took the tournament no less seriously than any postseason game with the Penguins or any time he had donned a Team Canada sweater. More than that, he raised the game of everyone in the Canadian lineup, not by simply wearing the captain's C and cheerleading, but by the way he played.

September hockey doesn't tend to do any favours for players at any level, whether it's a minor-hockey tryout, junior training camp, NHL preseason game or even an invitational event like the World Cup, where future Hockey Hall of Famers rub shoulders with mere franchise players. The notion has always been that NHL hockey in October is about 75 percent of the game that is played by the time Christmas holidays roll around; that NHLers are, after ever-briefer training camps, shifting gears up from third to fourth and finally fifth through the autumn months. And that figured to be the case, particularly for the likes of Crosby, who was, when the Canadian team gathered, barely 90 days removed from raising the Cup after the last game of the final in San Jose—those last off the ice at the end of the NHL season were figured to be at a considerable disadvantage by the time the puck dropped in Toronto for the start of the tournament. You would presume it to be true of any player in a Stanley Cup finalist's rank and file, but especially of one counted on for so much—in 24 postseason games, Crosby logged 20-and-a-half minutes of ice time, most among the Penguins' forwards, three full minutes ahead of Evgeni Malkin. This after missing only two regular-season games and with a workload virtually the same.

Yet the physical and emotional tolls seemed non-existent. No one arrived at the World Cup more prepared than Crosby and it was the rest of this best-possible field that had to play catch-up to him. You could read between the lines when talking to Marchand at the tournament—the Bruins left winger had developed into one of the more unlikely all-stars of his generation, and yet playing beside Crosby forced him to raise his game. "He just reads the game and executes at such a high level and so quickly that you do need to react a little differently," Marchand said.

For Carey Price, the World Cup was his second chance to play with Crosby at an international event—they had been teammates at the Olympics in Sochi two years earlier. From his vantage point in the Montreal Canadiens net in seven seasons, Price had also seen an eyeful of him. Nonetheless he would say that Crosby's play in Toronto came as a revelation to him. "He's probably the best player of our generation," Price said. Added defenceman Drew Doughty, who had played with Crosby on the 2010 and 2014 Olympic teams, "The three tournaments I've had the opportunity, I would say he's playing unbelievable. Things are working for him now. He's hot. Not that he didn't play well at the other tournaments, he just didn't get this hot."

It's a pity that, when all is said and done, almost no one will remember Crosby for his play at the World Cup, at least to the degree that it will be front of mind. That's just how memory and hockey work.

Of all the world's sports, hockey has to be the one with the most curious political history. International hockey launched before the NHL was founded, but oddly excluded North America. The International Ice Hockey Federation was created in 1908 and staged its first championship tournament with a pool of four teams drawn entirely from Europe: Germany, Switzerland, Great Britain and Belgium. A world tournament drawing on both the eastern and western hemispheres, one that the IIHF lays claim to as its own, came along a couple of years after the birth of the NHL: improbably enough, the ice hockey competition at the 1920 *Summer* Olympics in Antwerp, Belgium, where the Winnipeg Falcons won the gold. The IIHF staged its first world championship in 1930, and again Canada won with an amateur club team, the Toronto CCMs. Canada would continue to send club teams and, through to the '50s, win the gold most of the time—the score for championships being Canada 15, Rest of the World 4. The dynamic changed somewhat with the entry of the Soviets in 1954 and the rise of their amateur powerhouse in the '60s, one that won eight straight world championships.

Canadian amateur ice hockey officials grew disenchanted with the IIHF and the International Olympic Committee and, for a time decided not to send teams to international tournaments, as if the country's absence somehow devalued the events.

Through all these decades, the NHL was separated from the international game—a matter of amateurism. NHLers and those in the high minor leagues affiliated with the NHL were deemed professionals and thus ineligible, which is why Canada had sent either senior-league outfits or, in the '60s, a national squad of those untainted by NHL contracts.

The first crossover event where the elite pros of the NHL met the best of the amateurs was, of course, the Summit Series in '72. When it was organized, it seemed to be a one-off—no structure was put in place to make any similar event a fixture on the hockey schedule. Farther into the decade, the concept of the made-for-TV sports event came to the fore, and the great wall between the professional and amateur sports worlds began to ever so slightly erode.

Into one small breach in that wall the hockey-gloved hands from Canada and the USSR reached, presumably clenched into fists rather than open for shaking. The Summit Series proved that bringing together the world's best could be done, but it wasn't easy. Consequently, it wasn't tried frequently and the results were all over the place. The 1974 series between the Soviets and the WHA's Canadian all-stars was better than you might expect. The Soviets didn't send a good number of their first stringers to the '76 World Cup, likely for fear they might defect. The '81 Canada Cup was the Soviets' most dominant performance; the '84, '87 and '91 instalments were opportunities for Canadian pride to recover. All of these, however, were autumn tournaments, preseason events. However intense and drama-filled they might have been, the players were out of season. For all the care you take in putting together a fruit salad, it can only be so satisfying when the ingredients aren't ripe. For decades a true in-season championship bringing together all the world's best seemed to be only a fan's fantasy.

More to the point, though, the first best-on-best international tournament featuring NHL talent—not one staged as an NHL-endorsed autumn invitational, but a true, in-season event—didn't occur until the Nagano Olympics in 1998. Yes, it took only 90 years after the creation of the IIHF to get everyone on the same sheet of ice.

Because of this twisted history and administrative dysfunction, many of the greatest players in the history of the NHL had a limited chance to play on the international stage. Now, appreciate that the lists that the *Hockey News* and TSN compiled were drawn up to rank the best NHL players of all time, and not the world's best players, so they exclude a lot of great players from consideration—or at best shortchange them, overlooking the greatest career achievements. Where would Viacheslav Fetisov figure on an all-time ranking? How would he compare to, say, Doug Harvey? At his peak Fetisov was surely a more game-defining presence than Lidstrom. Where would Vladislav Tretiak fall among the all-time greats? But enough with the hypotheticals—let's deal only with those whose names we have to this point been considering.

Gordie Howe was well into his 40s and had come out of retirement when he played for the WHA all-stars against the Soviets in 1974, so you could only imagine what he might have done in international competition in his prime. Regardless of age, Howe showed flashes of greatness, physically wasting and terrorizing Soviets who clearly hadn't read the scouting reports. Over the course of the series they gave him an ever-wider berth. And Howe's performance only left to the imagination what the legends of his generation— Maurice Richard, Doug Harvey or Jean Beliveau—might have done on the game's greatest stage.

Bobby Orr missed out on the Summit Series because of injury, and by the time the '76 Canada Cup launched he was physically diminished to the point of being unrecognizable as the player who had led the Bruins to two Stanley Cups. His performance was heroic but also bittersweet, again like Howe's in '74—one could only imagine what it would have been like if he had been able to play for his country at the height of his game.

The first player on the list to have a significant international career would be Gretzky, and his resumé was a decidedly mixed bag. Most memorably, he combined with Mario Lemieux on the overtime goal that won the '87 Canada Cup. (For a sense of the concept of *tempus fugit*, it's worth noting that this famous moment happened a month after Crosby's birth.) Gretzky also served as a cornerstone of the teams that won the Canada Cup in '84 and '91;

but as his career wound down in the mid- and late '90s, disappointments outnumbered highlights, with a loss to the Americans in the '96 World Cup and a fourth-place finish at the '98 Olympics in Nagano. It seemed cruel that the image we're left with is the sight of him sitting on the bench, watching his teammates get stoned by Dominik Hasek in the shootout in Canada's semifinal loss to the Czechs. A glorious book with a heartbreaking final chapter.

For Lemieux, there was glory in '87 and then a long silence, as he passed up playing in the Canada Cup in 1991 and the World Cup in '96. By the time the Nagano Olympics rolled around Lemieux had retired, but he returned to the game in time for the 2002 Games in Salt Lake City. What is remembered from that tournament, what ultimately decided the gold medal game, is the last great moment of Lemieux's career, and perhaps the one that defined him as a player: with the game tied at one, Chris Pronger sent a pass in Lemieux's direction as he crashed in on the US net. But instead of trying to play the puck, he allowed it to pass through his skates and onto the stick of Paul Kariya. American netminder Mike Richter only saw No. 66 coming down on him, and by the time he realized the puck had passed through his skates, he was sunk. It was as if Lemieux had seen the play unfolding as an out-of-body experience and processed the physics of the pass, his skates and Kariya in flight, all in a split second.

What is not remembered about that tournament is Lemieux's mostly desultory performance in earlier games in the Olympic tournament. He had joined the team as a late addition—having been sidelined with a hip injury in the weeks before, leaving his participation in doubt. A rumour circulated that he was so disappointed by his play in an opening-round loss to Sweden and a narrow win over Germany that he had packed his bags with the intention of flying back to Pittsburgh. All those hard times, of course, were erased in the time it took for the puck to travel from Pronger's stick, through Lemieux's skates, over to Kariya and finally into the back of the US net. Canada had the lead, never surrendered it and pulled away for a 5–2 win over the Olympic home side.

Lemieux would go on to play for the Canadian team that won the World Cup of Hockey in 2004, but that really wasn't much more than a curtain call, ahead of the soon-to-be-cancelled NHL season. It was the play Lemieux made in Salt Lake City that lingered in the memory—less than two years before, it would never have even occurred to anyone that Lemieux would play in the event, having been out of hockey for three complete seasons and the better part of two more. A dream conclusion to his international career after it had seemingly ended 15 years earlier—and, coincidentally, a foreshadowing of the Olympic debut of the young player who would briefly be his teammate.

Suffice it to say that the *Hockey News* ranking was no less than 95 percent formulated on performance in the NHL—whatever weight you'd give Gretzky, Orr, Howe and Lemieux for international play would be entirely eclipsed by any run through the Stanley Cup playoffs. And in this way, Crosby stands apart. With two Olympic gold medals, a world junior title and a world championship, Crosby's international accomplishments already outstrip those of his predecessors, in number, consequence and drama. Yes, there's the benefit of timing—he came along in an era when opportunities to play were more frequent. (If you presume that this put Crosby at some advantage, consider the favourable terrain that past greats skated through in establishing their legacies through postseason glories—it would have been far easier in a six-team league for Howe and contemporaries, or even the much-diluted

12-team and 14-team league Orr dominated. The ranks of the league had swollen by the time Gretzky and Lemieux came along, but not to the degree—a 30-team loop—in which Crosby's Penguins won three Stanley Cups. Further, there were the market forces— the others played when teams either had players over a barrel or could spend as freely as they pleased, while Crosby's entire career has been played in the salary-cap era, which effectively levels the playing field leaguewide.)

Back in his rookie season, Sidney Crosby didn't put up any public protest when he was passed over by Wayne Gretzky, the general manager of the Canadian team going to the 2006 Winter Olympics in Turin. There might have been hope that Lemieux would return for a second trip to the Olympics and that he'd ride along with Crosby, but in early December he was pulled from the Penguins lineup with an irregular heartbeat that would force him to retire for good just weeks later. Early in the season, Gretzky had assured Lemieux that Crosby was in the mix for the team, and while the Penguins were struggling on the ice, their rookie kept up a point-a-game pace through his first three months in the NHL. Ultimately, though, Gretzky's decisions about the Canadian roster came down to experience—returning players and those who had played in the 2004 World Cup and world championship tournaments were given the priority. The youngest player on Gretzky's list, Rick Nash of Columbus, was only three years older than Crosby, but he had led the 2005 world championships in goal scoring. Carolina's Eric Staal, also 21, was leading the league in goals, but was only named to the reserve list, ostensibly because he had only one full season of NHL experience and had never appeared in a playoff game.

As with any Canadian team selection, several of Gretzky's choices were second-guessed. The most controversial was the selection of Vancouver's Todd Bertuzzi, who had been suspended in the spring of 2004 for the balance of the season and the playoffs for his attack on Colorado's Steve Moore. And, as is often the case, some questioned the inclusion of role players like Kris Draper, who had been a key checking-line centre on three Red Wings championship teams. That said, Gretzky received more criticism for the veterans who had been excluded (Brendan Shanahan, Patrick Marleau and Alex Tanguay, who were among the league leaders in scoring) than he did for passing over the young phenom. Even the most generous of media critics would only go as far as to make the case that Gretzky could have selected Crosby as a 13th forward, mostly just a backup, to get some experience that could help in Olympics down the line.

When the Olympic roster was announced, some of the buzz around Crosby was static—he was being taken to task by commentators, opponents and even some of his teammates for whining to officials on the ice. Philadelphia coach Ken Hitchcock had gone farther, calling Crosby "a diver."

Even if he wasn't concerned about the appearance of complaining too much, Crosby put up a diplomatic front. "It's important for me to move on," he told the Associated Press. "I try to go out and give myself an opportunity to play there and if not, I'm not second-guessing any guy there because they all deserve to be there. It's tough because I thought I had a chance, but it's not tough because I think I should replace someone else, it's not like that at all."

Lemieux was also loath to criticize Gretzky for leaving Crosby off the roster, but Pat Brisson did speak up on his client's behalf.

"Regardless of their decisions, it was going to create some kind of controversy with the talent pool," the agent said. "However, as I've said before, in my opinion Sidney thrives under pressure and could play with anyone in the world and make a difference."

Any sting Crosby felt in being passed over was compounded by the fact that the Russians selected Ovechkin and Malkin, the latter in his last season with Metallurg Magnitogorsk. That was more red meat for fans who were cheering on Ovechkin over the perceived overhyping of Crosby, but it also served as an incentive for the slighted—in the six games after getting the disappointing news, Crosby scored seven goals and five assists. There was talk that injuries might open up spots on the roster, and Crosby made his case for them.

Ultimately, Gretzky and the players he selected were roundly roasted for Canada's most embarrassing performance in Turin, one that made the disappointments in Nagano seem minor by comparison. Canada was undone by a paucity of scoring, shut out in opening-round losses to Switzerland and Finland and in a quarter-final elimination game against Russia. Crosby might have been able to, as Brisson said, make a difference, but he couldn't have cured all that ailed that team. Still, his play after the snub continued to make it seem he had raised his game in response—in the 23 games left in the Penguins' season after the Olympic break, Crosby racked up 11 goals and 26 assists and earned a spot on the Canadian team that went to the world championships in Latvia.

Crosby's play in that tournament fuelled second-guessing about his omission from the Olympic roster. Playing beside Patrice Bergeron once again, Crosby scored eight goals and eight assists in nine games, becoming the youngest player ever to lead the tournament in scoring and be named as its top forward. In no game was he more impressive than in a 5–4 loss to the eventual champion, Sweden, in the semis. In that contest, a couple of suspect goals early in the game put Canada in a deep hole, and late in the second period the Swedes had a 5–2 lead. When Crosby put a rebound past Johan Holmqvist to bring Canada within two goals with 30 seconds left in the second period, he threw his hands up in the air—a pretty standard "celly," no taunting, nothing over the top. Swedish defenceman Mika Hannula either spontaneously took umbrage or did some moral calculus and cross-checked Crosby in the face, sending him down in a heap against the boards behind the net—Canadian coach Marc Habscheid called it "a blantant take-out." Hannula was hit with a major penalty and a game misconduct, although Canada ended up on the power play for only three minutes because of a minor for unsportsmanlike conduct when Crosby's teammates roughed up Hannula. Crosby was down for over a minute and had to be helped up and off the ice—he told the medical staff in the dressing room that he was dizzy, and his return to action seemed unlikely. He did re-enter the game during the third and, just seconds after stepping on the ice, was off on a breakaway. He later set up a goal by Bergeron, but the Canadian rally ended there. Canadian captain Brendan Shanahan was suitably impressed, and after the game he tweaked those skeptical of Crosby. "It said a lot to us the way Sid came out and played the third period because he was in rough shape during the second intermission," Shanahan said. "It says a lot to hockey fans and the people of Canada who are still trying to figure out what kind of heart and desire he has."

The next Olympics were still four years off at that point, but everyone presumed that those questions would be answered in full in Vancouver in 2010.

———

Before Crosby came along, the most momentous goal scored in international hockey history was Paul Henderson's stuffing the puck past Vladislav Tretiak in the dying seconds of Game 8 of the Summit Series in 1972. Never mind limiting it to a sports criterion, some would make a case that it was the seminal moment in Canadian history for citizens of a certain age. Regrettably, I'm old enough to have been around for it, but thankfully only old enough to remember it vividly. The Summit Series games in Moscow were played out when it was daytime in North America, in conflict with my high-school classes, but I listened surreptitiously to them on a transistor radio, an earpiece buried under hair worthy of a roadie for Mott the Hoople. For the eighth and deciding game, our school, like virtually all others, cancelled classes and the game was screened in the auditorium. For fear of getting outed, I'll admit that I actually rooted for the Soviets—it was just a reaction to the likes of *Globe and Mail* columnist Dick Beddoes's vow to eat a newspaper column if the USSR won a single game from Team Canada. Who wouldn't put love of country behind the opportunity to see a biliously over-confident jackass eat newspaper? Beyond that, I thought it was patently unfair and unwise for the NHL and Alan Eagleson, head of the players' association, to shut out Bobby Hull, Derek Sanderson and others who had signed with teams in the WHA.

For the next 38 years, Henderson's goal would have only one rival in terms of drama and significance: Mike Eruzione's game winner for the US in their dramatic upset of the Soviets at the 1980 Olympics in Lake Placid. Which was more impressive? It's tempting to give points to 1980 because of the backdrop of political tensions—the US, Canada and a number of other nations would boycott the Summer Games in Moscow later that year because of the Soviet invasion of Afghanistan. But on Henderson's side, there was a certain finality. Eruzione's goal didn't actually win the gold for the Americans, but left them needing a win over Finland in the final game of the tournament to seal the deal.

You don't need to have come along after '72 or '80 to include Sidney Crosby's "Golden Goal" at the 2010 Vancouver Olympics in this conversation. Granted, Crosby's overtime winner over the US lacked the Cold War intrigue of the Summit Series or the game in Lake Placid. And in Vancouver, that gold medal game featured a collection of NHLers well known to all; the Soviets were a mystery to fans in '72 and only slightly less so eight years later. On a number of counts, though, Crosby's goal carried far more psychic weight.

In the history of the game at its highest level, a championship being won or lost by a single goal in live play is far less common than you'd probably presume. Only twice has a Stanley Cup gone to overtime in Game 7: in 1950 Detroit's Pete Babando scored in double overtime against New York's Chuck Rayner; and four years later Tony Leswick gave the Red Wings another Cup, putting the puck past Montreal's Gerry McNeil after less than five minutes of extra time. In international play, probably the closest thing to a precedent would be Peter Forsberg scoring the postage-stamp winner in the shootout over Canada at the 1994 Olympics — but again, that was a shootout, and it wouldn't only be traditionalists who would downgrade it on that count.

And really, look at the names we're throwing around here. Forsberg is a Hockey Hall of Famer, yes, and a Hart Trophy winner with a couple of Stanley Cups on his resumé as well as two Olympic golds — with Nicklas Lidstrom, he'd be among the first names that you'd throw out there on a list of the greatest Swedish players of all time. But Pete Babando and Tony Leswick? Two journeymen, at best. Paul Henderson, if the truth be told, was a good but not great player, an unlikely choice for Team Canada 1972, who summoned the best he had in the Summit Series; every year, a devout cult of Henderson loyalists campaigns for his election to the Hockey Hall of Fame, but I doubt any of them could cite his second-best moment in the game outside of those games against the Soviets.

On the list of the NHL's 10 greatest players, the only one who scored a championship-winning goal in overtime is Bobby Orr, and it has been freighted with significance—in a fan vote conducted by the NHL in the league's centennial year, Orr's overtime Cup-winning goal against St. Louis in the 1970 final finished second to Mario Lemieux's five goals scored five different ways in a game in 1988. No matter; Orr's goal provided what is likely the single best-known image in the hockey history: Blues defenceman Noel Picard hoisting a jubilant Orr fully airborne after he put the puck past Glenn Hall. But Orr's goal wrapped up a four-game sweep of an expansion team—to that point, none of the teams added in 1967 had won a playoff game against an Original Six franchise.

It's impossible to predict where Crosby's goal against the US will stand in the game's lore. It did inspire the flowery best of *Sports Illustrated*'s Michael Farber: "The golden goal in Vancouver is embroidered on the tapestry of hockey, part of a Crosby legacy that will one day veer into legend." And the magazine did name it as its play of the year—this from a magazine that mostly kept hockey in a niche well behind the NFL, major league baseball, the NBA and the NCAA.

What can be said with certainty is that the overtime goal against the US in Vancouver in 2010 was the most *visible* climactic moment in hockey's history. It drew a record number of viewers in North America. According to BBM overnight ratings, 26.5 million Canadians watched at least some part of the game, and two-thirds of the country—22 million—were watching the moment that Crosby yelled "Iggy," skated in on the American net and beat Ryan Miller. To put this in historical context, Henderson's goal was seen in real time by 13 million Canadians. The audience in the US actually outstripped that in Canada. NBC's live broadcast of the final drew an average viewership of 27.6 million, the largest live hockey audience since the US's gold medal–clinching victory over Finland in Lake Placid (32.8 million), back when the nation's three major networks operated with virtually no opposition on the dial. (The Americans' win over the Soviets in the penultimate game in 1980 wasn't even broadcast live, but on a three-hour tape delay—with the outcome already widely know, ABC's broadcast drew an audience of 34 million.)

The US market with the largest rating was Buffalo, which edged out Pittsburgh, Detroit and Minneapolis–St. Paul. That stood to reason: Buffalo native Patrick Kane was the Americans' best scoring threat and the Sabres' Ryan Miller was in their net. That weekend, I was on assignment and had been watching the Minnesota state high school tournament. On the Sunday morning, I flew out of Minneapolis–St. Paul and made it to Buffalo a half hour before the puck drop. I figured I might be able to get home to Toronto in time for the second period, but at that point the game might be already decided. I wound up at a downtown watering hole a short walk from the Sabres' arena, the Washington Square Tavern, and if the standing-room crowd there was any measure, then the Nielsen rating undersold the reach of NBC's broadcast. The locals had come out to see what they hoped would be the most momentous American hockey victory since 1980.

I didn't talk to the other patrons, for fear that I might slip up and say "about" or slip into the northern patois. I feared being mistaken for a lurking Canadian fan when, in fact, I was nothing of the sort. With three decades in the game, I've grown incapable of taking off my reporter's fedora. I look at every game I work as a trial, and my job is to be a fair juror. I've been at it long enough that I no longer root for team or even country, and I had dealt with players on both sides of this gold medal game. I only hoped that no one got hung out to dry as the goat. I wouldn't wish for anyone to become another Scott Norwood or Bill Buckner.

It's now a decade in the rear-view mirror and detailed memories of that game slip away. (For you perhaps a little more than me, because I actually have my notes from watching the game at the Washington Square Tavern, which may have made me suspicious-looking, but probably discouraged anyone from striking up a conversation.) And I did track Sidney Crosby in that game—just a habit I had picked up since first covering him seven years before.

Here's what people forget about that gold medal game and about that Olympic tournament: Sidney Crosby was *that close* to being a scapegoat, if not *the* goat. If Canada didn't win that game, its players would have been crucified, but none more than Crosby.

The Canadian team had been projected to win the tournament not just by the pundits in the host nation, but by the independent arbiters, most notably *Sports Illustrated*. A Canadian Olympic team featuring a lineup of future Hockey Hall of Famers playing in Canada: you can make a case that other international teams had rosters that might have matched that squad in Vancouver, but none ever enjoyed a greater home-ice advantage. Scott Niedermayer, a holdover from the 2002 Olympic championship team, would wear the captain's C, but in the words of coach Mike Babcock, Crosby was "the face" of the team and, as such, the face of the tournament.

I remember being in Washington when Crosby and the Penguins came in to play the Capitals for an NBC matinee game on Super Bowl Sunday, on the eve of the Olympic teams heading to Vancouver. Crosby looked to be not just in peak form but raising his game to all-new heights. The Penguins' flight from New York to Washington had been cancelled due to the worst snowstorm in the capital's history, so they had to crawl into town on a marathon bus ride with barely any time to spare. Advantage: Washington. Yet Crosby came out and staked his team to an early lead almost single-handedly, scoring two goals in the first 10 minutes. Though the Penguins would predictably fade and Washington would come back to win the game with Ovechkin scoring a hat trick and assisting on Mike Knuble's overtime winner, it augured well for riveting mano a mano between the rivals at the top of their games in Vancouver.

The opening round started promisingly enough: an 8–0 blowout of Norway with Jarome Iginla getting a hat trick and Crosby picking up three assists, playing on a line with Rick Nash and Patrice Bergeron. Thereafter, though, the qualifying round in Vancouver felt like Turin redux. Just like four years before, the Canadians weren't blowing anyone away. Switzerland figured to be a tune-up for serious stuff down the line, but the hosts were stoned by Swiss goaltender Jonas Hiller—held off the score sheet in regulation, Crosby scored on his second attempt in the shootout to win the game, if not put the country at ease. Then came existential dread when the Canadians lost to the US in their opening-round contest—Canada had the balance of play, but again a hot netminder, Miller, turned them away.

"Like every team in the tournament, we're now playing to survive," coach Babcock said.

Crosby (in the front row at right holding banner) celebrates with his Shattuck-St Mary's teammates after winning the national championship at the prep-school level. Said Coach Tom Ward (back row, left): "At Shattuck, Sid was just Sid . . . and really he didn't get any special attention. He just blended in and he liked that a lot. And even at 15 at some level he knew this was the last time it was going to be like that. He was an old soul."

On a break from Shattuck, Crosby led Team Nova Scotia to a fifth-place finish at the Canada Winter Games, the best ever performance for a provincial team at that level. In the seasons since he led Dartmouth to the Air Canada Cup final and represented the province at the under-17 level, teams from Nova Scotia have been a growing factor in minor hockey. Says his coach in Cole Harbour Paul Gallagher: "Players see what Sidney has done and it's made them believe that they can get there too, maybe in a way that 20 or 30 years ago, kids just didn't think about."

Crosby's Rimouski Oceanic swept his hometown Halifax Mooseheads in the final as his QMJHL career wound down. He won the CHL Player of the Year in both his major-junior seasons. In his final season with Rimouski, he scored 66 goals and 168 points in 66 games, and led the Oceanic to the Memorial Cup final with a line-up featuring only one other player who made it to the NHL.

CP PHOTO/Jonathan Hayward

Crosby celebrates alongside teammate Mike Richards (right) after Canada's victory over Russia at the 2005 world junior championship in Grand Forks, North Dakota. Crosby played wing on a line with future Olympic Games teammates Patrice Bergeron and Corey Perry. The 2005 under-20 team is considered arguably the most dominant in the history of the tournament. Said one scout: "The other guys were beaten before they stepped on the ice."

CP PHOTO/Ryan Remiorz

Crosby reaches Alexander Ovechkin in the handshake line after Canada's 6-1 victory over Russia in the 2005 world junior final. Ovechkin could only watch the final two periods of the championship game from the bench after sustaining a shoulder injury. Crosby levelled Ovechkin with a huge open-ice hit in the neutral zone on one of the last shifts the Russian star would take in that game.

Despite expectations of joining a veteran-led Stanley Cup contender after the NHL lockout, the Penguins in Crosby's rookie season proved to be a mess, winning just 22 games and finishing with the league's second-worst record. The promise of the young star going to school as a teammate of Mario Lemieux abruptly ended in mid-winter when the Hall of Famer had to retire because of an irregular heartbeat.

AP Photo/Mark Humphrey

As the 21-year-old captain of the Penguins, Crosby hoists the Cup for the first time after Pittsburgh beat the Red Wings 2-1 in an incredibly tense Game 7 in Detroit. The victory over the defending champion Wings avenged the Penguins' loss in the final the previous spring. Said Wings captain Nick Lidstrom: "The difference in speed and strength in the young players like Crosby and Malkin from one season to the next was pretty dramatic. They learned a lot from that first series against us."

Crosby celebrates after taking a pass from Jarome Iginla and putting the puck past goaltender Ryan Miller to defeat the U.S. in overtime of the gold-medal game at the Vancouver Olympics in 2010. It was almost certainly the most watched hockey game in history: 26.5 million Canadians tuned in, while the NBC live broadcast of the final drew an average viewership of 27.6 million in the U.S., the largest live hockey audience since the Americans' gold-medal clinching victory over Finland in Lake Placid (32.8 million).

THE CANADIAN PRESS/Paul Chiasson

Back in the 2010–11 campaign, Crosby was having the best season of his career and seemed a certain winner of the Hart Trophy until this mid-ice collision with Washington's David Steckel in the Winter Classic at Heinz Field. Few noted it at the time, though *Hockey Night in Canada's* Craig Simpson picked up on it almost immediately. While many thought that Steckel had no intent to injure Crosby, the Penguins captain would later claim the Capitals' journeyman knew exactly what he was doing.

Matt Niskanen takes a stick to the helmet of Crosby in the first period of Game 3 of the 2017 Eastern Conference semi-final. Crosby had to be helped off the ice and did not return to the game. The Penguins would announce that their captain had a concussion and fears rose that his season was at an end. Yet less than a week later he returned for Game 5, and a few weeks down the line he would win the Conn Smythe Trophy and raise the Stanley Cup for a third time.

In the 2017 Stanley Cup final, the Penguins faced the Nashville Predators, who had gone into the playoffs at the eighth seed in the Western Conference. Here Crosby is taken into the boards by the Predators' P.K. Subban. In Game 5 of the series, Subban and Crosby would tussle and the Penguins' leader would take a stick to the back of the defenceman's helmeted head while he was down on the ice.

When the author met him in Cole Harbour, Nathan MacKinnon (here with the medicine ball) was a 15-year-old enrolled at Shattuck St-Mary's, like Crosby had been before him. At that age, MacKinnon had yet to meet Crosby, but a couple of

seasons later he was the first overall pick in the 2013 NHL entry draft. Today he's Crosby's neighbour on a lake outside of Halifax and his most frequent training partner. Here MacKinnon works out in his home gym with Andy O'Brien (right) whose work with Crosby has made him the most in-demand personal trainer in the NHL.

Darren Calabrese

Courtesy of Ellen Hughes

Jack Hughes (centre) was the first overall selection in the 2019 NHL entry draft. Here in a family photo going back to his minor hockey days in Toronto, he's framed by younger brother Luke (left) and his older brother Quinn, a first-round draft pick of the Vancouver Canucks in 2017. The Hughes brothers are just a trio in the legion of next-generation players influenced by Crosby and, not coincidentally, Quinn and Jack signed with CAA, the agency that represents the star whose sweaters they wore in hockey, on the ice or the street.

People wondered exactly when Canada's "face" was going to show up. Crosby, who went goalless in the run-up to the quarter-finals, was having a forgettable tournament, and at a press conference after the loss to the US, Babcock pointed out that Crosby had gone minus-3 for the game, just in case anyone had missed it. Perhaps some cut Crosby some slack because he was only 22 years old, but then again 20-year-old Drew Doughty, perhaps a small surprise to be selected, was a revelation on the Canadian blue line.

The loss to the US appeared to give Canada a difficult route to the final, and in the quarters the hosts ran into Russia—in a matchup many had expected to occur in a high-drama gold medal game, offering another thrilling instalment in the Crosby–Ovechkin rivalry. Neither came to pass in any way, shape or form: Canada routed the Russians 7–3, while Crosby and Ovechkin were basically sidemen. In the third minute, defenceman Dan Boyle rushed deep into the Russian end, fairly adventurous in a scoreless elimination game, and found Ryan Getzlaf in the slot; on the backcheck Viktor Kozlov just waved at Getzlaf, who fired it into a wide-open net. That goal and some ferocious hitting set the Canadians on their way. They ran out to a 6–1 lead through the first 24 minutes of action. Though Crosby led all forwards with over 17 minutes of ice time, he was held off the score sheet. It was the lines of Mike Richards, Jonathan Toews and Rick Nash and Corey Perry, Ryan Getzlaf and Brenden Morrow, along with some huge hits by Shea Weber on Ovechkin and clutch saves by Roberto Luongo, that left the Russians at sea. Still, with Canada through to the semifinals, no one was much questioning the play of Crosby—it evoked, if anything, his play and role with so many of these same players at the 2005 world juniors.

The darlings of the tournament, the Slovaks, had not only upset the Russians with a shootout win in the opening round, but seemingly saved the hosts a difficult ride in the semis by knocking off the defending Olympic champions, Sweden, in the quarter-finals. Canada got past them, but it was tense — after running out to a 3–0 lead on goals by Patrick Marleau, Morrow and Getzlaf in the opening 40 minutes, Slovakia roared back in the third period and pulled within one goal with five minutes to play. Again, what lay ahead for Canada, the rematch with the US, became the over-riding narrative rather than "whither Crosby."

The Golden Goal has probably been dissected like no other in the history of the game of hockey, but the prior events of that particular game have become about as obscure as the Dead Sea Scrolls. In short, Canada ran out to a 2–0 lead on goals by Toews, who would be named the tournament's top forward, and Corey Perry. The hitting in the contest was much like it had been in the Russia game, but it cut both ways. For Canada, Perry and Weber were dropping bombs at both ends of the rink. Maybe the biggest hit by an American came on the shift after Toews's goal, when Joe Pavelski turned Crosby upside down and left him crashing to the ice on his neck. Another time, Ryan Kesler decked Crosby. Unlike the Russians, the US pushed back. Crosby was held off the score sheet again, but he did have his moments: on a power play, he sent Eric Staal in all alone on Miller, but Staal struggled to control the puck and the goaltender came well out of his net to force the issue. Though goalless since that opening game against Norway, Crosby never lost Mike Babcock's confidence — he was creating chances and winning faceoffs at both ends of the ice. It wasn't a case of the other Canadian centres, Toews and Getzlaf, usurping Crosby or that he didn't have his game going—Babcock balanced the ice evenly among the top three lines.

In the second period, Canada had a couple of chances to put the game away with a third goal, but Miller made a couple of clutch saves, including turning aside Iginla, who almost pushed him into the net with the puck. Any hope for breathing room vanished when Kesler deflected Patrick Kane's shot from the wing with six minutes to go in the second period. It was a white-knuckle ride the rest of the way. Canada was clearly taking a safety-first approach, and you watched the highest of high-end players in the game assuming the work ethic of third-liners protecting their jobs—Crosby diving in front of a shot by Brian Rafalski with six minutes to go in the third period was of a piece with the tense third period. On his next shift Crosby stripped Kesler of the puck in the Canadian zone and, with the Americans pressing, the waters parted: a breakaway, albeit a rolling puck to chase. Kane desperately pursued Crosby and managed to give his stick a knock at the very last moment.

Crosby was on the bench and watching like the rest of the hockey world when Zach Parise cashed in a pinballing carom of a Kane shot to tie the game with just 24.4 seconds left in regulation. A tie at that point seemed eminently fair—despite Canada's rousing start, the US surged late. Shots were even at 32 apiece and scoring chances were about a wash. You could make a case that the US was better in this game than they had been in the win over Canada in the first round.

A couple of breaths before Crosby's winner, Pavelski almost had a Golden Goal of his own: Scott Niedermayer, the Canadian captain, turned the puck over to Pavelski, who was in a solo forecheck during a Canadian line change. Pavelski turned directly and fired the puck, with Luongo getting a shrugged shoulder in front of it, looking far from certain that he'd made the save.

And then it was Crosby's time.

Through 67 minutes, you had a sense that the US blueliners were wearying under the onslaught—whether it was Getzlaf and Perry dropping big checks or Crosby and Toews forcing defenders to chase around their own end, that's a heavy toll for any defencemen. The Americans' lead pair, Rafalski and Ryan Suter, would log almost 28 minutes and more than 31 respectively. By comparison, Chris Pronger was the big minutes-eater on the Canadian defence, and he finished with 23 and a half. In a game played at such a frenetic pace, at the end of a compressed schedule of games and with the stakes so high, fatigue had to set in. And that's basically what led to the goal that won the game and the gold medal for Canada.

Rafalski was one of the best-skating defenceman of his generation, effective in the wide-open post-lockout game that puts a premium on mobility rather than size and strength; but when he was chasing Crosby along the boards, he overcommitted and couldn't find the legs to recover. Crosby yelled, "Iggy." Iginla hit him with a pass. Miller stuck his stick out to pre-empt a shot, but too late and just out of reach.

The ride for Crosby and the Canadians was at times terrifying but in the end exhilarating, and the scene at the end was right out of a movie. Crosby took his place at the end of the line when IOC president Jacques Rogge draped the medals around the Canadians' sweaty necks. Because the men's hockey final was the last event of the Games, Crosby was the last of the champions at the Vancouver Olympics to receive a gold medal. And if that was straight out of a movie, so too did lines from the principals seem to be perfectly scripted. Crosby's anointment as a Canadian hero was immediate and thoroughgoing. "Sid's got a little destiny to him," GM Steve Yzerman said. "His entire career, throughout minor hockey, junior hockey, the NHL and now this . . . it's just another monumental moment in his career. And he's what, 22 still? He's a special, special guy."

Crosby, in turn, deflected any personal praise. He did what he could to take a place in the ranks, if not in the background, saying "that it could have been any of us" who scored the overtime goal. "I never saw myself as the guy, the one who had to get it done," he said, which might have reflected his true inner thoughts, but not those of many—if not most—Canadian fans. And Crosby was equally quick to put his own and his team's victory fully in context: the win over the US capped the most successful Olympics in Canadian history. Canada's 14 gold medals led all nations in Vancouver, and in fact set a new record for a nation in a single Winter Games. "I'm as proud of us setting that record as anything," Crosby said. "It's been a great experience all around, with all our great athletes."

The NHL returned to the Olympics in 2014 and this time Crosby wore the captain's C. He and his team had a very tough act to follow, especially when the event-defining moment had him in the centre of it. And it was the roadie to end all roadies for Canadian hockey players: Russia. Perhaps there'd be some sort of symmetry if Olympic hockey had been played in Moscow's Luzhniki Palace of Sports, an echo 42 years removed from the Summit Series. Instead, the tournament would be in Sochi, where the Russian government had plowed billions into the development of pop-up Olympic venues.

Even though Sochi is hundreds of miles from Moscow, the Olympics played out in the shadow of the Kremlin, Russian president Vladimir Putin positioning the Games as a propaganda tool. Though a team of Russians last captured gold in '92,[1] it was tempting to grant the Russians status as the gold-medal favourites—unlike Vancouver, games in Sochi would be played on the larger international ice sheet and presumably benefit the European sides. Said Russian team captain Pavel Datsyuk on the IIHF website, "The pressure is enormous, and it's growing every day. Everyone is expecting only one thing from us. And we won't have the right to make an error." On the Russian hockey federation's website, Vladislav Tretiak, the national hero of the Summit Series, evoked the Soviet era. "In our time, we did everything for the victory. We glorified the USSR, our people and our sports. Don't let Russia down, guys!"

And, once again, the 2014 tournament was expected to feature a showdown between Sidney Crosby and Alexander Ovechkin. Once again, it didn't play out that way.

Early on, the arc of the Canadian team's tournament looked familiar: the defending champions struggled to score against a seeming lightweight (winning 3–1 against Norway in their opening game) and didn't impress in a tune-up against a squad made up of journeymen of the European leagues (a 6–0 win over Austria). What figured to be their only truly tough game of the opening round, a meeting with Finland, stuck to the template: dominance

---

1   A quirk in the record book: Because of the dissolution of the USSR in fall of 1991, the members of the Soviet Union's national team played in the Olympics in Albertville, France, under the name and banner of the Commonwealth of the Independent States (CIS).

in possession, and shots that didn't translate into scoring. Drew Doughty broke a one-all tie with a shot from the point three minutes into overtime to send Canada into the elimination round undefeated but perhaps beatable, a No. 3 seed with eight out of nine points and a goal differential of eight. The only seeming advantage here was that, with the win over Finland, Crosby and company could only face Russia in the final, and that would be the Russians' fourth game in six days if it were to come to pass. The big game that loomed more immediately looked to be a semifinal against the Americans, who had knocked off Russia in a shootout in group play—coach Dan Bylsma sent T. J. Oshie out six times in the extended shootout, with Oshie finding the back of the net four times, including the winner.

Through the opening games, Canadian fans wondered when Crosby was going to take over, as if he were just picking up where he left off in the gold medal game four years before. Three games into the tournament, though, Mike Babcock was still trying to find a winger to complement Crosby and replicate the chemistry he'd had with Iginla and Eric Staal in Vancouver. There hadn't been as much controversy over the selection of the roster as there had been in the past—no surprise omission like Mark Messier's in 1998 —but if there was any debate it probably focused on Chris Kunitz, Crosby's everyday winger in Pittsburgh at the time. The 34-year-old Kunitz hadn't been in the mix for the 2010 roster, and he had no significant Olympic or international experience. Though he was widely perceived to have piggybacked on Crosby's success, he had made the NHL's First All-Star Team in 2012–13 and would go on to rack up a career-best 35 goals that season. If Kunitz's history with Crosby had landed him a spot on the roster, his play didn't automatically win him a spot on Crosby's wing. Babcock tried cycling others through, notably Jeff Carter and Jamie Benn, but going into the elimination games it didn't seem the team's brain trust had quite figured it out. Crosby maintained that there was no cause for concern—he was staying the course even if the coach was changing tack from shift to shift. "I don't think I'm out there thinking about where a guy's going to be or second-guessing a play because I haven't played with that guy," Crosby says. "I would do the same things I would do in Pittsburgh."

Once again Canada ran into a hot goaltender in the quarter-final: Latvia's Kristers Gudlevskis, who bounced between the AHL and ECHL. In Canada's 2–1 victory, perhaps the most one-sided one-goal game in international history, Gudlevskis stopped 55 of 57 shots and kept the Latvians in the hunt, at least theoretically, until seven minutes were left in regulation, when Shea Weber scored on a shot from the point. Carey Price faced only 16 shots, a fair indication of the balance of play, but the Canadian media's takeaway was mostly pessimistic. A *National Post* headline was an effective thought bubble on press row: "Canada limps into the semi-final." The obvious narrative: Crosby, he of Vancouver's Golden Goal, had yet to score in Sochi. Even though it seemed that Babcock had settled on Kunitz and Patrice Bergeron as the captain's wingers, some were suggesting that the revolving door on Crosby's wing was an indictment. Yes, the claim (and not the first time it would be made) was that Crosby was a difficult line-mate to play with. Yes, as unlikely as it sounds, the idea floated that Crosby was not *adaptable*. Those on the outside viewed this as his personal failure, but his teammates saw it an entirely different way. Said Rick Nash, "He's a tough guy to keep up with. He's so fast. The way he thinks about the game seems like it's far beyond everyone else's thought process."

As in Vancouver, winning has a way of fixing everything and erasing fresh dread. Canada's 1–0 win over the US in the semifinal was a game of a far higher quality than even the thrilling gold medal game four years before. "That was as fast of a game as I think I've ever been a part of," Dan Bylsma said. While scoreless in the first period, a few chances were traded and you had a sense that an American goal could put Canada in dire straits. As time wore on, though, the gap in speed and skills grew more apparent, and after Jamie Benn tipped a puck past Jonathan Quick early in the second, Canada maintained an ever-tighter grip on the game until the buzzer. Crosby's line generated 9 of 37 shots on Quick and dictated the play on seemingly every shift.

As in Vancouver, the Canadians caught breaks on the other side of the draw: first, the potential matchup with Russia in the final blew up when the hosts crashed against Finland in the quarters; and then the Swedes ran out of bodies by the time they advanced to the finals, with Henrik Zetterberg going down to injury and Nicklas Backstrom getting tossed from the tournament for a positive drug test—not a performance-enhancing drug, but an over-the-counter allergy medicine. Backstrom's suspension was handed down just before the final and cast a pall over his team— he and Zetterberg might have been the two players the Swedes could least afford to be without. They didn't even have a forward they could activate to take Backstrom's place.

The final in Vancouver had been high drama, the final in Sochi a clinic. The Canadians were ruthless in their efficiency. And as in Vancouver, Crosby authored the most electric moment —Toews's goal in the first period is the official winner, but Crosby's with five minutes to go in the second period gave the Canadians a 2–0 lead and felt like all the insurance they'd need for the gold.

Crosby stripped defenceman Jonathan Ericsson of the puck at Canada's blue line, headed off on a 120-foot breakaway and neatly deked Henrik Lundqvist. That Kunitz would add a goal in the third period to complete the scoring was vindication in full. In the end Canada got enough done, and the rest of the world could get almost nothing done against them—the Swedes, Americans and Finns, in their tournament games against Canada, managed a total of one goal and were easily outchanced nearly two to one. GM Steve Yzerman called it "the greatest defensive performance" he had seen in international hockey, and a lot of the defence the Canadians played they did while playing keep-away—they protected leads by possessing the puck, and no one was better on this count than Crosby.

In Sochi, Crosby didn't pick up where he left off in Vancouver. At the World Cup in Toronto he did pick up exactly where he had left off two years before in Russia. Okay, the World Cup didn't carry the historical or psychic weight of the Olympics, and no one was using the games in Toronto as a propaganda tool, unless you count the NHL marketing department. On the ice, though, fairly fresh off his second Stanley Cup victory, Crosby was at his imperious best. There was no debate about those playing his wing—Bergeron was there from Sochi, as he had been in Grand Forks 11 years before, and Brad Marchand offered not just the speed to keep up, but a spiky attitude, a level of grit and eagerness to do whatever dirty work was necessary. Marchand's time with Crosby in his summer sessions over the years no doubt contributed to his fast rise from third-line pest in Boston to all-star and seamless fit alongside the Canadian captain in the World Cup lineup.

Before the tournament, you might have predicted the Europeans would want to match Zdeno Chara against Crosby's line, but whether it was his age or the speed of the game or the preseason start, the former Norris Trophy winner struggled. Instead the Europeans matched their best defenceman and probably their best skater in the tournament, Roman Josi of Nashville, against Crosby. Little did it occur to people that this game-within-a-game matchup foreshadowed another that would play out in the Stanley Cup final eight months down the line.

In the second game of the World Cup's best-of-three final, Team Europe took a lead early when Chara skated in from the left point and wired one of his ever-potent slapshots that found the far top corner on Carey Price. Europe managed to clog up the neutral zone and take Canada's speed out of the game. In goal for the underdogs, Jaroslav Halak came into the tournament expecting to compete for the backup job behind Frederik Andersen, but when the Toronto netminder went down with an injury on the eve of the event, Halak stepped into the void and stole games. And it looked like Halak might do it again in Game 2 of the World Cup final — with three minutes to go in regulation, Europe's 1–0 lead was still standing up. But Bergeron scored on a late Canadian power play with an assist from Crosby, and with about a minute to go in regulation Marchand scored on a penalty kill to effectively close out the tournament.

The 2016 World Cup of Hockey didn't generate a fraction of the interest of the Olympic tournaments or the Canada Cup tourneys. Even among the World Cups it ran a poor third. It left me wondering, though, if this might be the last game that Crosby would ever play on the world stage. I'm not suggesting that somehow the World Cup and the tournament's MVP award provided him with some degree of closure. Nor was the idea that this would close a chapter on his career prompted by a postgame statement —his quotes in the aftermath were fairly interchangeable with those in the wake of Canada's victories at the Olympics. He didn't drop any hints—there was no long lap of the rink to drink in the memories. And there certainly wasn't a falloff in his game, not like when Bobby Orr collected his award at the Canada Cup. In Orr's case you wondered if he would ever play another game of any sort.

No, for Crosby it's first a matter of politics. The NHL wasn't going to Korea in 2018, and its future participation in the Olympics beyond that is uncertain. The IOC awarded the 2022 Games to Beijing, and the league's head office in Manhattan has been aggressively trying to develop an audience in the world's largest market. If the players had their druthers, they'd go; in fact, they're desperate to do just that. In counterpoint to those who begged off from the World Cup with injuries, stars have tried at no small risk to race back from injury in time for the Olympics, the instructive case being that of Steven Stamkos, who tried in vain to come back from a broken leg in time for the Games in Sochi. The other principals—the NHL franchise owners and the IOC—are another matter. The owners don't like the idea of putting the league on hold for a couple of weeks during their high season, and they would like to get a fair return from the IOC for the value that they believe NHL players bring to the Games.

Even if the NHL and IOC get together for the Beijing Games, there's the matter of math. By then Crosby will be 34 years old. He will have been in the NHL practically half of his life. If he stays reasonably healthy, he'll have blown past 1,200 career games— after missing more than a full season's worth of games due to postconcussion syndrome, he has been remarkably durable, appearing in at least 75 regular-season games in each of the seasons since. Add to that playoff contests—at the time of this printing, he has played 164 playoff games, the equivalent of two more full NHL seasons. Add to all that two Olympics, two world championships and the World Cup. It's wear, but it's also age—in Vancouver only two Canadian players were older than Crosby would be in 2022: defencemen Chris Pronger and Scott Niedermayer were 35. Iginla was the oldest Canadian forward at 32. At the 2016 World Cup, the oldest player in the Canadian lineup, 37-year-old Joe Thornton, was able to play a supporting role, but it doesn't seem likely we'll see another forward his age play for one of the gold medal contenders at the game's summit. Mario Lemieux was 36 in 2002, and 37 when the World Cup was played 18 months later, but that was pre-lockout—the former version of hockey, one more favourable to the older player, not the track meet of the modern game. In every year that Crosby has played in the NHL the game has grown faster. Being able to keep up in 2002 or even 2010 would not mean that you'd be able to keep up in 2016, and one can only imagine what it will be like in 2022. By then the fastest players in the NHL today, Connor McDavid and Nathan MacKinnon, will be 25 and 26 respectively—as fast as they are at this printing in 2019, they will be, barring injury, even faster down the line. By statistical norms, they wouldn't even have reached their peak by 2022.

As competitive as Crosby is, it's hard to see him passing up an opportunity to pursue a third gold medal. The question is: If he is passed or usurped, would he be willing to take a complementary role? No doubt he could do it, but would he rather give another deserving player a shot at glory, possibly his only shot at an Olympic gold? Or would Crosby, as others such as Mario Lemieux and Ray Bourque have done, pass up an opportunity to play in an international tournament and focus on his NHL season? There's no use speculating because the Olympics are no sure thing at this point, and there's no knowing what Crosby's circumstances will be down the line.

The World Cup didn't have the feeling of a coda in Crosby's career. If the tournament was somehow muted, it wasn't for lack of effort and excellence on his part. He didn't fade away. He didn't walk off into the sunset.

Easy to forget: only five years before, many feared that gold medal goal in Vancouver would wind up being the last time we'd ever see Crosby on the international stage. In the direst moments it seemed that he would, like Bobby Orr, have to walk away from the game far, far too soon and never fully realize his greatness. For Orr, it was his knee and his bad luck to come along before advances in orthopaedic procedures were made that might have minimized the effects of his surgery; he wasn't the first star whose career was cut short by an injury of this sort, one that now would be far more easily and less invasively treated. For Crosby, though, it was far more complicated because it was a brain injury he suffered; it came at a time when concussions, many of them career-ending, were an epidemic in the National Hockey League, almost certainly on the rise in step with the accelerating pace of the game every season.

CHAPTER 9

"HE'LL BE OUT ABOUT A WEEK"

January 1, 2011

The darkest hours of Sidney Crosby's career did not commence with the drop of a curtain or with the house lights dimming. It wasn't a single moment of a significance that was plain to all at the outset; nothing catalytic nor catastrophic. There was seemingly not a dramatic turn at all. No, it was the slow-motion unfolding of events over a series of days at the start, and then weeks and months, with concern rising incrementally and then crossing over into despair. And the effect was akin to an *It's a Wonderful Life* reimagining of the game: What would hockey be like without Sidney Crosby?

Even casual hockey fans can recall when events were set in motion, mostly because of the timing: the NHL's biggest signature event outside the Stanley Cup playoffs, the Winter Classic, the annual outdoor game played on New Year's Day. It's the most-watched regular-season game each season, and the 2011 game was likely the most anticipated in the history of the event. It provided a dream matchup: Crosby and the Penguins hosting Alexander Ovechkin and the Capitals—the two biggest names, the fiercest rivals. It was Crosby's return to the Winter Classic after his star turn in the first-ever outdoor game on New Year's Day in Buffalo in 2008. No surprise, then, that the television audience in the US, 4.4 million, set a record that still stands. In Canada more than 2 million were tuned in, and 68,000 came out to the ballpark in Pittsburgh.

All were watching and waiting for something sublime—like Crosby bearing down on the Capitals net and beating one defenceman with a deke and then another, or Ovechkin setting up in his office and wiring a one-timer on the power play. In Pittsburgh, they were hoping at the very least for Crosby to give another heroic turn like the one at Ralph Wilson Stadium in Buffalo, when he scored in the third and final round of the shootout to give the Penguins the 2–1 victory.

As has most often been the case with the NHL's outdoor games, conditions were less than ideal—the skies couldn't make up their minds whether to rain or sleet. And at least partially as a result, the play on the ice didn't really come close to matching the spectacle in the stadium. The Winter Classic was a classic in name only: a forgettable 3–1 victory for the Capitals. Neither Crosby nor Ovechkin made a mark on the score sheet. Malkin opened the scoring in the first for Pittsburgh, but then the Capitals' journeymen took over, Mike Knuble tying the game and Eric Fehr scoring the winner and an insurance goal.

The play would be discussed and dissected for months, though it received only passing mention in newspaper accounts and was barely noted on the broadcasts. On the last shift of the second period, Crosby was skating in the Washington zone, circling on the right wing, trying to find the puck along the boards. David Steckel was between Crosby and the Washington net. The fourth-liner spotted the puck clearing the zone before Crosby did. Steckel started towards the puck in a straight line, intersecting with Crosby. The six-foot, five-inch Steckel didn't drop his shoulder as he might have if he intended to drive Crosby backward. But he didn't skate around him either.

Steckel caught Crosby high with a shoulder. Crosby's head turned sharply and he was knocked into a spin around the faceoff dot. No penalty was called, even though the puck was 100 feet away. Crosby might have shot a ref a disgusted look as he skated back, but it didn't go further than that. Dan Bylsma didn't ride the zebras about not calling a penalty on the play. The Associated Press account of the Winter Classic did cite the play, but only in a single line: "The shoulder hit did not look premeditated." As it turned out, a Cup contender's season went up in smoke and the career of the league's best player took an awful turn on what at the time might have easily escaped notice.

Later, when the implications of the hit became clearer, an honest if sometimes partisan debate ensued, with many inside the game claiming that Steckel knew exactly what he was doing—not that there was premeditation per se but rather intent formed in the heat of the moment. Years later, people who track the NHL even casually can recall the image of Crosby going down in that game, but those who saw it in real time are far outnumbered by the millions who would see it replayed in heavy rotation for months after. No more than a handful had any suspicion of the long shadow it was going to cast. The play was probably more remarkable for what it *wasn't*. It wasn't a violent, seismic event, like Scott Stevens's hits on Eric Lindros and Paul Kariya. It wasn't a head-on collision, not a hammering into the boards, not a fall into the boards. It wasn't an obviously calculated head shot like the cross-check to the head Crosby had absorbed from Mathias Joggi in that game against Switzerland at the summer under-18 tournament. In fact, Steckel's head was turned and he was looking back, heading up ice, when Crosby curled into him. If Steckel were six feet tall, he might have caught Crosby shoulder to shoulder, but at six foot five, and being an upright skater, his shoulder caught Crosby at chin height. No, what happened on that shift in the Winter Classic in Pittsburgh was seemingly incidental contact, a glancing blow, albeit from his blind side—watching it the first few dozen times, you were inclined to think, *If Steckel had really wanted to drill him . . .*

It's strange how memory works, what sustains, what fades. Steckel's hit on Crosby is etched into the cortexes of hockey fans, by virtue of it being played hundreds or even thousands of times during Crosby's indefinite hiatus. "I see it every day, whether I want to or not," Steckel told the *National Post* a year after the fact. With the passage of time, many will have forgotten about Crosby's season to that point. More renowned as a pass-first playmaker than a finisher, Crosby had never scored as many as 40 goals in his first four seasons, but he burst through that threshold in 2009–10, racking up 51 goals along with 58 assists. Henrik Sedin of the Vancouver Canucks barely edged him for the Hart and Art Ross Trophies, but no matter. You had a sense that he wasn't close to the peak of his skills. Through the first three months of the 2010–11 season, the 23-year-old Crosby again raised his game. Going into the 2011 Winter Classic against the Capitals, Crosby was on pace for 64 goals and 132 points. He seemed like a lock to win the Hart and Ross, and no one would have bet against him leading the Pens back to a Stanley Cup—at 25–11–3 the Pens were on course for 110 points, maybe more, maybe enough to give them a shot at the Presidents' Trophy. Crosby wasn't just the best player in the game—no one else was even close. He wasn't inserting himself into the conversation about the greatest players of all time—those who have been part of that conversation were the ones including him. "What he's doing now is much more impressive than what I did years ago," Mario Lemieux said of Crosby in the run-up to the Winter Classic.

Memory will start to fail some when it comes to the other principal, the player who caught Crosby unawares. It wasn't Alexander Ovechkin, Nick Backstrom nor one of the other players at the top of the Capitals roster. It wasn't a physically punishing defenceman, nor was it one of the league bad boys, someone with a long rap sheet of suspensions. No, the antagonist in this piece was a fourth-line centre, an earnest workman, a role player. To be frank, Steckel might have been the most wooden skater in the NHL. Los Angeles had selected him in the first round of the 2001 draft, but after four years at Ohio State and a single season divided between the AHL and the ECHL, he washed out with the Kings. He signed a minor-league deal with Washington, where he found second life, becoming a favourite of Bruce Boudreau, then the head coach of the Capitals' affiliate in Hershey. When Boudreau was promoted to the same job with the big club, Steckel came along with him and filled the role of a fourth-line centre, a faceoff and penalty-kill specialist—he would joke that teammates kidded him about being a blood relative of Boudreau, and possibly not a legitimate one. Steckel would wind up playing over 400 NHL games across nine seasons, never scoring more than eight goals nor registering more than 34 penalty minutes in any campaign. "Everyone in the game knows I don't play [to hurt other players]," he told the *National Post*. "If someone with a reputation [for cheap shots] had hit Crosby, he'd probably be facing retribution to this day. I haven't had any problems with opposition players; they know it was an accident. I just don't like seeing the replay all the time because it is violent and I'm not a violent player." Steckel was simply a journeyman who happened to skate into the frame for a moment that turned a season around—Crosby's *and* the league's—and maybe had an even more lasting effect than that.

What the replay of Steckel's hit on Crosby didn't capture is what is almost certainly forgotten. First, after the horn at the end of the second period, Crosby went over to the bench, folded over at the waist, head low, in obvious distress—something that was picked up on the *Hockey Night in Canada* broadcast. Crosby was neither checked for a concussion during the second intermission nor after the game. But HBO's series 24/7 later showed footage of Crosby in the Pittsburgh dressing room during the second intermission, looking obviously dazed. Nonetheless, Crosby stayed in the game after the Steckel hit and didn't miss a shift. In fact, he played 24:56, a staggering workload.

Craig Simpson, the colour commentator on *Hockey Night in Canada*, might have been the only person who noticed anything out of the ordinary in real time, as the game unfolded. During the broadcast, he pointed out that Crosby seemed not to notice goaltender Marc-Andre Fleury coming over to the bench in favour of a sixth attacker with about a minute left in regulation. It was a subtle observation that could only have been picked up by someone with a decade's worth of NHL experience. Such an oversight might not have been notable—much less cause for alarm—for most players, but Crosby has never been "most players." In ordinary circumstances, Crosby's levels of vision and awareness wouldn't just be in the league's 99th percentile, they would be exceeded by none. He would be the last guy to space out in a game. If the Penguins staff—who would've seen examples of his hypervigilance on a daily basis, his functioning baseline as it were—picked up on what Simpson had noted on air, it should have been cause for concern at least and probably a concussion exam.

According to the experts, this was a big whiff. Physicians are usually loath to second-guess, especially when they haven't directly examined a patient or scrutinized his file. Nonetheless, Dr. Charles Tator, a neurosurgeon and professor in the medical faculty at the University of Toronto, didn't hesitate to call into question the handling of Crosby at the Winter Classic. "It isn't clear why they managed the situation the way that they did," Dr. Tator told me in 2011.

In hindsight it may seem the Penguins dodged a bullet when Crosby managed to avoid a big hit from one of the Capitals in the third period. Even so, according to Dr. Tator, further damage could have been done just by having Crosby out on the ice for a skate. "It's not simply the risk that the player and the team are taking if he had been hit [in the third period]. Simple exertion could exacerbate [the concussion]. So could a whiplash effect without any contact to the head," said Dr. Tator.

Crosby would later say that he had no big complaint during or immediately after the game. He did allow that he had a sore neck but really thought nothing of it—and certainly no sense of a profound injury. "It seemed to be all neck-related," Crosby said. "I've gotten hit a lot over my time playing hockey and had sore necks. That's kind of what it felt like at the time."

That by itself should have been cause for further investigation by the medical staff, another specialist told me. "Along with headaches, sore necks are a very common physical complaint for an athlete who has suffered a concussion," said Dr. J. Scott Delaney, team physician for the Montreal Alouettes and an emergency and sports physician at McGill University. "It's reason for follow-up and baseline testing."

It may seem harsh to dump all this on the Penguins' staff— they would have known Crosby better than anybody, and thus they would have known that Crosby would be inclined to tough out any hardship, to play through the heavy weather on the ice without complaint. It's in his nature not to back down, but to bore ahead without fear. This ethic had taken him to the heights of the game. Players at all levels of the game have long looked down upon those who land in the trainer's room too often without obvious cause. Crosby was a top-level example of that sentiment. Such were his standards and his code, and as it turned out, they indirectly placed his career under grave threat.

January 5, 2011

Crosby had felt *off* after the Winter Classic. He would later say that he thought he was coming down with a case of the flu. He'd also say that his neck continued to be sore, citing the Steckel hit. The day after the game, the Penguins were given the day off but were scheduled to practise on Monday. He could have asked for a rest day, a practice off—the kind of thing that these days gets called a "maintenance day." It would seem in line with his having played just under 25 minutes—outdoors—against the Capitals. He could have taken two days off. And if he didn't feel better, the Pens could have easily sat him for a game, which happened to be against the Tampa Bay Lightning. Instead, Crosby skated in full practices on

Monday and Tuesday before facing the Lightning at the Mellon Arena on Wednesday.

The second hit on Sidney Crosby in that short timespan was not seen by as many people as the one in the Winter Classic, but it might stick as vividly among those who viewed it. A couple of common threads ran through the hits—both happened on shifts late in the second period; both times, Crosby collided with a taller player; and both times, Crosby stayed in the game and played in the third period. Nonetheless, the second hit provided a stark contrast to Steckel's skate-by on a few counts.

This time the perpetrator was more memorable, a long way from a journeyman like David Steckel: Tampa Bay's Victor Hedman was a former second-overall draft selection, a towering, six-foot, five-inch Swedish defenceman who was at that point still an emerging talent. Though his size prompted comparisons to the ever-dangerous Chris Pronger, Hedman styled his game after two defencemen more noted for skills than a physical game: Nick Lidstrom and Ray Bourque. Like the three aforementioned, Hedman would go on to win a Norris Trophy and is prominent in any conversation about the best blueliners of his generation. And matched up against these three Hall of Famers in their primes, Hedman would no doubt be the swiftest and most mobile skater—given the accelerating pace of the game played in his generation, Hedman has to be.

While you could debate whether Steckel's hit was intentional (Crosby would take the "pro" side in that debate), Hedman's hit was not incidental contact; rather, it was a hockey play. That's not to say that Hedman made a premeditated attempt to injure Crosby; just that he was physically taking Crosby into the boards behind the Lightning's net. Crosby did have his back fully turned and was up against the boards with his head turned to his left, able with his peripheral vision to pick up Hedman pouring in towards him—that is to say, unlike the Steckel hit, Crosby did see Hedman coming—but really wasn't in any position to brace himself. Hedman went into Crosby flush, not turning and dropping a shoulder or a hip. Instead, he had his gloves up and drove them squarely into the numbers on Crosby's sweater—it wasn't a shot focused on Crosby's head, but you could see on impact that his helmet was up against the plexiglass. And this time Crosby's distress was obvious—he seemed to be in trouble from the first breath after the hit; even though he didn't fall to the ice the way he had four days earlier in the outdoor game, he did drop to one knee. His anguish was even clearer when he stood up and skated away.

Unlike Steckel, Hedman was penalized on the play: a minor for boarding. But like the Winter Classic, Crosby stayed in the game and played all of the third period, even though the Penguins would go on to an 8–1 win. And again, there was no assessment in the second intermission or in the aftermath of the game for concussion symptoms. In days to come, Pittsburgh management would say they had no real cause to perform one. "He actually had a really good game that night," Ray Shero, the GM, said later.

Within an hour after the game, the Penguins' equipment was packed up and Crosby and his teammates had boarded a bus to head out to the airport. They were bound for a flight to Montreal, where they had a game the next night.

January 6, 2011

Crosby had told the Penguins' team doctors that the flu-like symptoms and sore neck had returned and that he was also suffering headaches. The Penguins decided not just to scratch him from the lineup but to get him back to Pittsburgh for examination posthaste. By the time Dan Bylsma filled out the lineup card, Crosby was already consulting with physicians in Pittsburgh. The Penguins weren't coy about the situation. They did report that their captain had been scratched from the lineup with an upper-body injury, but Bylsma didn't obfuscate. "I have not talked to Sid about this, I just got the report through the doctors that he went home and had a mild concussion," he told reporters before the game. When asked how long he expected Crosby to be out of the lineup, Bylsma tempted fate and, in retrospect, read too much into "mild." Said the coach in words that would haunt him: "He's got to be symptom-free, but I'd say he'll be out about a week."

"About a week" became, when all was said and done, more than a season's worth of games. Thus commenced the learning curve about the nature of concussions—for Crosby, Bylsma, the Penguins, hockey fans and anyone else tracking the very uncertain future of one of the game's best players, who was, it should be pointed out again, only 23 years old.

Crosby spoke to the press over the course of the next few days and was, like Bylsma, optimistic about a quick return. "I'd like to think I'm cautious with every [injury], but probably a little more so [now]," Crosby said. "You have to rely on the doctors and what they say. It's important to let them know your symptoms and everything going on. There will be a lot of communication that way. There's got to be no symptoms."

If Crosby seemed at all reluctant to do a deep dive on his concussion, he went at Steckel and Hedman with both barrels. Crosby's indignation was plain, but his take was clinical, not personal. He didn't name the players or the teams. "I didn't like them," Crosby told reporters. "You talk about head shots and dealing with them, that's been something that's been a pretty big point of interest from [general managers] and players. When I look at those two hits and we talk about blindside and unsuspecting player . . . there's no puck there on both [plays]. A direct hit to the head on both of them. When you go through the criteria, I think they fit all those."

Crosby found an ally, perhaps an unlikely one, in a former critic: on "Coach's Corner," Don Cherry was more critical of the hit by Steckel than he was of Hedman's. "I come on right after that and I said, 'The kid [Steckel] meant to hit him. He saw him.' I didn't say he set it up, but he hit him. The old story is if you hit something, you look back [wondering,] 'What did I hit?' He knew he hit him. And I said Crosby was hurt, because you could just tell [with] his head. He got up and played the period and then he played the next game. But I said, 'This kid is hurt,' because you can just tell after you're in the game a long time—you know when it's a real good hit to the head."

Hedman, for one, seemed surprised by the furor around the hit. It wasn't like he was playing to the jury in the NHL offices in a bid to avoid a suspension. The league didn't even call him in for a hearing. "I don't really remember the play," Hedman told the *St. Petersburg Times*. "It was just a hit. I never am going to go in and try to hurt somebody. It's too bad he got a concussion. It wasn't on purpose. I obviously laid into him. But it's just playing the game."

The severity of Crosby's concussion woes weren't known or even suspected when his originally projected return passed and one week bled into a second and then a third. The second-guessing began to mount even in those first days. The Pittsburgh media would ask Bylsma for an update on a daily basis, and he'd have nothing in the way of an update, saying that he hadn't talked to Crosby directly, only to the team physicians. Ray Shero probably anticipated some blowback, criticism for not sitting Crosby after the hit by Steckel in the Winter Classic or pulling him from the lineup ahead of the game against Tampa. "If Sid had felt something out of the ordinary, he would have said something to our training staff," the GM said. "Our trainer spoke to him and didn't notice anything wrong. And if Sid's teammates noticed anything wrong with him, they're supposed to go right to the trainer."

If the Penguins were alarmed by Crosby's prognosis, they hid it well. Seemingly no one with the team had any idea how serious Crosby's injury was. And beyond that, his absence wasn't just a cause for despair around the league; it was a development that went beyond merely drawing attention to a full-blown crisis and really threw it into the forefront. Among the coverage of Crosby's concussion, a few opinions and commentaries threw in asides about, say, Eric Lindros's career being compromised and ended too soon as a result of an awful series of concussions, but few mentioned that one star, Paul Kariya, decided to sit out the entire 2010–11 campaign in the hope of getting past his history of brain trauma. Playing for the St. Louis Blues the previous season, the 35-year-old Kariya had missed a couple of weeks with a concussion from Christmas through New Year's, but managed to log 75 games and finish the season with 18 goals. Whether Kariya's hiatus was any benefit can only be guessed at—on his return his game barely resembled his days as one of the league's most gifted scorers.

Likewise, no one was connecting the dots between Crosby's concussion and a spate of head shots across the league that month.

Calgary's Tom Kostopoulos broke the jaw of Detroit defenceman Brad Stuart. Perhaps more gruesome than the play was the reaction of Mike Milbury, former player, coach and GM, who in his role as a commentator and self-styled upholder of old-school values on the league's broadcasts on NBC, told viewers he thought the hit was "great."

Colin Campbell, the NHL's vice-president in charge of hockey operations, dropped the hammer on Kostopoulos—though he had been assessed only a roughing minor in the game, Campbell dealt him a six-game suspension, a relatively heavy sentence that took into account his prior history of recklessly endangering opposing players. Campbell also suspended Toronto forward Mike Brown for three games for a head shot on Phoenix Coyotes defenceman Ed Jovanovski and a four-game suspension to Scott Nichol of San Jose for a high, reckless hit on another Coyotes defenceman, David Schlemko. Both Brown and Nichol were repeat offenders, fourth-liners who were kept around for their toughness.

Did these measures effectively address the issue of dangerous play that placed stars like Crosby at risk? Not really. It was as if a bank had been knocked over and the authorities started arresting previously convicted shoplifters—more of a response to some bad publicity and an exercise in profiling than effective policing.

Something that *did* attract attention came to pass three weeks after Crosby went down: Colorado defenceman Matt Hunwick delivered a hard, legal check that knocked Boston's Marc Savard unconscious. For Savard, a skilled centre, it was his second major concussion in 10 months—near the end of the previous season he had been levelled by Crosby's Pittsburgh teammate Matt Cooke. Though Savard was placed on the injured reserve list, no one had any illusions about him ever returning to play—Savard would later say that he realized as much on the night of Colorado game. For the Bruins, Savard was the first of two key players they'd lose to a career-ending concussion in awful succession—forward Nathan Horton would be stretchered off in Game 3 of the 2011 Stanley Cup.

Over the summer of 2010 the league had implemented Rule 48, which prohibited blindside hits to the head that were deemed avoidable. Those found in violation would be subject to a major penalty, ejection from the game *and* a suspension—which represents the limit of what the league could drop on players. But the rule was having no real effect in making the NHL a safer workplace—in fact, based on various surveys, the incidence of concussions from one season to the next increased significantly. According to a study later issued by St. Michael's Hospital in Toronto, there were 77 concussions, suspected concussions and facial fractures in the 2009–10 season, but that number soared to 120 for the 2010–11 season and 126 for the season after that. According to internal league documents that would surface several years later, Crosby's and Savard's concussions were two of the 86 documented in the league in 2010–11. (Crosby was one of 31 players who either returned to play or didn't miss any time in the game during which they suffered a brain injury.) The study also showed that about a third of those injuries were caused by plays that were deemed illegal, resulting in a penalty and/or suspension. Of course, correlating the numbers of brain injuries with their causes was difficult business —some, most notably Crosby's, weren't the result of a single impact, but a cumulative effect.

With Rule 48 in place, Campbell was dealing out more suspensions related to blows to the head—the number increased from just seven in 2009–10 to 18 (of 38 suspensions overall) in 2010–11, but again, it was a chicken-or-egg proposition: did that spike in numbers reflect a greater vigilance by the league or more dangerous play on the ice? What was inarguable was that, despite the efforts of those who write the NHL's rules, the league was becoming ever more hazardous to a player's health. And when Sidney Crosby is forced to the sidelines, when his career is threatened, it bodes ill for the league's health.

One week became two, and in that time evidence surfaced of a side effect not noted in any medical journal: rumours. It started with word that Crosby was going to boycott the NHL All-Star Game in Raleigh, North Carolina, at the end of January. The All-Star Game is mostly derided by dedicated fans as an unwatchable shinny contest, and more than a few players have been quietly disappointed at being selected to fill out rosters rather than getting a four-day midseason break. For those at the head office in Manhattan, though, the All-Star Game and its accompanying skills competition serve as a trade show attended by all the league's corporate partners. Bottom line: it's a meaningless game except to those who want to get Madison Avenue to notice a league in the shadow of the NFL, MLB and the NBA.

If Crosby boycotted the game in protest, it wouldn't have been as in-your-face a gesture as, say, kneeling on the sidelines during the national anthem; nonetheless it would have relayed his discontent with the league's decision not to punish Steckel or Hedman and, more broadly, its perceived failure to protect star players. Crosby's absence or any sort of snub would have been a terrible look for Gary Bettman. That Crosby had been the leading vote-getter on the public ballots would only have given the story more oxygen and exacerbated the damage: the NHL's marquee star undertaking a protest around the league's midseason marketing bonanza.

Of course the rumour seemed apocryphal—airing out any grievance would have been out of character for Crosby, who had no previous history of courting controversy and was cautious about offending. When convenient, the league likes to refer to its relationship with the players as a partnership, but it's a fairly accurate characterization where Crosby is concerned. Whenever called, he shows up. He wasn't inclined to bite the hand that feeds him. He emphatically denied that there was anything to the reports of a boycott: "Not even close."

According to the NHL's vice-president of hockey and business development at the time, Brendan Shanahan, Crosby had in fact called to reassure him that he would be in attendance if he were cleared to play. Of all the games ever played, the NHL All-Star Game would be the least physically risky. No one can remember the last time a check was thrown in anger.

Crosby sounded far from alarmed about his recovery. "[The effect of a concussion] is something you probably have a little bit greater of an opinion on after going through it," he told the Pittsburgh *Post-Gazette*'s Shelly Anderson. He said his progress was "kind of on and off." He said that he was still suffering from occasional headaches. "Some days you feel good, you feel like you've had progress, and there are other days that are a little bit tougher."

Dan Bylsma joined the optimistic chorus, perhaps wishfully, claiming that his star showed no signs of fogginess when he came out to watch his team at the arena. "I've actually remarked several times about how he's alert, normal, thinking about the game, helping out the coaching staff," Bylsma said.

The optimism expressed by player and coach wasn't well founded, however. Crosby wasn't going to be practising with the team anytime soon. He was not even cleared for workouts by the time the All-Star Game rolled around. In fact, he'd miss not only the rest of January, but all of February. The word was out that Crosby was suffering the full gamut of symptoms. He was fatigued and foggy. Hopes were adjusted. Management held out hope that Crosby was going to be back for the end of the season. Then he was going to be back before the playoffs.

In Crosby's absence, the Penguins treaded water—as Bylsma said, they knew how to play without Crosby. They had also figured out how to play without Malkin, who went down with a torn ACL. Nonetheless, Pittsburgh was still contending for top spot in the division, so the team was still entertaining prospects of Crosby returning and making another run in the postseason. Then a dark cloud blew in and fans were prompted to imagine the Penguins having to go forward without their captain.

Some unfounded claims were floated in Toronto, the hockey media hub, alleging that those in Crosby's circle were pressuring him to retire. Crosby's agent, Pat Brisson, tried to scuttle the talk, but no half measures would suffice; thus did Crosby and his father, Troy, come out to state that no one was talking about retirement. However, this seed, once planted, was difficult to unearth, and every day he spent on the sidelines made fans wonder if they'd ever see Crosby play again.

A return for the playoffs looked promising when, in mid-March, doctors cleared Crosby to work out; his prognosis looked even rosier a week later when they cleared him for non-contact practice with the team. That, however, lasted about a week before the symptoms flared up again: headaches after exertion. Crosby was shut down once more. A new timeline was set, with Crosby scheduled to return for training camp in September—or, at least, pencilled in for the fall. And again, another cycle of rumours, speculation and innuendo ensued: the Penguins were either taking appropriate caution or being overcautious in the extreme; Crosby was buying into the team physicians' treatment plan or seeking other expert opinions; Crosby was going to return only when he was the same player who had torn up the league before January 1, 2011; or we'd never see that same player—or even a reasonable facsimile—again, just a much diminished player, a compact model of Eric Lindros.

Even without Crosby and Malkin, the Penguins didn't stagger down the stretch. Their record stood at 26–12–3 when Crosby went on hiatus at the halfway mark of the season. Through the spring, they went 23–13–5. Those latter numbers, however, flattered the team—Pittsburgh won four straight games late in the season in shootouts. It had to rate as something of a surprise that the under-manned Penguins took the Tampa Bay Lightning to Game 7 in the opening round of the playoffs. The Penguins' leading scorer against the Lightning was career grinder Arron Asham—he had five goals in 44 games in the regular season, but three in the first six games of the series. Tampa Bay won Game 7, 1–0, and the Penguins' year of what-might-have-beens came to a disappointing close.

The second-guessing of the team's handling of their captain's concussion, however, was around its midpoint.

What was more interesting to me, and certainly more significant, were the first impressions of neurologists on the cutting edge
of concussion research. I spoke to several that summer while
Crosby's prospects were still very uncertain — the last word out of
the Crosby camp was that his return for the start of the 2011–12
season was unlikely and that his symptoms had returned during
summer workouts.

Charles Tator suggested that the Penguins' medical staff had
dropped the ball on the Steckel hit in the outdoor game. If they
hadn't picked up on it in real time, then certainly after the game,
after viewing the video, they should have examined Crosby. "On
the replay it was clear to me that he was concussed," says Tator.
"The blow had a rotational rather than a translational element.
That's the type of hit that is more conducive to a concussion [and
to] a more severe concussion."

Just the force of the Steckel hit might have caused a concussion, but the context within the game further exposed Crosby.
"Given that it was a blindside hit, something like a sucker shot,
[Crosby] didn't have a chance to contract his neck muscles and
absorb the shock of the blow, [which would] lessen the likelihood
or the severity of a concussion," says J. Scott Delaney. In other
words, with no way of knowing what was coming, Crosby had no
chance to brace himself for the blow.

It's not clear whether Crosby suffered one concussion or two
in succession — there's no unscrambling that egg. Even if it was
just one concussion, sustained on the Steckel hit, he would have
put himself at mortal risk by trying to play through it and tough
it out. "Second impact syndrome: if you suffer a second concussion before you've recovered fully from a first concussion, you can

die—it's just that simple," says Tator. "Some who've survived are wrecked neurologically. It goes beyond persistent post-concussion syndrome as we know it."

September 7, 2011

A lot of hockey had been played, and history made, since Sidney Crosby skated off the ice after that game against Tampa Bay nine months earlier. Daniel Sedin of the Canucks had won a scoring title and led Vancouver to the Presidents' Trophy. Corey Perry of Anaheim claimed the Hart Trophy. The Bruins had beaten the Canucks in Game 7 in Vancouver to win the Stanley Cup. But though Crosby was absent, he wasn't out of mind for those who track the game—it was the season that played out without him. The question as NHL training camps opened was when the Pittsburgh captain could come back. When the Penguins staged a press conference at the start of training camp, many presumed that the team was going to be able to offer some clarity, a timeline, reassurance. None was forthcoming.

In addition to Penguins GM Ray Shero, Crosby was flanked by two specialists: Dr. Michael Collins, the director of the University of Pittsburgh's sports medicine concussion program, and Dr. Ted Carrick, a chiropractic neurology specialist who had worked extensively with Crosby using treatments outside the mainstream. Dr. Collins's opening statement gave the nuts and bolts of Crosby's condition when he checked in on January 6. It also suggested that the Penguins' initial projections of a week on the sidelines came out of the team's hopes rather than the doctor's prognosis. "Sid was having very consistent symptoms, consistent with a significant cerebral concussion," Collins said.

He was foggy. What that means is . . . it feels like you're one step behind yourself. It feels like you're in slow motion. He had headaches. He had fogginess. He had difficulties with fatigue. He had light sensitivity. He had noise sensitivity. He had a hard time thinking. I evaluated him with a tool called ImPACT, which is a neurocognitive test. His testing showed significant problems with his cognitive functioning. His findings were entirely consistent with what we see with a concussion. When I saw Sid's profile of symptoms, when I saw the deficits and impact, I knew that we were in for a long recovery. The types of symptoms Sid had initially are exactly the type of symptoms we see that end up taking the longest to recover . . . I wasn't, nor am I now, surprised that it's taken this long for Sid to start improving.

Collins laid out the nature of Crosby's brain trauma: a vestibular concussion. Stripped down to the basics, a vestibular system in the brain integrates sensory information; the more complicated the information, the greater demands upon the system. Crosby's concussion compromised his ability to orient and focus when he either wasn't in a fixed and set position or he had to process an environment in motion—which is to say, it might have been an annoyance to an artist painting a still life, but it ravaged Crosby's ability to play the game. Making the challenge of tracking Crosby's progress even harder for the specialists was the fact that what might be judged "normal" vestibular performance did not apply in this case. "Sid is a Ferrari. His vestibular system is better than anyone else's," Collins explained. "That is why he is the most elite hockey player in the world. That system is where Sid excels at. That system is why Sid is who he is. It makes sense that with where his injury was, it's going to take a while to rehabilitate this."

Though Collins represented the neurological establishment, he readily admitted that Crosby turned a significant corner when he started consulting with Carrick at his institute in Cape Canaveral, Florida. Carrick's practice has been described by some medical publications as "controversial," and the mainstream media goes a fair bit further—ABC News questioned whether his incorporation of chiropractic approaches into neurological therapies was "a miracle method or a placebo." Carrick's bedside manner—or at least his mic-side manner—was the polar opposite to Collins's. "It's Christmas for Sidney Crosby and for people that care for him," Carrick said. "Sid shouldn't have any sequelae, or problems, in the future. The incidents of head injury are epidemic. This case is one of the good outcomes. Some cases are not as good as this one. We're fortunate today to have technology that allows us to quantify things in ways we only dreamed of yesterday. It's a good time to have a head injury now compared to a few years ago, but hopefully we won't have to go through these things in the future."

When Crosby spoke, he put to rest that idea that he had ever contemplated walking away from the game: "Retirement? No. I think I've always thought about the consequences of this injury and making sure I'm smart with it, because at the end of the day that's the last thing I want. But with that being said, I think no, I didn't really give a whole lot of thought to that."

What was notable about the press conference was the stuff that wasn't discussed. Events in January were well established, hashed and rehashed over and over again. Through 40 minutes the names of Steckel and Hedman were never raised. Likewise there was no discussion about the league's policy and enforcement of head-shot rules intended to protect players. No questions were posed about how the Penguins had not exercised greater caution, how the warning signs had been missed, how Crosby's stiff neck had not been addressed. The media knew that second-guessing and assigning blame was a minefield for player and GM and outside the purview of the physicians. The only person in the world more cautious with his opinion than the doctors behind the microphone was Crosby in his default mode.

Collins laid it out for the media that Crosby wasn't cleared for full practice yet and that he'd be eased into contact in practice when he hit certain benchmarks. Despite all the optimism and talk of progress, the situation was still very much unsettled, a point that was captured in a single sentence. When a reporter asked him for a timeline for Crosby's return to game action, Collins didn't take the bait. "I have no earthly idea," he said.

So it was that, at the start of training camp, the Ferrari was as yet not roadworthy.

When I was in Pittsburgh in the fall of 2011 for the start of the Penguins' season without Crosby, I sought out a player who was on the bottom half of the roster but was of particular interest with the team awaiting Crosby's return at a still-undetermined date. The paradox: Crosby was sidelined, still indefinitely, a victim of the physical threat posed by the NHL game's inherent violence, and yet the Penguins employed Matt Cooke, a journeyman who would have topped any poll that asked respondents to name the league's dirtiest player. A winger on the third or fourth line, a grinder and penalty killer, Cooke had two years to run on a three-year deal, but he understood that he was going to have to reinvent or reform himself to hold on to his place on the team—and probably in the league.

He gained a level of infamy for a blindside hit on Marc Savard in March 2010, one that knocked the Boston centre cold for half a minute, the penultimate concussion of Savard's career. Rule 48 tracked back to that hit on Savard, even though the league deemed that it didn't merit a suspension, even though he had been suspended three times previously and had taken down a long list of NHLers with elbows, knee-on-knee hits, blindside hits, boarding, sucker punches, steamrolling of goaltenders and even kicks that Colin Campbell decided did not rise to the threshold of offences meriting suspension. But in the spring of 2011 the league threw the book at Cooke, suspending him for four games for boarding Columbus's Fedor Tyutin, and then 10 regular-season games and the first round of the playoffs for an elbow to the head of the Rangers' Ryan McDonagh. "[Cooke,] a repeat offender, directly and unnecessarily targeted the head of an opponent who was in an unsuspecting and vulnerable position," Campbell said upon handing down the suspension, which also cost Cooke almost $220,000 in forfeited salary.

Penguins GM Ray Shero valued what Cooke brought to the team—he had been an integral part of the league's best penalty-killing unit in the 2010–11 season—but, factoring in the seven post-season games, he was unavailable for almost a quarter of the season due to his reckless play. When Campbell dealt Cooke his suspension after the hit on McDonagh, Shero didn't defend his player; rather, he called the play "exactly the kind of hit we're trying to get out of the game." Thus was management giving him an ultimatum: having been too often a liability to the team, and with Brendan Shanahan taking over for Colin Campbell and promising to better protect the players, Cooke was going to have to shape up. It was hard to do for any player; harder still for a 33-year-old who had already logged 12 seasons in the NHL.

I had first talked to Cooke when he was a member of Canada's team at the world junior championship in Finland in 1998—ironically, he missed the last games of the tournament with a concussion. He seemed to revel in the role of the agitator and disrupter. When I reminded him that I had talked to him at the under-20 tournament, it didn't register with him, which wasn't really a surprise. When I asked him how he had suffered a concussion at the world juniors, he didn't think it was a fitting topic for small talk. "That was a long time ago," he said.

Cooke was more open about talking about this mid-career metamorphosis he was undertaking. He had spent hours reviewing game video with the Penguins' coaching staff, looking for adjustments he could make. "I can play this game," he said. "I just have to play differently. There are spots to play a physical game, and that's what I've done, but the game has changed and I have to too."

Effectively, it was like a Darwinian exercise, although it played out in real time, Cooke being a dodo bird and being advised that, due to natural selection, he was going to have to adapt almost overnight or go extinct in short order. Cooke wasn't bristling at change —he *was* changing, albeit not necessarily out of conscience. No, as he told it, he used to glory in the almost unfettered physical game the NHL had once allowed, but he was wiser now that he had a family and was thinking about life after hockey like he never had before. And he was affected by Crosby's concussion (though you might have had trouble convincing Tyutin or McDonagh).

Cooke said that players have played with concussions before and will likely do it again, that he had been on the wrong side of big hits in his career, sitting out games four times with concussions and playing with them on a few other occasions. "I wouldn't do that now, but I did before and a lot of guys have," he said.

"[Third- and fourth-line] guys feel they're risking their jobs if they don't get back in there."

It was hard to envision that Cooke could go clean, but mellow? Well, perhaps. That said, that this was even a conversation he was having reflects a fast-paced evolution set in motion by the spate of career-ending concussions and punctuated by Crosby's time on the sidelines.

There wasn't any real suspense in the run-up to Pittsburgh's first game of the 2011–12 season, a date against the Canucks in Vancouver, the first of a three-game road trip through western Canada. Though Crosby was working out, he hadn't appeared in any preseason games, hadn't been cleared for full practice and hadn't offered up any firmer timeline for his return to the Penguins lineup. If the team was trying to focus on the players they had on the ice rather than the conspicuous absence of their captain, it didn't help that they were starting off the year in the arena where he'd had the highlight of his career to that point. The Penguins came away with a 4–3 shootout victory, and the early results on the remaking of Matt Cooke were fairly spectacular, with the former bad boy scoring a pair of goals—one on a power play, the other shorthanded. And Evgeni Malkin seemed to be in fine form—his goal in the second round of the shootout proved to be the winner. Still, the two points were earned in the very significant shadow of the star who remained on the sidelines. Shutting down Crosby for the duration of the previous season might have been viewed as well-exercised caution, but the uncertainty around his status in October, with every passing game, was more than troubling and fuelled the whispers that maybe, *maybe*, he might never play again.

For all that they gave the game and the fans, the greatest players in history deserved a fitting send-off, but looking back you can see that circumstances are often beyond their control—they don't always get to write the script. In fact, the well-staged exit seems to be the exception rather than the rule.

Even casual hockey fans of a certain age will claim to vividly remember Wayne Gretzky's last game back in the spring of '99. They'll remember Gretzky, helmet off, in his Rangers sweater. They'll remember Gretzky skating a big loop and waving to fans, a turn in the spotlight at Madison Square Garden. Really, though, what most people mostly remember is *image*. Not the opponent that day (Pittsburgh). Not the outcome (a Ranger loss). Not his team's dismal season (13 points out of the playoff race). Not Gretzky's struggles that season (nine goals in 70 games). Not the seeming haste of his decision to retire (coming together in the last week of the season, with only a road game in Ottawa and Game 82, at MSG, remaining). Gretzky's was a rush to the exit that caught most people by surprise, rather than an extended farewell tour freighted with memories.

Go down the list. Bobby Orr's knees and Mario Lemieux's arrhythmia denied them a chance for a moment like Gretzky's. At age 52 and with his intentions to retire announced, Gordie Howe recorded the last goal of his career at the Montreal Forum in Game 2 of an opening-round series against the Canadiens—remarkable stuff, sure, but somehow, seeing Howe wearing Hartford green instead of Detroit red in an NHL game diluted the moment, as did the fact that it was the penultimate game of his career, with the Whalers losing the final, little-seen game of the best-of-five series at home in overtime two nights later. Howe's was nonetheless better than Maurice Richard's, the Canadiens not so gently suggesting that his time had passed, holding the door open for him. So it is, going down the line. Ray Bourque finally raised the Stanley Cup, the grail he chased for more than two decades, after the last game of his career in Colorado, but that glorious farewell is the exception.

More than any great NHL player before him, Crosby's career had seemed precisely stage-managed, every turn a matter of planning and calculation. As Gretzky's game was suffused by wonder and magic, Orr's by speed, Lemieux's by elegance and Howe's by durability, Crosby's was defined by control—the game that evolved in his era was growingly defined by possession, by keeping the puck away from opponents. And now his hockey life was beyond his control, off his stick, kept away from him.

In performance, we only see the surface and the very end product of an athlete's gifts. What underlies it all we don't know, and we can't. In fact, even the performers often don't. Maybe Gretzky and Howe (at last) fully realized that their games were eroding away, that they were unable to do what they once had—if they did, they would have known before any of us on the other side of the glass. But when Orr underwent his first knee surgeries, did he really full appreciate the threat they posed to his career? He couldn't have known that he'd only play 36 games after turning 27. Certainly Lemieux, in his last game—an overtime loss in Buffalo in which he and Crosby assisted on a goal by Ziggy Palffy—didn't know that his heart was going to lose its cadence and he'd be forced to walk away. Sports have a secret life that is sometimes a secret even to the principals themselves.

Through this stretch, I talked to Dr. Charles Tator and tried to fathom how Crosby's recovery, had stretched into almost a year. He pointed to history. "You are more likely to recover after one concussion than after 10 concussions," he said. It was tempting to imagine that this could be the secret life of Sidney Crosby's genius, and perhaps his undoing—really, there was no knowing if he had suffered concussions when he had thought he had simply had his bell rung and played through it, as Matt Cooke and hundreds of others had. I thought of that first game when I first saw him at the summer under-18s in Switzerland—that cross-check to his head was a far more blatant attempt to injure than the hits by David Steckel and Victor Hedman, and seemingly with a far greater immediate effect. And how many times had that scenario played out in his two seasons with the Oceanic? How many times had someone in the Quebec league drifted an elbow up to Crosby's helmet or run him from behind? In the run-up to the NHL draft, there hadn't been any talk in the scouting community about Crosby having a history of concussions—nothing that showed up in his paperwork from Central Scouting in his draft year—but then again, at that time, such stuff was really left to players and their agents to self-report, and that is not to suggest that Crosby was anything less than forthcoming. There could only be supposing, no knowing, because not even Crosby himself could have known for sure.

In November, positive reports started to flow out of the Penguins camp: Crosby skating with the team and having no symptoms after the fact; Crosby being cleared for full-on practice with contact and again being asymptomatic. After so many false starts and hard stops, it was hard to be too invested or optimistic about a possible return, and you had to wonder if, in the event of a return, Crosby would come back in some sort of diminished version—an athlete broken, like Eric Lindros had been with every concussion, like countless boxers who were seeming indomitable but, once tagged and knocked out, wound up on much lower and too often tragic career trajectories. Crosby's greatest asset was always his brain, his hockey sense, vision and anticipation. Through dedication to training and work ethic, he physically caught up to the original elite aspect of his game, the ability to see plays before anyone else, to see plays that others miss entirely.

Crosby did not return in time for the start of the season, but there was much relief when he did make his return to action in late November, 320 days after the ill-fated game against Tampa Bay. And in the history of players coming back from a major injury, none performed as spectacularly as Crosby did, scoring on his third shift, not six minutes into the game, adding another goal and two assists in a 5–0 win over the Islanders in Pittsburgh. He logged what was, for him, a light load, less than 16 minutes (he has averaged more than 20 in recent seasons), but no matter. It set off a celebration in the hockey world. It was cause for collective relief, a sense that Crosby and even the game itself had dodged an awful bullet—that he had provided a scare that the NHL needed. As Kevin Paul Dupont wrote in the *Boston Globe*, "The game became a better, safer place in Crosby's absence, because it became painfully obvious—minus the face of the franchise for the second half of the last season—that the NHL had to clean up the ugly truth about its head woes. Now it has Brendan Shanahan and friends in the Player Safety Dept., keeping a keen eye on the kind of concussive hits Crosby suffered . . ."

If Crosby's return to action wasn't premature, the celebration was. Seven games later, on December 5, Crosby was on the sidelines again, with a recurrence of concussion symptoms. The team didn't cite any single play as the cause, and it wasn't anything that had happened obviously and in real time, as had been the case with Steckel and Hedman. A review of the video suggested that two plays seemed to be the catalyst. Early in the game, Bruins centre David Krejci, not a reputed headhunter nor even a physical player by any stretch, was standing at the boards and trying to keep the puck in at the Pittsburgh blue line with Crosby giving chase —just at the last second, Krejci turned to seal off Crosby, who ran into an elbow and shoulder and reeled into the boards. And in the third period Crosby collided with teammate Chris Kunitz. Crosby was examined for baseline testing and it seemed to be all clear, but the next day, the symptoms returned.

The Penguins announced that Crosby was going to sit out the next two games. He didn't play again until mid-March. By that point, he would have played eight games in more than 14 months. If fans were worried once more that Crosby would have to walk away from the game, their ranks grew by one: Crosby himself. Back in the fall, he had expressed bluff confidence about returning to the game. "Don't bet on it," he told reporters about the chances of retiring. This time, though, the future seemed even cloudier and he was shaken. He'd later tell the CBC, "I'd be lying if I didn't say that I thought about [having to retire]."

During this second round of convalesence, Crosby's spirits were raised by what seemed like a breakthrough diagnosis—namely, that his symptoms might have issued from a neck injury, a swelling around the top two vertabrae, rather than a concussion. A CAT scan and MRI performed by a specialist in Los Angeles revealed no fracture, just soft-tissue damage. After receiving a cortisone injection, Crosby sounded a note of optimism after a year of almost unbroken frustration. "From what I've been told, this is something pretty commonly linked with concussion symptoms, and in a way that's encouraging," Crosby said. "There's no magic to get rid of it but, if this is contributing, this is something we can obviously treat and work on and hopefully it will go away." Some in the media stirred the pot, suggesting that Crosby's soliciting the opinions of doctors outside the Penguins organization might have caused a rift between the captain and management, but he denied that there was anything to the rumours. "The team has been very encouraging and there's not a lot of answers with this stuff," he said.

When Crosby finally returned again, for a game in New York against the Rangers on March 15, he was joining the hottest team in the NHL. It might have seemed like Dan Bylsma didn't want to disrupt a good thing and wanted to ease Crosby into the mix, putting him on the ostensible third line with Matt Cooke and Tyler Kennedy. The result: Cooke again had two goals (on his way to a career-best 19 for the regular season), with Crosby picking up an assist in a 5–2 Pittsburgh win. Crosby wouldn't miss a game down the stretch, and his play seemed to be exactly where he had left off before the Winter Classic the year before—he accumulated six goals and 19 assists in 14 games, even though his ice time was down (less than 18 minutes in most contests). It looked like Bylsma was priming the franchise player for the playoffs. Pittsburgh racked up 108 points during the regular season, good for the fourth seed in the Eastern Conference, despite having their captain only for about a quarter of the schedule.

It should have been regarded as a good-news story, not just for Crosby and the Penguins, but for the NHL: the return and form of the league's marquee player. Yet it prompted a strange reaction, and not just among fans of Pittsburgh's rivals: a groundswell of criticism of Crosby. A small faction of media personalities voiced their absolute disdain for the Penguins captain. Some of it was predictable—Mike Milbury went on the attack late in the regular season after an incident in a Pittsburgh–Philadelphia game. Any game between those teams has been a small-scale war, but the teams were even edgier in the weeks leading up to the playoffs, when they knew they were bound to collide in the first round. It started with Crosby slashing Brayden Schenn, a bit of stickwork that had serious intentions but came in the flow of play and was not obvious enough to draw a whistle. Schenn struck the second blow: a cross-check across Crosby's lower back away from the puck, when he was skating to the bench on a line change. Those are routine circumstances for discreet digs at an opponent, but Schenn crossed the line and Crosby dropped to his knees. It wasn't close to a dive, but Crosby did look for a ref.

Milbury aired it out on Philadelphia sports-talk radio, which is a sort of no-think tank. "Little Goody Two Shoes goes into the corner and gives a shot to Schenn," Milbury said. "Schenn was late to the party, he should have turned around and drilled him right away, but I guess better late than never. So, you know, Crosby gets cross-checked, big whoop. He said after he came back from his 35th concussion, 'I'm not going to do this anymore, I'm not going to get into these scrums, I'm going to stay away from that stuff.' He couldn't help himself because there's a little punk in Crosby."

Milbury issued a league-pressured, job-saving apology, but like all damage control, it came too late and was too half-hearted to matter. And he wasn't a single gunman shooting off his mouth alone. The league doesn't lack for little minds in love with the sound of their own voices, and New York Rangers coach John Tortorella led a chorus of profanity-splattered name-calling,

labelling Crosby and Evgeni Malkin "f—— whining stars."
Maybe that's more to be expected, the coach of a rival team trying
to get under the skin of an opponent's stars.

Crosby tried to take the high road about the knocks. "I'm not
surprised," he told reporters before Game 1 of the Philadelphia
series. "I'm not ready to get into a battle about it. I don't feel like it's
necessary to get in these battles in the media. The game is played
on the ice."

Standing there in the scrum of reporters, I was struck by
Crosby's refusal to engage and respond in kind, but discouraged by
the playground name-calling. Anyone with a shred of empathy had
to have hoped the spate of concussions around the league would
spur a conversation about preventing brain trauma—a little too
much to hope, I guess. Loath as I am to admit bias, I'll cop to it
here: I had hoped the Penguins would make a good run in the
postseason, because Crosby's comeback had the makings of both
a good story and a shot across the bow of his critics. The Penguins
had looked like a fringe contender without Crosby, but stood as
one of the favourites to win the Cup with him. That's what I thought
when I went to Pittsburgh for Game 1 of their opening-round series
against the Flyers, a rival that had given the Penguins trouble
during the regular season.

For the first few shifts of Game 1, played entirely in the reeling
Flyers' end, it looked as though the league was going to have to
play catch-up with the Penguins. In his first playoff action in two
years, Crosby seemed to raise his game to another level—he looked
like his former self in that half season leading up to the 2011 Winter
Classic. On an early power play the Penguins threw the puck around

the perimeter and cycled the puck along the wall with impunity, and then Crosby skated to the left side of Ilya Bryzgalov's net, in the filthiest part of the dirty ice. Pascal Dupuis threw a pass over to him from the far wing and hit the tape of his stick. Even when the pass was on its way, everyone in the building knew it was as good as a goal, and that included Flyers' defenceman Nicklas Grossmann. Philadelphia had acquired the six-foot, four-inch, 230-pound Grossmann at the trading deadline from Dallas ostensibly just for the playoffs' heavy weather, but he was more imposing than fleet, more suited to the game in 2002 than 2012, and he was too slow and too late to mark Crosby or break up Dupuis's pass. The puck was past Bryzgalov when Grossmann levelled a head shot that didn't quite catch Crosby flush. With Crosby down and the red light on, Grossmann delivered a downward cross-check, more out of frustration than intent to injure, but also with more malice than Steckel's drive-by hit or Krejci's raised shoulder.

The Consul Energy Center erupted—the most meaningful goal that Crosby had scored in such a long time was surely worth celebrating—but in the tumult, for one awful moment, you could see Dupuis leaning over and looking down at Crosby with a sense of dread, as if to say, "Not again." Still on all fours, Crosby gave him a fist bump and a sense of relief. And, as with Steckel and Krejci's hits, no penalty was called.

Crosby and the Penguins looked like world beaters for a period, carrying a 3–0 lead into the intermission, but for 40 minutes and a couple beyond, the team's weaknesses were exposed—namely a suspect defence and even more suspect goaltending from Marc-Andre Fleury. Daniel Briere led the way for the Flyers with two goals and Jakub Voracek scored the winner in overtime. In the wake of the 4–3 loss, Crosby was stoic and resolute, but he would be a lot less so as the series unfolded and the Penguins' season quickly unravelled. Game 2 was an absolute mess. The final score —Philadelphia 8, Pittsburgh 5—flattered the Penguins. Fleury was abysmal and the defence in front of him was no better, wilting under the Flyers' forechecking. It was a deep hole and the odds weren't with the Penguins, to be sure, but Crosby, seemingly for the first time in his career, went into a full emotional meltdown in Game 3, a resounding 8–4 loss.

Crosby had displayed class, even in previous defeats, but he showed only a sad lack of it on the road against the Flyers. The Penguins fell behind a couple of goals early, Fleury's struggles continuing, and their captain acted out like a spoiled ninth-grader, really setting the tone for the team. The collective emotional melt-down started at the top.

The first sign of bad things to come might have escaped the notice of a casual viewer. A Pittsburgh teammate was locked in a tussle with Flyers tough guy Zac Rinaldo and Crosby pushed his glove in Rinaldo's face. It didn't quite rise to the seriousness of a cheap shot, but it was shabby, without real cause and without any danger of Rinaldo returning fire.

Crosby later ended up in a couple of sessions with Flyers star Claude Giroux, whose performance represented a coming-out party as Philadelphia's franchise player. In the first exchange, one that looked like just a little bumping behind the net that would blow over after a couple of profanities, Crosby put his glove in Giroux's face and shoved him helmet-first into the glass. Giroux, like Crosby, had missed time with a concussion that season, but no matter. Crosby clearly subscribed to a variation on the Golden Rule: do unto others as they have done unto you. Crosby and Giroux, a more willing participant this time, would end up trading punches and rolling around on the ice as Crosby's and his team-mates' frustration boiled over and fights spilled over into something approaching a line brawl. It was ugly, it was unnecessary and it was ultimately ineffective.

To an extent it was also inexplicable—at least, Crosby couldn't explain it, or didn't feel like bothering after the game. "I don't like them," he said. "I don't like any of them." It was either out of character for the image-conscious star or a glimpse behind a face he puts on for the public.

Yet Crosby came off looking the worst because of something so innocuous that it might have passed unnoticed had it not been in view of a wide-angle shot. During a stoppage of play, just when it looked like hostilities had been quelled, Voracek bent down to pick up his glove and Crosby, like a grade-school brat, pushed it out of his reach, a bit of acting out just provocative enough to raise tensions once more.

Crosby snapped at reporters after the game. "There's a lot of stuff going on out there," he said. "There's no reason to explain why I have to sit here and say why I pushed a glove away. They're doing a lot of things out there too. You know what? We don't like each other. Was I going to sit there and pick up his glove for him, or what was I supposed to do? Skate away? Well, I didn't that time."

The Penguins would rebound and make a bit of a series of it —winning the fourth and fifth games, the former by the football score of 10–3, the latter 3–2 on home ice, an outcome more typical of playoff action. Still, even with those wins, you had no confidence that the team was built for the long haul, Crosby's return to form notwithstanding. The storybook season was not meant to be—there was going to be no Golden Goal, no raising of the Cup. When the series made it back to Philadelphia for Game 6, the Flyers put an emphatic end to the Penguins' season with a 5–1 rout. Crosby would be on the wrong side of the handshake line. Yes, he made it back into the game to stay, it seemed, after missing more than 101 regular-season games and seven playoff contests. But he hadn't returned to a team ready to contend for a Cup, nor to a league that seemed to have drawn any lessons from his experience.

A dark cloud had hung over the National Hockey League while the career of its greatest player was threatened at a cellular level. To all outside Crosby's medical team, those in the organization and his network of friends and associates, his brain injury was invisible, untrackable, unpredictable, mysterious and really unknowable. We look to sports for a story that plays out, unscripted, in real time. Crosby's hiatus was akin to a script penned by Samuel Beckett —we waited for him as Vladimir and Estragon did Godot, and in the meantime, not a look, not a word, not a hint, albeit without a bit of the black humour, I suppose. We all heaved a sigh of relief when he returned to the game, evidently none the worse for wear —in the years that followed, he would win another gold medal, a Hart Trophy, another Art Ross Trophy, two more Stanley Cups and a pair of Conn Smythe Trophies, as well as making the First All-Star Team three times and the Second Team twice. You could make the case that he has had two Hockey Hall of Fame careers, one before that Winter Classic against Washington and another since coming back.

But did Crosby's brain injury and convalescence represent something more than a crisis averted, an awful scare? I'd suggest they did, and there is significant evidence to back me up on this count.

It starts with a narrative as old as sports itself: people will glamorize players who suffer injuries and play hurt, saying that they've taken one for the team. Sidney Crosby didn't volunteer for the task — it was, of course, a matter of unforeseen and unfortunate circumstances — but he did take one for the game, for sports in general when he was out of the lineup. His time on the sidelines kept post-concussion syndrome and brain-trauma injuries in the news and forced a conversation about them. To put this in an awful context, consider the death of Bill Masterton from a brain injury suffered in a game in 1968 — the league's response to that was effectively limited to the naming of a trophy after him. The players' association went to the league with a request to elevate player safety as an issue and make helmets mandatory, but league president Clarence Campbell brushed off the suggestions and wouldn't even grant official league sanction to a benefit game for Masterton's family.

Of course, it was a different time. Masterton's injury was witnessed by those in the arena, but not beyond it. There was no video played in a constant loop, only written accounts. And eyewitnesses in the arena offered versions that were at once vague and conflicting. And Masterton's was a name known only to fans of the Minnesota North Stars and a few dedicated followers of the game in the expansion era. Prior to the NHL's first round of expansion in 1967, his career was a minor-league journeyman's. A 29-year-old Winnipeg native and graduate of the University of Denver, Masterton was playing in his first season in the NHL and in just his 38th game when he absorbed what seemed to be a routine hit from Oakland Seals defenceman Ron Harris. But he struck his head when he hit the ice, was taken off the ice on a stretcher, never regained consciousness and died 30 hours later.

Over the years a few media outlets have reopened investigations into Masterton's death. Twenty years after the fact, with most of the North Stars and executives available, the *Chicago Tribune* rooted around and came away with a clouded picture—teammates talked about Masterton having suffered a blow to the head in an earlier game and being bothered by headaches, but the pathologist who performed the autopsy reiterated that the cause of death was the single blow in the game against Oakland. The *Toronto Star* took an intensive look at Masterton's death and, with access to his autopsy and the benefit of expert opinion, postulated that he had suffered a brain trauma of some sort, possibly even cerebral hemorrhage, before he came in contact with the ice. To put this in context, the *Star* undertook this investigation in 2011—forty-three years after Masterton's death.

While the NHL mourned Masterton's death, he wasn't among the league's elite, one whose loss would be guaranteed to provoke widespread soul-searching. It would have been an entirely different story had it not been Masterton but, say, Bobby Hull or Jean Beliveau, Hall of Famers who were the faces of the league. Without a doubt, the league looked at its options in the wake of Masterton's death and decided that investigating the tragic accident and legislating to prevent any recurrence would be tantamount to an admission of culpability or even liability. The NHL waited 11 years after Masterton's death before it took what would have seemed like a common-sense measure: league president John Ziegler mandated that all incoming players be required to wear helmets. Even so, with veterans grandfathered in for exemptions, some NHLers were still playing without helmets in the mid-'90s, almost three decades after the tragedy in Minnesota. What took so long?

By contrast to the glacial pace of change on helmets, the effect of Crosby's brain injury was almost immediate at a macro level, and it mounted quickly with every passing week. In March of 2011, two months after Crosby was sidelined and just days after Montreal's Max Pacioretty suffered a concussion and a neck fracture on a terrifying hit by Boston's Zdeno Chara, commissioner Gary Bettman announced that the league was moving immediately to tighten its concussion protocols for players. "There's no one single thing causing concussions," Bettman said at a meeting of league general managers. "There is no magic bullet to deal with this. I know that it's an emotional, intense subject, particularly for our fans. We get it. But dealing with this issue is not something you can do whimsically or emotionally. You really have to understand what's going on."

At that point, it was a vow to act, a promise to phase in, rather than make an immediate and thorough intervention: protocols for those who were suspected to have suffered concussions would be tightened, and tightened again in the seasons to come; likewise the head shot became the nearest thing to a capital crime in the league, not quite eliminated, but certainly subject to more severe punishment. When you factor in the virtual disappearance of those fourth-liners who were kept on to fight and do little more, it's fair to believe that today's league, while not a safe place by any stretch, is a safer one than it was a decade ago.

You could understand if Dr. Ted Carrick watched Crosby's return with a particular interest, and maybe even a proprietary one. Many in the media didn't know quite what to make of his fusion of neurology and chiropractic. And in some of the coverage, voices from the medical establishment had been skeptical, even critical of his innovative therapies. While Sidney Crosby, the Pittsburgh Penguins and the National Hockey League were all at least qualified winners with his return to action, even if the team's postseason was a bust, Carrick could take a degree of satisfaction and pride in Crosby's comeback, if not comprehensive vindication—while Crosby was just one of the patients who came to the clinic, he was by far the most famous, and his recovery played out in real time, suspenseful if not dramatic. Carrick tried to frame it not as a win for his methods and therapies, or even for the clinic, but for concussion awareness.

"In broad strokes, when you have a celebrity who is known that has an injury or a disease, it raises public awareness," Carrick said. "It was true of, say, Michael J. Fox when he went public to talk about Parkinson's disease, and this was true of Sid. More people, the public and medical professionals, became aware not just of the issue, but also of evolving treatments. And no doubt, whenever there's a high-profile case we see a spike in funding, more money going into research. While the details of Sidney's case are confidential—I can't discuss a lot of the particulars—it started a conversation. Because of his case, more people are aware that traditional approaches—with patients basically resting until they got better and then toughing it out—are nonsensical. There's a greater awareness of the role of neck instability—how every concussion is both a brain injury and a neck injury. Honestly, it was a very tough time for Sidney, to be sure, but no doubt because of the resultant attention to his concussion, some athletes or people in other professions were able to identify risk or symptoms and sought out treatments that have become available. There's no counting how many lives he touched that way."

CHAPTER 10

BE LIKE SID

To some extent Crosby's career is at once the product of physical gifts, dedication and invention. The first two have been well explored in these pages (and elsewhere) for years, but the latter mostly flies under the radar. "More than people realize, it wasn't just talent that was behind Sidney's success," agent Pat Brisson says. "It was a vision that he had of how he could become the best possible player. And really it took imagination. He was going to do stuff [in training and conditioning] that no one was doing then, definitely not as a teenager. What he did was out of the box at the time, but now it's the standard."

For all the impact he has had on the record book, for all the Stanley Cups he has raised and Olympic medals he has won, Crosby's greatest influence on the game at the NHL level has been behind the scenes, out of the public view, but it touches the lives of his peers every day. "Be Like Mike" was the advertising tagline to a commercial featuring celebrity baller Michael Jordan back in the '90s. The encouragement was simply to drink Gatorade like Jordan, a nonpareil player who might have inspired many but was beyond imitation. No company has launched a Be Like Sidney campaign, nor has any similar slogan gained any traction within hockey. Crosby is a singular player and talent, to be sure, but he was seemingly a self-made young man. He brought no special physical giftedness to the game—not, say, Eric Lindros's height, or Zdeno Chara's strength, or Mario Lemieux's reach. Seemingly, he was far closer to the NHL's median player in raw athletic stuff— even his longtime personal trainer Andy O'Brien will note that Crosby's "physical makeup is not built naturally for pure speed." Thus he was a more reasonably aspirational figure than Michael Jordan was—trying to be like Jordan was an invitation to disaster and embarrassment, while following Crosby's lead held the promise of actually being a player like him, or at least the best player you could possibly be. There's long been a debate about athletes being role models for youth, but over the course of his career Crosby became a blueprint—not just with his career decisions, but more to the point with his self-actualization, his self-creation.

I don't have to rely on young NHL stars telling me stories about the effect that Crosby had on their approach to the game when they were growing up. Such testimonials might be puffed up. But in the case of one of the most prominent, I watched it play out in real time as close-up as you possibly could be. This is a player who not only was inspired by Crosby, but basically used his youth as a personal template. Maybe not coincidentally, he may turn out to be, if not a reasonable facsimile of Crosby, then a player whose impact might someday approach his.

In December 2009 I sat in the living room of Kathy and Graham MacKinnon in Cole Harbour and watched the announcement of the roster of the Canadian Olympic team. I had gone out to Crosby's hometown to do a story on the MacKinnons' 14-year-old son, Nathan. Though the MacKinnons lived only a few blocks from the Crosbys, Nathan had never met the hometown hero. He had seen him work out at rinks in Cole Harbour and Halifax. He made it out to games when the Mooseheads hosted Crosby's Rimouski Oceanic—at the time, the MacKinnons were billeting Fred Cabana, one of the Mooseheads' players. And MacKinnon had stood on the parade route when Crosby brought the Stanley Cup to Cole Harbour on his 22nd birthday the previous June. He hadn't hung up posters of Crosby in his bedroom, but he did have a copy of the book I had written about Crosby before his rookie year with the Penguins. It turned out that the family's beloved pet had got at it and used it as a chewing toy, leaving it more dog-*teared* than dog-eared.

Though there had been no direct contact between them, not even so much as an encouraging word, the influence Crosby had on MacKinnon was comprehensive. He was skating along the same career path, stride for stride. He enrolled as a freshman at Shattuck-St. Mary's, a year younger than Crosby had been back in the winter of 2002–03. He had gone to school on Crosby and paid homage through imitation of his single-mindedness. When I was in Cole Harbour on Boxing Day, MacKinnon's parents gave him the gift he had put in a special request for: an hour of ice at an arena in Dartmouth. Instead of inviting friends over for a pickup game, he used the time as an opportunity to work out—skating alone, going through puckhandling drills, and then sort of bag-skating himself. Any resemblance between that and Crosby's renting ice for himself during the All-Star break of his rookie season was purely intentional, or at least Being Like Sid.

Crosby's influence on MacKinnon became pretty well known not long thereafter, when he was the first player selected in the 2011 QMJHL draft—breaking from Crosby, MacKinnon refused to report to a team in a francophone town, in this case the Baie-Comeau Drakkar, forcing a trade with the Mooseheads. And when MacKinnon wound up going first overall in the NHL draft two years later, Crosby as the aspirational figure and trailblazer became a recurring theme in coverage—before Crosby, no player who developed in the region had been the No. 1 pick, and now there were two in quick succession.

Underplayed if not unmentioned at the time was that Crosby had a more direct impact on MacKinnon, one that dated back to the summer after I met the family and watched the announcement of the Olympic team roster. Just a few months later, MacKinnon started working out regularly with Andy O'Brien. A Charlottetown native with a degree in kinesiology, O'Brien was a Halifax-based personal trainer who had worked with Crosby going back to age 13. Anyone who has covered Crosby over the years can tell you the degree to which he has physically transformed himself. Hockey players are famously . . . oh, let's say "hard to fit," and none more than Crosby with his hyperdeveloped glutes and quads. That happened over the course of a decade, but MacKinnon, to my eye anyway, was an even more extreme example. When I went out to Halifax to write a story about him in early September of 2011—he had just celebrated his 16th birthday days before, just like Crosby at the summer under-18s in 2003—I didn't recognize him, even though I had spent a couple of days with him just 20 months before. He had filled out seemingly overnight—in fact he didn't resemble Crosby at 16 so much as Crosby in his rookie season with Pittsburgh.

Saying this, there's no real way of knowing precisely the level of Sidney Crosby's conditioning when he came into the NHL in 2005. With the top incoming prospects, you can usually get a decent if not authoritative read based on their results at the NHL Central Scouting Service's combine, which puts them through a battery of tests. Crosby did check in at the combine in May of 2005, though nothing he did there, not even a flag-burning, could have adversely affected his status as the No. 1 pick. He did opt out of several tests, however. Because he had played games against the Ottawa 67's and London Knights at the Memorial Cup the weekend before, he was given a pass on several of the stations at the combine.

That's standard procedure for any invitee who's played in the Memorial Cup tournament. Such players have surely taken a bit of banging around and are bound to arrive at the combine nicked up. This would have been especially true of Crosby—even though the Oceanic had rolled through the playoffs, he was nonetheless playing more than 20 minutes a game and skating through a gauntlet of slashes. On his form at the combine, physicians listed left hip and right knee bruises that "will resolve."

The combine is never quite fair and balanced. Most players have weeks to recover from a season's exertions and prep for it, effectively cramming for the drills the way other kids do their SATs or LSATs. They'll practise the tests that they'll face, particularly the gruelling anaerobic and VO2 tests on the stationary bike. The value of the combine is a matter of continuing debate, and the tests and standards have evolved over the years. They probably are a better, though still hardly authoritative, measure of work ethic than of upside. Scouts will tell you the only sure takeaway is that an unproductive player who scores well on his fitness tests is probably out of upside. There were still a few interesting takeaways from Crosby's abbreviated combine numbers, though.

Players' measurements, as they appear in team programs and media guides, are a source of constant dispute. These self-reported numbers are generally exaggerated and overly flattering. Numbers at the combine, though, are definitive—no one can get up on his toes with his back to the wall when the measuring tape comes out, and while some have tried sneaking weights into their socks, they have not gotten away with it. So we know for sure that Crosby measured 70.3 inches in height (a little over five feet ten) and 191 pounds—the latter being a little surprising, at least to me. When I saw him at the summer under-18s, I'd have put him in the low 170s, mid-170s at the very high end. His body fat reading at the combine, 8 percent, was well below the average of 9.6 percent among forwards. Physicians also rated his physical development —more of an eyeball test—as AA (above average) for both upper and lower body. (Only 11 out of 59 forwards tested were rated AA, while six were graded below average—among them future NHL First Team All-Star James Neal.) Some of the data is only of cursory interest: the lowest body fat percentage in Crosby's year belonged to forward Christian Hanson, the son of Dave Hanson of *Slap Shot* fame, and no NHL team bothered to draft him; the highest, a whopping 14 percent, was registered by Bobby Ryan, and he'd wound up going second to Crosby and having a long NHL career.

Crosby's numbers in upper-body strength were around average, maybe slightly lower than those in the field. I thought he might shine through in the hand-eye coordination test, but he was just slightly above average. The one thing that caught my eye, though, was Crosby's reading in flexibility. The test at the combine was called "sit and reach," and it focused on the lower-body and core muscle groups—individual teams had their own tests for a lack of suppleness in the groin and hamstrings, which was a predictor of potential injury issues down the line, but the sit and reach test was a place to start, perhaps flagging a tight-muscled teenager for follow-up. Given that he wound up tied with Russian defenceman Andrei Zubarev as the most flexible among more than 100 prospects—most surprisingly of all, outstripping all the goaltenders, who are always presumed to be bulk-free and so loose-limbed as to be almost double-jointed. For all the acrobatics that Ben Bishop, Carey Price and Tuukka Rask would display in earning NHL All-Star honours, Crosby outperformed them in flexibility tests at the 2005 combine. I was struck by this for one reason: any player at the combine could improve his performance in the flexibility test, just as he could have worked on an issue identified in most of the tests at the combine; but working on flexibility generally offers no immediate or measurable return. It's not a matter of putting another plate on a weightlifting bar, or of adding an inch to a biceps measurement or vertical leap. In a word, stretching is a bore for many outside a yoga studio—especially for a teenager. Further, in Crosby's case in particular, the degree of difficulty would have had to spike: it's hard enough to maintain flexibility while putting on muscle mass, never mind trying to get bigger *and* more flexible at the same time. Crosby's flexibility couldn't be put down to genetics alone: it had to be the product of work and planning.

There's no knowing what marks Crosby would have registered if he had been subjected to the full battery of tests at the combine —however goofy and unnecessary some prospects have considered the stations at the combine, Crosby would doubtlessly have approached them with the seriousness of the Olympic decathlon, looking not just to post the best marks but to break records that would go unchallenged. That's simply a function of his competitive streak. Within a couple of seasons, though, the results would have been mostly of academic or historic interest, such was his continued physical transformation even by the time he hoisted the Stanley Cup for the first time at age 21. Those AA ratings on physical development wouldn't start to cover it. Only a few times, not as often as once a year, would a prospect at the combine be designated EX, for "extreme," in development, but Crosby would surely have qualified a season or two after the fact. One of hockey's worst-kept secrets is that the standard hockey uniform is like Clark Kent's office wear—almost implausibly managing to make the Superman who dons it blend in with the everyman.

For the record, I'm not suggesting that Sidney Crosby brought the concept of off-ice conditioning to the National Hockey League. Players were already taking off-ice training more seriously during the '90s and early 2000s, and the trend gathered some public attention. Conditioning became ingrained in the daily ritual. When I was covering the Ottawa Senators back in those days, postgame interviews were conducted with the team riding stationary bikes as if they were in the pack at the Tour de France, and occasionally the likes of Daniel Alfredsson or Marian Hossa would head over to the squat rack for prescribed workouts. In Toronto, Gary Roberts, who mounted a comeback with an ambitious conditioning regimen after a neck injury that threatened seriously to end his career, was mixing protein smoothies for his teammates on the Toronto Maple Leafs, fairly dictating their diets and getting them to embrace the weight room the way they once had the golf course. Roberts was the most prominent of the game's conditioning apostles, but every team would find the religion at some point—the catalyst might have been the addition of a given player to the roster or the hiring of a strength and conditioning coach. Upon his retirement, Roberts even turned his commitment to training into a going business concern, building a training facility in suburban Toronto where players from various organizations—including all-stars Steven Stamkos of Tampa Bay and P. K. Subban of Nashville—have signed up for his summer workout sessions. In fact, he regularly has a waiting list of NHLers hoping one of the slots opens up. Within the NHL, a subculture of self-improvement took hold—understandable given that the results were tangible and fairly immediate, with improved performance putting players in line for bigger paydays.

I had also seen up close the work that Swedish and Finnish teams at the club level, from the pros down to junior, were doing in the off-season. And of course, what the Soviets had done in terms of year-round conditioning with the Big Red Machine back in the '60s and '70s was a central part of hockey lore.

With regard to conditioning, Sidney Crosby didn't invent it, but he raised the bar. And he benefited from seemingly the earliest possible exposure. Before the likes of Roberts and the Senators, even before he had played a junior game, he was approaching hockey with a level of sport science greater than most of the pros. He didn't just hit the squat rack or run intervals; working with Andy O'Brien, he dedicated himself to a much more sophisticated

conditioning program, one designed with very specific applications to the game. Some of it looked like the old-fashioned grunt
work—during the summer, Haligonians would often see Crosby
run Citadel Hill in the noonday sun. But O'Brien brought a kine-
siologist's eye to the demands of Crosby's game and how he could
best prepare him for success. They organized a training plan for
off-season and in-season workouts and kept a running log of performances in those sessions.

We've seen the "test-tube athlete" go sideways terribly—for
example, Todd Marinovich, the son of a coach with the Oakland
Raiders, made it to the show, but soon thereafter was addicted to
heroin, presumably because he had been rebelling against the suf-
focating pressure placed on him by his father. Crosby profited from
a scientific approach, but in contrast to Marinovich or others *pro-
grammed* for success, he undertook his journey organically. He was
never just an experiment; rather, he was an active participant in the
research and development of a better player—namely himself.

"When I started out with Sid, he was curious about anything
that might make him a better skater or help him in any aspect of
the game," O'Brien says. "It wasn't a matter of him going to school
on somebody's experience or following any formula that was out
there. And the only pressure that was ever on him was self-imposed.
There was never any danger of burnout, not that I could see. That
wasn't the situation at all and not his personality. He was *engaged*
—even at 15, Sid kept a log of his workouts as meticulously as a
lot of NHLers."

It may come as a surprise that, for all his athleticism, Crosby's
physique (length of legs, flexion in ankle) and his body composition
(the ratio of fast-twitch to slow-twitch muscle) don't lend themselves to speed—in broad strokes, he doesn't set up for raw speed.

"Sid's strength as a skater is below the circles, on the cycle," O'Brien says. "We didn't focus on any single aspect to the exclusion of everything else, but it's not striking a perfect balance either. It's making the adjustments to avoid deficiencies from becoming weaknesses." While you would put Crosby in the 90th percentile of NHL skaters in open-ice speed, he'd be in the 99th percentile in strength on the puck along the wall—with his strength and low centre of gravity, it's hard to think of anyone who'd be in the same category when adjusted for size.

Nathan MacKinnon wasn't just able to go to school on Crosby's example; he had early access to the same teacher, Andy O'Brien. MacKinnon did meet him with once when he was in Grade 6 or 7 —his recollection of the experience is somewhat faint and it didn't make a big impression on him. "I did one workout with him, mostly lunges and that sort of thing. Andy asked what I did for workouts and my dad told him I used to run telephone poles on the way home from school with my backpack on. That was my sprint work. That was all I did."

MacKinnon did start working with O'Brien in earnest the summer after I met him, so a bit more than a full year before making it to junior hockey. He was pretty puffed up when he first went to O'Brien that summer. "I had this video of me at Shattuck and thought Andy would watch me skate and be impressed," he says. "When I was 14 or 15, I thought I was a sick skater. Andy looked and said, 'Look how bent over you are when you're skating.' Mechanically I had a lot to work on. I got humbled quick."

The regimen that followed was not what the teenager expected. O'Brien reprised the role of Mr. Miyagi in *The Karate Kid*

—you know, the learning-to-walk-before-you-run proposition. That's exactly what he had MacKinnon do: walk. All summer long. For hours. On a treadmill. MacKinnon had skipped too far ahead when he was running from telephone pole to telephone pole.

It was as boring as it sounds, but a little more intense than you might imagine. He wasn't going for strolls; he was attacking a steep incline. "We focused on flexing his ankle and positive shin angle," O'Brien says. "My experience is that it's hard to train technique later. If you're three, four, five years in, it's hard to retrain and correct technique. You can wait for the power. Other than Sid, Nate was the only teenager I worked with where I had the benefit of taking that approach and being able to be patient with the process. If you're in the NHL, you don't have the luxury of time."

The best measure of Crosby's influence (and O'Brien's), on MacKinnon in particular and the NHL in general, plays out every August in the run-up to NHL training camp. Crosby used to work out on his own or with MacKinnon and other NHLers who were summering in Halifax. And he would work out often with O'Brien coaching from the sidelines and taking notes, or with one of O'Brien's assistants. But a few summers ago, O'Brien launched a late-summer intensive program, by invitation only, bringing together NHL stars for off-ice and on-ice workouts that are as fiercely competitive as Stanley Cup playoff games. The summit brings together the likes of Crosby, Taylor Hall, Jeff Skinner, Jason Spezza and John Tavares, among others—all of them CAA clients and all of whom retain O'Brien as a conditioning advisor in the off-season. Beyond the famous names and cornucopia of hockey skills, it's a collection of all-around athletic talent probably without equal, outside of All-Star Games or the Olympics, regardless of discipline. Those who turn out for the intensive camp are the few who could in any way measure themselves against Crosby, the few who could regard him not just as an inspiration but as an example to which they can aspire. The past couple of seasons, they've congregated in Vail, Colorado, which offers not just spectacular scenery but also the aerobic challenge of high altitude.

It's easy to imagine that what started out at Crosby's camp will someday, several years down the line, become Nathan MacKinnon's. Not that there will be any formal passing of the torch. And to some degree a period of transition has already started. MacKinnon came to this camp for the first time a couple of weeks before he turned 18, just before heading to the Avs' rookie camp. Exactly where MacKinnon was in terms of his athletic development would have been a bit of a mystery to all but O'Brien and Crosby. Like Crosby, MacKinnon had gone to the NHL combine fresh off the Memorial Cup tournament—in contrast to Crosby, MacKinnon had scored a hat trick and added two assists in Halifax's win over Portland in the final. Crosby had passed up the bike and jumps at the combine, but MacKinnon pulled out of all the physical tests. The Vail camp was the first sustained period he had spent around a bunch of NHLers—he had skated with Crosby and a few other pros in Halifax in summer workouts, but then headed back to his parents' home after practice. Vail was an entirely different story. Looking back, he was basically thrown into the shark tank for his first swimming lesson. "I just tried to fit in. It helped that by then I was around Sid a bit, but still it was pretty intimidating, that first trip," he says.

In ensuing years, though, MacKinnon didn't just learn to swim; at some very early point he became a shark. That is to say, he didn't just fit in with the rest of the A students, he did things they couldn't, things that left them scratching their heads. MacKinnon will say that Crosby is the best all-around athlete in the NHL. ("Sid can basically do anything, any game," he says. "And he's probably the most competitive you'll ever meet.") But it was MacKinnon doing things that were completely out of the box in Vail.

The example O'Brien always cites came during a running drill up a steep incline, an anaerobic test that leaves lower bodies awash in lactic acid and has a direct carry-over to the game's fundamental skill. "It puts you in a biomechanical position very much like skating," O'Brien says. In one session, MacKinnon ran 14.9 seconds. The second-best time was 15.9; others finished in the 17-second range. By itself, pretty remarkable, but that was only the start. Like Crosby, MacKinnon has never been short on drive or focus in the gym. The rest of the field started to tail off as the reps went on. By the fifth or sixth trip, the other campers were dropping a second or more behind their best times. MacKinnon, though, didn't fade — he kept clocking 14.9, again and again, like clockwork. "Only on the last rep was there any change, and it was 15 flat or maybe another tenth, barely anything at all," O'Brien says. "That hill-running drill, it just shouldn't work out that way. If your muscle composition is built for power, you should fatigue more rapidly than the average and if your composition is for endurance, you shouldn't be able to explode as well."

Given the choice of Column A or Column B, somehow MacKinnon alone can order up both. This was a long way from walking on an incline on a treadmill, and no odometer can really measure the distance that MacKinnon has travelled under O'Brien's direction.

For any player, an NHL season plays out not just over 82 regular-season games and an indeterminate number in the postseason, but also over 50 or 60 off-season workouts and practices with his team. That is to say, there's the game that plays out in front of a crowd and then a lot of stuff that goes unseen. In the unseen game, MacKinnon can do stuff that others couldn't think about. "They're all exceptional athletes [at the Vail camp], but Nathan is an exception among the exceptions," O'Brien says.

The grinding hill work is just one example. When you watch videos of their cone drills, the agility tests, you can see that most of the stars in Vail will take quick crossover steps in lateral movement, whereas Crosby and MacKinnon sometimes burst sideways, more of a split-second plant-and-jump—something that would take the legs out from under average NHLers or even NHLers who average $8 million a season.

Says O'Brien, "I don't like to do projections about what any player is going to do, at least when it comes to performance in the NHL, but early on with Nathan, on a purely physical basis, I could see Nathan had great genetics to work with . . . I started seeing a certain level of limb speed with Nathan that really kind of made me take notice. He has a sprinter's body composition. By the time he was old enough to compare to some of the NHL clients I was working with, I had a nice perspective of what he was capable of. He isn't just able to turn his feet over really quickly, but he has length of stride—in some part because of a significantly longer-than-average thigh bone and long lower body in general. It's true both when he's moving forward and when he's moving side to side. The distance that he creates with a crossover step is like no other player I've worked with. That's why he has such good separation when he goes east–west on a rush. Some athletes are long like Nathan, but they don't have the turnover [on their skates] or the power. He has all of that."

O'Brien will stress MacKinnon's genetics, but discretion has to factor into that decision. O'Brien doesn't want to be seen as taking too much personal credit for MacKinnon's athletic gifts and break-through performance. That's commonplace for the test-tube ath-lete, the victory supposedly belonging to the mad scientist behind the scenes rather than the talent. Yet doubtlessly, MacKinnon ben-efited from the early exposure to O'Brien's training techniques, which has evolved over the years. No, MacKinnon isn't Crosby 2.0, but the next-gen star is working with technologies and equipment that weren't available for the original almost two decades ago. Work that was once done with a barbell or dumbbell is now done with sophisticated cables and pulleys, which track not just the load of a lift or movement but also the speed, which has meaningful application in hockey—"a higher-quality movement replicating the game," O'Brien says. Heart rates in exertion and recovery can be tracked in real time and a profile can be compiled across a full workout rather than sporadically. "There's just so much more that we can do and track than there was when I was starting out with Sid, and that's benefiting him today as well as others," O'Brien says. "We just have more data to work with . . . we can evaluate it criti-cally and develop strategies for areas that we're looking to improve. It's not just the eye test or gut feelings that we can go with now."

When you look back on the list of the 10 greatest players in the history of the NHL, you have to believe that none had put in the time and effort away from the rink that Sidney Crosby has dedi-cated to the game. Probably not even a fraction. Yes, some proba-bly had gained a level of conditioning through life circumstances rather than any conditioning regimen. Gordie Howe had lugged bags of cement as a teenager and Bobby Hull had done hard phys-ical labour on the farm. But application of workplace toil to their respective games was more coincidental than calculated. If you dug deeper on the list, you might make a case that across the span of his career, Nick Lidstrom might have logged more hours working out than Crosby has, simply by virtue of longevity—but that would be an only-so-far proposition.

Crosby stands as the brightest star of a league that today requires a level of fitness from its players that far outstrips bygone times, when summers were dedicated to rest, recovery and golf. Those days aren't exactly ancient times either. You'd only have to go back to the '90s to find an era when getting in a few weeks of skating in advance of training camp was standard summer preparation. Consider that only 10 NHL teams had strength coaches in 1996. In fact, more than a few NHL teams didn't have staff dedicated to conditioning when Crosby was already working with O'Brien—Anaheim, for instance, didn't hire a strength coach until 2003.

When I was covering the league back in the '90s, there'd be a couple of players on every team who put in time in the weight room, but usually it was a tough guy looking to bulk up, doing beach lifts. One that stands out for me: I remember watching Marty McSorley, then with the Kings, doing incline squats with a rack fairly groaning with an arm's length of 45-pound plates on either side. Great if you were looking to push a car stuck in the snow, or maybe win a posedown; not so useful if you were trying to catch up to Pavel Bure. Which is to say, there wasn't a lot of work done, and a lot of the work that *was* being done wasn't done scientifically or even smartly. Crosby was not only a trendsetter in this regard, but he has worked—and continues to work—on conditioning's cutting edge. It seems a safe bet that whoever inherits Crosby's role as the game's best player in years to come—whether it's

Nathan MacKinnon or Connor McDavid or someone not even in the league yet—will have followed Crosby's lead in conditioning. And even as he's 13 years deep in his career, Crosby is still looking for an edge. "Every off-season, Sid has made an assessment of what he wants to work on," Andy O'Brien says. "[In the summer of 2018,] Sidney saw the speed that Nathan and McDavid were bringing to the game and said that he wanted some of that. I told him that he would have to give up some of that strength below the circles —his bread and butter. It was something that we had to assess. He's never going to settle for doing what is safe, what he's done before. Nathan has picked up on that. So have the players who go to the camp in Vail. That's just the way Sid is."

And the way the NHL has become.

CHAPTER 11

THE FUTURE GENERATIONAL TALENTS

It's seemed like Jack Hughes had already skated miles by the time practice hit the one-hour mark at the USA Hockey Arena. You could have looked at just about anybody on the ice and, with the knowledge that he was 17, recognized him as a professional prospect, or with a few, even a certain NHLer. Focus on one for a stretch and he'd show a flash of *something* and a scout would put a checkmark beside *skating* or *puck skills* or *shot* or some other quality on his shopping list. With Jack Hughes it was another story entirely.

In every line drill, his every turn and pivot was a marvel. When he took a sharp corner, no matter how tight, it seemed like he never slowed. He went from due north to due south without seeming to pause, as if he was a 170-pound stone slung out of a slingshot. NHL scouts had deemed him "special" only because of their poverty of language. *Nonpareil* would be better, maybe *sine qua non*. It's hard to describe what athletic genius is, or should look like, but you know it when you see it. You're left asking, "Did he just do what I thought he did? How did he do that?"

At the one-hour mark, the coach blew his whistle and the members of the National Team Development Program, the NTDP, skated to the bench and walked off through the open gate in single file—they didn't head to the dressing room, but through a tunnel to another freshly flooded pad in the building. A great convenience: a two-hour practice didn't have to hit pause while a Zamboni circled the rink. The staff believes that quality ice makes for quality practice.

Only when Hughes stripped off his helmet and took a squirt of Gatorade as he walked through the tunnel did his youth come fully into view. If he has ever shaved, it was never because a shadow fell across his face. By looks, he was 17 going on 14. Though he was about a year and a half older than Sidney Crosby had been when I talked to him for the first time at the summer under-18s in Breclav, Hughes somehow seemed even younger. And he seemed boyish in a way that Crosby never did. At that age, Sidney Crosby seemed like a man in a fresh package.

In the same arena the next night, in the NTDP's 3–1 win over the Waterloo Black Hawks in a United States Hockey League regular-season game, Hughes looked like a man among boys. His stats line in the game (secondary assists on the winning and insurance goals) only hints at his play. As in practice, he was moving faster than anyone on the ice, passing skaters in both directions on the same shift. In the early going he rang a puck off the crossbar and had a bit of a run of bad puck luck. He did make a semi-miraculous no-look behind-the-back pass on the insurance goal, but his finest moment might have been at the other end of the ice: on an American power play, one of the point men coughed up the puck and a Waterloo skater had a long breakaway, at least until Hughes, from way, way back, closed in and broke up the play.

For me, Jack Hughes evoked 2003, and a lot of NHL scouts I know are thinking along the same lines. It's not clear whether he is the second coming of Sidney Crosby, but the NHL GM that wins the 2019 entry draft lottery certainly is hoping he will be. If the consensus in the scouting community is to be trusted—a decent but not perfect batting average—Hughes can be the cornerstone of a franchise the way Crosby has proved to be.

In some ways, they followed similar courses, but then again, there are only so many ways to come up in hockey, I suppose. Who among them doesn't have ridiculous statistics from tyke and atom hockey, goals counted in the hundreds? All of the stars do, but so do an uncounted number who were expected to be stars and didn't pan out. At a more fundamental level, though, they run a parallel course: playing up. At the grassroots level Hughes, like Crosby, played up an age group—and even two age groups briefly. More-over, they didn't play up because they had physically outgrown their peer group—the he's-so-big-he'll-hurt-the-others approach—but in spite of a significant size disadvantage. Their family backsto-ries also match up: both their fathers played at a high level in their late teens and early 20s, but their playing careers didn't stretch beyond that; their mothers had athletic bloodlines of their own. Yet the backgrounds of Jack Hughes and Sidney Crosby are a stark contrast, and nationality is only a start and not the most meaning-ful one. It really comes down to time and circumstances—Hughes had the benefit of Crosby going before him. To make himself a player, Hughes could follow Crosby's lead and even use his hockey life as an instruction manual.

"You have to look at what the guys in the NHL did and what they're doing," Hughes told me when he sat down with me last season. "It's all part of learning the game . . . learning what works in a game and learning how to become a player at [the NHL] level."

Each sport has its own brand of hyperbole, and in hockey the most used, overused, misused and thoroughly abused is a term associated with talented teenagers: "generational talents." The foundation of this term isn't altogether wrong-minded—some of the very elite kids possess talent that doesn't come along every year. Just look back on a few NHL Entry Drafts and you'll find years that don't produce talent that shimmers so brightly (for example, Mario Lemieux was the best player born in 1965 and, arguably, Joe Nieuwendyk in '66 and Brian Leetch in '67—the latter two being good players, even NHL trophy winners, but a big drop-off from Lemieux). The notion of "generation," though, is seemingly tied to sport's short attention span or, maybe more fairly, short career spans. Lemieux was deemed a generational talent, as was Wayne Gretzky, who was born four years before him. Sometimes the gaps are bigger—after Crosby, who was born in 1987, you might pass over many *only* excellent players (including Steven Stamkos, John Tavares et al.) before you'd land on Connor McDavid as a '97. Sometimes the gaps are insignificant—Ovechkin being born less than two full years before Crosby.

Since Hughes, like Crosby, showed up on the hockey industry's radar at 16, he has been a name in the game; if he doesn't enjoy the highest profile among the media and public, then he is certainly universally known in industry circles. And, yes, Hughes has been labelled, for better or worse, a generational talent.

In his underage year, Crosby burst onto the scene at the summer under-18s, effectively a preseason exhibition and a preliminary read of talent for the upcoming draft, but really not much more than that; by contrast, in *his* underage year, Hughes stepped up to much tougher company when he joined the US team at season's end for the IIHF under-18s. The respective national federations were sending their best players, who were in much better form than they would have been in August and with much higher stakes on the line, namely their first shot at a real world championship and a last bid to impress NHL scouts before the entry draft that spring.

For scouts, Crosby had stood out on a below-average Canadian team, but Hughes effectively dominated play, leading the tournament in scoring and winning the MVP with a US team that came up a couple of goals short against Finland in the gold medal game. That Finnish team featured Jesperi Kotkaniemi, who would be selected No. 3 overall in the draft a few weeks later and, before year's end, at age 18, establish himself as a top-six forward for the Montreal Canadiens.

Like every kid on the ice with his under-18 team, Jack Hughes has never known hockey without Sidney Crosby. They were lacing on skates for the first time when Sidney Crosby was in Rimouski. They were in junior kindergarten when he was in his rookie season in Pittsburgh, in Grade 3 when he hoisted the Stanley Cup for the first time. More than they can know, they're playing a game that Sidney Crosby created or, at least, remade.

Of the game before Sidney Crosby, they may only recognize a few names or have seen a few highlights. They may have seen

Bobby Orr scoring the overtime goal against St. Louis—sure, the one that's in the commercials. But New Jersey's neutral-zone trap, the hook-and-hold slog of the '90s? That bears only a passing resemblance to the game they know. It might as well have been played on the sands in the Colosseum of ancient Rome for all they know. Jack Hughes and his teammates came into this world in 4 B.C.—that is, they were born four years before Sidney Crosby played his first NHL game. They and all generations to come are the game's real millennials, players in the game's second century.

Consider that the players on the ice with Hughes on this day don't know what it's like to play with two-line offsides. They came of age in a game that permits the 120-foot stretch pass. If they've ever knocked a stick out of an opponent's hands, it has resulted in a slashing penalty. Maybe the referees in youth hockey, or even up in high-tournament play, weren't as strict on penalty calls for hooking and holding as the referees are in the NHL today, but still, they've only known a game with a very low tolerance for the obstruction that was once accepted and expected.

The "generation" that came immediately in the wake of Crosby's arrival—Jonathan Toews, Steven Stamkos, John Tavares—were already players-in-progress in the early 2000s and as such entered the NHL in the early days of its transition period, as the league adapted to its new rules—they had their own hockey heroes. For instance, Stamkos, like Crosby, cited Steve Yzerman as his favourite player when he was a teenager. And when Toews, Stamkos and Tavares entered the NHL, they played with players who would be left behind by the game's paradigm shift. Ten years into the Crosby era, though, the game had fairly well sorted itself out—teams had effectively phased out the enforcers whose lack of skills or speed couldn't be hidden on the fourth line, or defencemen who just relied on their size and strength to clutch and grab their way around playing without the puck.

Connor McDavid and Jack Eichel, the first two selections of the 2015 entry draft, would have been in grade school when the impasse in collective bargaining led to the cancellation of the 2004–05 season—that is, there was no hockey to watch that year, even if they didn't fully understand why. They entered the league in what you can regard as the later stages of its evolution—in McDavid's case, he came into the league when it was faster than ever and he pushed the needle that much farther into the red. But for Jack Hughes and those who will come along down the line, all they will know is a game that puts a premium on speed and skill. Their hockey memories, ancient history, stretch back approximately to Crosby's first Stanley Cup victory. Crosby did not just represent the state of the art in hockey when they were growing up; he represented both the way the game was to be played and the way to make yourself a player.

Dick Irvin, the coach of the Montreal Canadiens between 1940 and 1955, had a motto painted on the wall of the home team's dressing room at the Forum in the early '50s: "To you from failing hands we throw the torch, be yours to hold it high." The line was pulled from the poem "In Flanders Fields," written by Lieutenant-Colonel John McRae in World War I, and if it didn't necessarily inspire some of the greatest teams in the history of the NHL, it was associated with them. What it certainly does, though, is neatly define what we expect from the outgoing and incoming stars during their briefly overlapping times. In the mind's eye the imagery comes to life as a narrative: a soldier, mortally wounded, giving way to an anonymous serviceman—a young kid, freshly enlisted, who recognizes the valour and feels a sense of duty to see the job carried through to its righteous conclusion. Likewise, we expect stars in the game, down to their last breaths, to sustain the game, to make it ever prouder. They more than anyone know their game and know that overstaying carries with it the significant risk of tarnishing their legacies.

The relationship between Crosby and the McDavids and Hugheses whose stars are ascending is a sharp contrast to that in other eras. It's no longer the way it was for the Canadiens when Irvin had that motto put on display at the Forum. In those days a young Jean Beliveau had tuned in Canadiens games on the radio, listening to the heroics of his future teammate Rocket Richard. He had known the legend of the Rocket, but not the man or his game at any intimate level. Likewise, for Bobby Orr, he would have seen grainy images of Beliveau or Bobby Hull on a black-and-white TV on a Saturday night in Parry Sound, but he couldn't really go to school on them—video replay and slow motion were still in their infancy, so everything would have had to be gleaned from a first reading. And even into Wayne Gretzky's teenage years up through to junior hockey, how much could he have seen of Orr, Hull et al., when their games were televised once or maybe twice a week until the playoffs rolled around, by which time he had his own busy schedule to keep?

In other realms, access is of a different sort. Think of art: the masterpieces hang in galleries where artists can study every brushstroke. Think of literature: writers can dive into the great books until they are memorized and their designs clear, enabling them to build on the works of those who went before. Think of science: researchers can search published papers on a given subject, giving them a running start on discoveries. Think of chess: aspiring players can study the documented games of past grandmasters and champions and recreate them. In each of these fields there is an accumulation, a direct and substantial building-on to what had gone before.

Now think of Sidney Crosby. While it's true that, in the '90s, there were dedicated sports television networks, and more NHL games were being broadcast than ever before. And games could be recorded and replayed on VHS tapes. Crosby had an access to the NHL game that Richard, Beliveau and those who came later in the modern era didn't have. Still, Crosby couldn't have had the understanding of the league and the game that Jack Hughes has.

It's not just that today's emerging stars are arriving in the NHL with a greater knowledge of those who went before them—they almost certainly know more about Crosby than Crosby did about the NHL circa 2005. I cite Jack Hughes here, mostly because he is an available and useful example, but you could substitute Connor McDavid or, a few years down the line, a phenom to be named later, some kid who is playing atom or peewee right now. And when I talk about knowledge, I'm referring not to the stats and the biographies, the stuff of history students, but rather the mechanics and very fundamentals of the game. At the risk of overstatement, Jack Hughes may actually know and understand more about Sidney Crosby's game than Maurice Richard did about his own. It is, I suppose, the difference between those who play the game and those who make a study of it—these categories can be sorted out generationally.

This goes to the heart of the difference between, on the one hand, fandom and worship and, on the other, impact and influence

—effectively, like the difference between a still picture and visualization.

As a grade schooler, Wayne Gretzky was famously photographed with Gordie Howe at a banquet in Brantford. The black-and-white photo has been trotted out repeatedly over time, and it offers context to a remarkable occurrence less than a decade later: two players, 32 years apart in age, playing in an NHL All-Star Game. But what influence did Howe really have on Gretzky beyond inspiration? How did No. 99 go to school on the Hall of Famer? It's impossible to pick up any common threads running through their games. There's not a bit of Howe's menace in Gretzky's game, nothing like Howe's ability to flip from a right-handed shot to left-handed as the situation demanded. If Gretzky's staking out the area behind the opponents' net as his "office" was inspired by someone, it certainly wasn't Howe.

Jack Hughes has a photo of Gordie Howe wrapping him in a headlock—evidently there wasn't a hockey stick available or they would have replicated the photo with Gretzky. Hughes has no shortage of souvenirs; given that his father coached for the Boston, LA and Toronto organizations, including a long stint as the Maple Leafs' player development director, Hughes had uncommon access to the NHL. But the photo with Howe is really just a treasured memento—where a hockey legend whose career began in the 1940s poses beside a kid who might be still be tearing it up in the 2040s.

Of far greater benefit to the development of Hughes's talent was the time he spent, as a middle-schooler, on the ice with his father, Jim, and even with a couple of young pros who would land in the Maple Leafs lineup: Connor Brown, whose father, Dan, was coaching Hughes in minor hockey, and William Nylander, who at

19 billeted with the Hughes family when he first moved to Toronto. This is to say, Jack Hughes had a proximity to the NHL game that less than 1 percent—and maybe even less than 1 percent of 1 percent—of youngsters have.

The Hughes family also has online scrapbooks full of photos of Jack and his brothers wearing matching Penguins No. 87 sweaters. On its face, this was homage and hero worship. Effectively, it amounted to an announcement of the brand: Jack Hughes wanted to be a player in Crosby's mould. He went to school on the Penguins captain. To an extent, that course of study continues to this day, even as Hughes is on the cusp of breaking into the NHL and playing against Crosby.

Consider Hughes's routine with the US National Team Development Program in Plymouth, Michigan. There are the expected constants: high school during the morning and early afternoon; practice and gym work later on. But in the midst of that—certainly when he's at the USA Hockey complex and very likely when he gets home, and perhaps even during spare minutes at school or in transit—Hughes will screen hockey video footage. It might be on a laptop or an iPad. It might be on a monitor in the coach's office or even on his iPhone. And it won't be a show of packaged news highlights. It will be either: sequences from NTDP games or sequences from NHL games, often but not always Sidney Crosby's. He views them with eyes trained to pick out the details, as you'd expect from the son of a coach. Says Hughes, "I watch a lot of Patrick Kane [of the Chicago Blackhawks] because we're physically pretty similar and have sort of the same skills, but I've picked up a lot from Crosby. The way that he uses his edges, his body position, the way he keeps his body between the checker and the puck, and the way he uses and finds his teammates . . .

technically, it's all that you want to do. I find things that I want to try [in the NHL video] and look for things that I can do better [with the NTDP video]."

Within a couple of hours after a game, a member of the NTDP staff will edit together videos for the players—general team footage, but also packages specific to individuals, readied for the coaches for review. The coaches will probably wait until the next day to screen it, but Hughes and a lot of his teammates won't. As soon as that video is up for sharing and streaming, Hughes will be all over it. "Sometimes I call Jack in to the office to watch some video—whether it's his game or NHL stuff—and other times he'll ask if he can come in," NTDP coach John Wroblewski says. "I do it with everybody, of course, but Jack is a sponge for coaching. He really wants it . . . anything where he can pick up an advantage. Every player who thinks there isn't room for improvement is going to flatline. Look at Auston Matthews—he scored all those goals last year and then spent a summer working on making his shot better.

"What we talked to Jack about was getting lost on the ice—we showed him video of teams sending two or three guys after him, trying to take him off his game or take him out. We're working on him getting lost in the fray, being the 10th guy away from the puck, taking inventory on the ice and not being the focal point of attention with the puck on his stick. We broke down video of Kane, [Mitch] Marner, [Johnny] Gaudreau and [Mathew] Barzal to show him how they'll get lost on the ice and let the puck go through someone else. He's a real student of the game. He watches video here and I know that when he gets home, he's breaking it down even more."

This routine—nay, ritual—does not stamp Jack Hughes as remarkable in his class, however remarkable his skills might be. In fact, this illustrates that even the very best player in his class is like so many other players who are emerging in the NHL's second century—the average pro prospect is enriching himself with this sort of video tutorial. For Hughes, for any other elite player, for those who only aspire to be elite, a game is first played and then watched and rewatched. When Hughes walks into Wroblewski's office, almost anything the coach screens is a second viewing for the teenager. The same applies for his teammates. Perhaps there are a few that remain incurious and casual about the game who excel, who reach the game at the highest level. No matter how committed they might be when the puck is dropped, their potential can't be fully tapped until they've effectively exhausted all means of preparation.

Of course, it's not just generational on the count of hockey. The fact is, the millennial—or, in the case of Hughes, the post-millennial—has a comfort level with technology, with video, with sports science, with analytics, that previous generations did not. They may not be any more worldly than teenagers of another time, but their knowledge and understanding of the game is certainly so. The viewing of a video doesn't wait for the day after the game —in midgame during stoppages in play, coaches at the NTDP will often lean over a player's shoulder and show him a play on an iPad and give him advice about a detail in his game.

All that Maurice Richard or Jean Beliveau would have seen would have been photos in a program or, at season's end, some grainy black-and-white highlight films. When Roger Neilson began his long NHL coaching career in Toronto in the late '70s, he was derided for using videotape as a tool for coaching NHLers, even though game film had been used in college and pro football for a generation. The conventional wisdom in the NHL was that systems were basic. Neilson was derisively nicknamed Captain Video, after a character from a TV sci-fi series in the '50s. At best, Neilson was considered an eccentric, at worst a quack, and that speaks to the prevailing mindset in pro hockey.

The league in those days observed something more than an orthodoxy. The game was a hidebound realm straining under a tyranny of traditions. Coaches operated on conventional wisdom and intuition. It's fair to say that coaching and teaching in the 1970s and '80s had more in common with the game as it was played four decades before than today.

Team-generated video available to Crosby and his teammates in Dartmouth, Shattuck or Rimouski would have been limited at best. Streaming of NHL games was a few years away. If the young Crosby were transported ahead in time a decade or so, and was entering an NHL dressing room as an 18-year-old rookie in 2019, his older teammates would not regard him as a hockey nerd—he would not be an outlier. In fact, he would lagging behind them, at least as far as video goes. Likewise, if Jack Hughes or any of his teammates had walked beside Crosby into the Penguins' room after the cancelled season, the general reaction would have been "What's with them?"

In hockey's first century the NHL provided jobs to hundreds of players who would have told you that hockey was a game; for the most deeply invested, a passion. Now, however, for those who are even reasonably aspiring to the NHL, hockey must be pursued with a professional rigour. The money is so great and chased by so many, that all must look for every small advantage. For generations, the sole concern was getting outworked on the ice, but that now is only the end point. If you are outworked off the ice, you may never get a chance to be outworked *on* it. And Sidney Crosby raised the modern standard for work to be put in—even lacking easy access to practice ice and other support when he was growing up in Halifax, he doubtlessly put in more hours of work—on skills, on conditioning—than any other player on the list of the NHL's 10 greatest of all time. No one looked for approaches away from the arena—diet, lifestyle choices—and no one looked for advantages like Crosby. He set standards not only put into place by teams, but also those set by the players themselves. Those who were early adopters flourished. Those who never came around fell by the wayside.

Moreover, Jack Hughes, born May 14, 2001, has only read about 20th-century hockey, only watched low-def video, only walked around the Hockey Hall of Fame and read the plaques. Jim Hughes told Jack and his brothers stories about his days playing college hockey back in the '80s, but it was nothing like the game circa 2019. They grew up in the game that Sidney Crosby not only starred in, but in fact shaped—the game that has de-emphasized the dump-and-chase, that has emphasized puck possession, that rewards elite speed and skill more than simple brute strength.

"It's a far better game now, one that's getting faster every season," Nick Lidstrom told me. "The change in the rules [in 2005] didn't make the game faster, though. The rules gave the players a chance to make the game faster. And once somebody is going faster, everybody has to catch up."

As Lidstrom lays it out, cause and effect might be tough to sort out here—did Crosby make the game faster, or did the evolving game compel him to find more speed? Regardless, he became the vanguard of the new NHL.

———

As noted previously, Jack Hughes doesn't name Crosby as his favourite player. Born in Florida to parents from New England and Texas, Hughes is an American citizen, and that's one factor in his high regard for Chicago's Patrick Kane. That they're similar in stature and skill set would also factor in. To an extent, Hughes's choice might be less emotional than analytical—there's more that he can glean and apply from watching Kane than he can find in video of Crosby. It might even be that, in viewing video of his own games, Hughes sees more of Kane than of Crosby. Then again, it might be a function of seeing Crosby mostly in midcareer rather than footage of his junior career or his first couple of years in Pittsburgh, before he physically matured, when he little resembled the powerhouse he is now.

On surveys that they filled out for NHL Central Scouting in their draft years, Connor McDavid and Jack Eichel both named Sidney Crosby as their favourite player. Central Scouting no longer asks NHLers to name their favourite players; instead, they're asked which one they consider comparable to themselves—effectively asking, "What type of player are you?" (When McDavid filled out his information sheet, he cited as a comparable player Tyler Bozak, a respectable centre but nobody's idea of an all-star, which suggests that McDavid's speed on the ice might only be matched by his sense of humour.) Among Hughes's NTDP teammates who are projected as first-round draft picks, Alex Turcotte, a centre who is the son of former NHLer Alfie Turcotte, compares himself to Crosby, but others on the team opt for NHLers who entered the league well after Crosby. Trevor Zegras, a centre projected to be a top-10 selection, compares himself to Clayton Keller, the Arizona centre who, back in 2016 when he filled out his own form while playing out of the NTDP, named Patrick Kane as *his* comparable.

All that you can conclude is that influence runs in tight circles and a youngster at 18 is much more comfortable comparing himself to a player in his 20s than one past his 30th birthday. That, and maybe common threads in background factor in.

Crosby always named Steve Yzerman as his favourite player, when many would have expected Wayne Gretzky or Mario Lemieux. To me, that made sense. When Crosby was 10 years old, Yzerman was captain of the Detroit Red Wings, who had just won their second consecutive Stanley Cup, while Gretzky was in decline with a Rangers team that missed the playoffs and Lemieux was retired. Timing, though, was only part of it. In choosing Yzerman, Crosby opted for a star who was highly regarded for character, hockey sense and an all-around game, a great player in a conventional sense. Gretzky was not an aspirational figure for the same reason that classical musicians don't aspire to be Mozart. Neither was Lemieux a player one could reasonably aspire to be. Genius is presumed to be out of reach. Likewise were Eric Lindros or Mark Messier not aspirational figures—they brought to the game physical gifts that were unmatched. What Crosby represents was the same as Yzerman—a player in the conventional mode, not a physical marvel, who by dint of diligence made the absolute most of gifts that weren't remote or unimaginable. For that matter, it's easy to see why young players would light to Patrick Kane, who overcame a significant size disadvantage to become a First Team All-Star. Any kid who feels the odds are stacked against him on at least one count could look to Kane for inspiration. Given what Crosby overcame at different points in his career, no doubt any young player could look at him likewise.

———

Though he looks first to Kane, Jack Hughes stands to benefit more directly from the trail Crosby has blazed by the time he skates in his first NHL game. Jim Hughes works as a player development consultant for CAA, the agency that represents both his son and Crosby, and Jack will join Crosby, Nathan MacKinnon and other CAA clients at Andy O'Brien's intensive workouts in Vail. It's not really like Wayne Gretzky borrowing skates to get on the ice with Crosby in Los Angeles all those years ago, and it would be way out of Crosby's character to hype Hughes and predict that he'd break NHL records. There will be no similar anointment.

Still, there are through lines, albeit ones that capture a point in time. Crosby at 14 probably would have had a lot in common with Gretzky at the same age — Halifax and Brantford might not have been different on a lot of counts. By contrast, Jack Hughes at 18 probably would have a lot in common with Crosby after he celebrates his 32nd birthday. Not that Hughes would think of himself as a peer — there'd still be a pecking order — but the degrees of sophistication are not as great as the difference in age, not in today's game at the elite level. It's just a matter of professionalism — Hughes grew up around the professional game, developed his game with a professional level of support. Whereas Crosby, unique among today's players, was self-made.

Look at Crosby's contemporary rival. Ovechkin had the support of Moscow Dynamo and a state-sponsored system in the Russian capital; he skated with pros from the age of 14. Look at those who have come along in the past decade: McDavid spun out of the Greater Toronto Hockey League, the largest minor hockey organization in the world; Rasmus Dahlin's father is a player development consultant with the Swedish hockey federation; and, as noted, Jack Hughes had experience not just in the GTHL and

USNTDP, but direct access to the NHL. These players had material support and surrounding talent that wasn't there for a kid in Halifax in the '90s. What sets Crosby apart is that his career, his creation, was very much his independent project. He very much did this on his own. It goes back to what Pat Brisson described as "vision" and what some new-age coaches in hockey and other sports might call "visualization." He at once saw what he might become and also how the game itself was evolving.

The lore about Gretzky as a child is well known: how he would sit in front of the television in his family's living room and trace the path of the puck across the screen with his finger, as if to find patterns within the game. The scene one imagines of young genius in action evokes A *Beautiful Mind* and anticipates Hughes's and other millennial players' use of their iPads. Whatever subtleties and intricacies Gretzky found are probably beyond the ken of an average fan, and perhaps even that of an average NHL player; in fact, they might only be so much data that bypasses Gretzky's conscious mind and sustains intuition. That is, if Gretzky knew better than anyone else where the puck was most likely to go in any given situation, if he knew better where his teammates and opponents were likely to be on the ice at any given moment, he might not be able to explain exactly how it was he came to know this. At a micro level, Gretzky saw things differently—if it could be explained, then it probably could be taught and everyone would have the knowledge.

In terms of hockey sense, Gretzky's IQ would be the highest ever recorded, to be sure. Crosby's genius is of another sort entirely, and it has played out at a macro level. That's not to give short shrift to his own vision and ability to process the play on the ice—it's second to nobody's in the NHL circa 2019. If he has been caught or passed by Connor McDavid or Nathan MacKinnon or anyone else, it's a tribute to their physical skills, not their vision or hockey sense. What he did that they haven't is to reimagine the game of hockey and what could contribute to excellence and success. It would have been challenging even with others helping out, but even more so with institutional resistance—from the officials in Cole Harbour who fought him in court to prevent him from playing midget hockey, to the Quebec league blocking his way to playing at 15, and even to the veterans on the Penguins who derided him as a hockey nerd. He was a kid who didn't know his place—at least that's what the adults in the room would have said, and sometimes loud enough to be heard. And some of them used their clout to block him along the way. For all the joy the game gave him, some of it couldn't have been fun for a kid or even a young man.

Watching Jack Hughes at the USA Hockey Arena, I found myself shaking my head and asking myself, *How did he do that?*

This was the question I've contemplated about Crosby across the arc of his entire career. Young players like Hughes might be fairly familiar with Crosby's games in Stanley Cup runs in 2016 and '17 that they've screened on iPads. They might have even read a bit of the backstory. Still, they can't possibly know the extent of the challenges that Crosby faced and overcame. Really, no teenager could possibly get it. No teenager has a world view expansive enough to appreciate the obstacles Crosby faced as a kid in Halifax. And even for Hughes and his teammates, they can't fully appreciate the advantages they enjoy in the USA Hockey program in Plymouth compared to Crosby at the same age.

It's tempting to presume that there was a levelling of the playing field when Crosby made it to the Quebec league, that the final stage of his development was going to be like that of others. Yet even in Rimouski, he was still playing catch-up. His peers were still in a position of advantage. The Q was in a very soft period, if not at an all-time low, definitely the third-best of the three Canadian major junior leagues. In the two seasons prior to his arrival, the Quebec league had turned out a paucity of NHL first-round draft picks: two skaters in the first round in 2003 (Steve Bernier, who'd go on to an NHL journeyman's career, and Crosby's Rimouski teammate Marc-Antoine Pouliot, who played less than 200 NHL games) and just one in 2004 (Alexandre Picard, a forward who didn't score a goal and recorded only two assists in 67 career games). Looking down the lists, occasionally a name pops up (Patrice Bergeron as a second-rounder in 2004, for instance). So, on its face, it looks like Crosby faced soft competition, and only a few of his teammates in Rimouski played any pro hockey, and at a lower level, after graduating from the Quebec league.

In Alexander Ovechkin's first season in Washington he was probably taking a step back from his Dynamo team in Moscow during the lockout season—in the KHL in 2004–05, he played with a dozen NHLers, including future Hall of Famer Pavel Datsyuk. In Connor McDavid's last season in junior, the OHL featured 24 NHL first-round picks from the 2013 to 2015 drafts. As a 16- and 17-year-old, Hughes was on the ice every day, practising and playing with seven other projected first-round draft picks.

When Crosby jumped from the Quebec league to the NHL, the bar was raised far more dramatically than for the aforementioned. *How did he do that?* is a question you can ask of any player who reaches the NHL and achieves stardom, but perhaps more than anyone on the list of the greatest players of all time, Crosby made his way from farther off the grid. If you pushed for a one-word answer, try *alone*.

Look back at our entry point, that long wait for another great player to come onto the scene in the 1990s, that time between Lidstrom's rookie season in 1991 and those of Crosby and Ovechkin in 2005. It doesn't seem like we'll have a wait like that again anytime soon. Barring injury, McDavid would be under consideration down the line. He's clearly the fastest player in the game when, as Lidstrom noted, the game now looks like video from 20 years ago on fast forward. Could Auston Matthews, with his otherworldly puck skills, wind up in the conversation 10 years into his career? Or Rasmus Dahlin as some sort of hybrid of Lidstrom and—well, let's say Coffey more than Orr? Or could Jack Hughes? The game is being played more places than ever before and by more people than ever before, and with ever-better coaching and applications of sports science.

In looking at that long list of great players, with only the barest of exceptions does the great player not burst onto the scene. Legendary careers spin out of great beginnings. The exception here would be Nicklas Lidstrom, who didn't seem to come into his own until he had been in the league several seasons, who had in fact been eclipsed not just by teammates but even those on the Detroit blue line—he didn't make a first or second NHL All-Star Team until his seventh season, at age 28. In that time two Red Wings d-men, Paul Coffey and Vladimir Konstantinov, had landed spots on the First and Second All-Star Teams, respectively.

In what can be fairly called the mature stage of Crosby's career, McDavid was voted onto the First All-Star Team twice in his first three seasons and was certain to win the Calder Trophy and be an all-star in his rookie season if he hadn't missed more than two months with a shoulder injury. I took a lot of heat for writing a magazine story that had scouts saying that McDavid, then a 17-year-old going into his draft year, was actually ahead of Crosby at the same stage. In retrospect, I wouldn't walk back that assessment. McDavid had enjoyed successes that Crosby hadn't. Like Jack Hughes, McDavid had been named the most valuable player at the world under-18s as an underager; he had played a more central role on a championship team at the world under-20s in his draft year.

I'm not talking about a victory lap here, and scouts shouldn't dance in the end zone. The Penguins made the Stanley Cup final in Crosby's third season and won the Cup in his fourth, while in his first four seasons McDavid's Oilers have won a single playoff round, the only time they've qualified for the postseason. Nonetheless, pro scouts still marvel at McDavid's skating and skills. When TSN's Steve Dryden recently described him as "hockey's most highly evolved of all time," it sounded painfully awkward, but Dryden was trying to boil the truth down to a handle of convenience. As one NHL pro scout told me, "Crosby never brought the speed to the game that McDavid does, but that might be unfair. There's never been a player in the history of the league with McDavid's speed, and really the only player in the league right now on that count, with dynamic skating like that, is MacKinnon, who brings almost the same most north–south speed but a little better lateral movement. And McDavid can still use all of his skills when he's going full speed."

McDavid hasn't caught a torch thrown from Crosby's failing hands so much as snatched it when skating by. And just as Crosby compelled a generation of NHL players to adapt or die, so is McDavid imposing his standards on the way everyone will have to play the game. And even Crosby, through his thoughts and actions, indicates just that.

In this way, the "In Flanders Field" line does not really apply. The poem is in the voice of the soldier who is by his own admission failing, looking for someone to uphold his standards. Crosby is loath to admit that he has peaked, much less declining. He's still clearly covetous, clearly desiring not just to hang on but to excel. In a counterpoint to the line about McDavid being "the most evolved player," Crosby believes his game is still evolving. He will be 32 when this book is printed, which by all measures should put him not only on the back nine of his career, but with the clubhouse in view. And yet he's still grinding. If or when he ever actually does fail, when excellence is no longer within his grasp, it won't be because of a failure to work, compromises he has made or shortcuts he has taken.

Crosby knows that some of the game's greats had glorious runs late in their careers. On that list of the game's greatest players, Beliveau was the most obvious case when he led the Canadiens to the Stanley Cup in his last season at age 39. Lidstrom won his last of seven Norris Trophies at age 41. For some others, though, the fall-off was precipitous. Orr's last season consisted of a handful of games in Chicago at 30, and he played those after sitting out the entire previous season. Gretzky had racked up fourteen 100-point seasons by age 32, but just one after that, and he scored only nine goals in 70 games at 38.

Then again, Alexander Ovechkin won his first Stanley Cup at 32 and beat Crosby and the Penguins along the way. Ovechkin's game had been conspicuously trending downward—he failed to make either the First or Second All-Star Teams in two consecutive seasons, but raised his game for a few weeks in the spring of 2018. Not that Ovechkin turned it off or coasted or saved himself—that would be ill advised for a player whose teams had never previously advanced out of the second round of the playoffs. And of course, if you've read this far, you know that there's no cruise control for Crosby. If anything, perhaps, it will fall to the coaching staff in Pittsburgh to conserve the energy in Crosby's bank during the regular season, to avoid overusing him.

CHAPTER 12

HIS RETURN AND HIS NEMESIS

When Sidney Crosby lay on the ice at the feet of Matt Niskanen in April 2017, when the trainer ran out onto the ice and leaned over him, when a hush fell over the crowd in the Penguins' arena, hockey fans would have been recalling his collision with David Steckel in that 2011 Winter Classic game; they would have flashed back to Victor Hedman running Crosby into the end boards in the next game; they would have had just cause to fear the worst because Niskanen's hit seemed to be a much more serious blow. My memory ran in a different direction, though, unlike anyone else in the arena that night unless Crosby's parents were in attendance, because they alone would have witnessed it. The sequence eerily evoked that scene in Breclav 14 years earlier, when I saw Crosby live for the first time, when he was cross-checked upside the head by Mathias Joggi in the opening-round game against Switzerland at the summer under-18 tournament. It also evoked the semifinal against the US in that same tournament, when Niskanen and his teammates went after Crosby in the hot arena in Piestany.

The game of hockey just puts talent in harm's way. Those who pose the greatest threat to an opponent's chances to win expose themselves to the greatest physical peril on the ice. If they're at all shy about that, if they've tasted it and want no further part of it, the terrorists win, I suppose. And it was just as the scouts had told me from those days when Crosby was 16: he was bold, seemingly fearless, maybe even recklessly so. He would fend for himself. But that was impossible to do when he lay on the ice, concussed.

Niskanen's hit on Crosby was one of those incidents that would lead a perpetrator to be cuffed and booked if it had played out in the streets. In the hockey arena, though, it's just put down as the game as we know it, just another risk you assume, just a pretty tough way to make a living. Someone who only casually followed the NHL might have been shocked by the league office's decision not to punish Niskanen—or even summon him in for a meeting or make a conference call with the league's player-safety officials. "Nothing to see here" seemed like a strange position to take after the best player of his generation was helped off the ice, concussed —*again*—this time for a blow dealt after the play was whistled dead. Give the NHL credit for being inexplicably consistent: if it's not working from an entirely different rule book in the playoffs, it definitely is using another set of sentencing guidelines. An egregious regular-season offence that merits a suspension of several games (and with it, a loss of salary that can run into six figures) might sideline the perpetrator for a single game in the postseason.

The Penguins had been explicit about Crosby's injury in the wake of Game 3. Teams aren't much inclined to offer too much detail about injury to talent at any time, and in the playoffs they are treated as state secrets—injuries are risibly designated either "upper-body" or "lower-body," and in the postseason an upper-body injury could range from bruised ribs to a fractured skull. Thus was Mike Sullivan's postgame press conference out of the ordinary— the Penguins coach went on the record as saying that Crosby had a concussion, delivering a message—or maybe even a plea—for the league to step in and do something, anything, to protect him.

Maybe the league didn't quite appreciate Sullivan's prompting —the statement from the media relations department offered no explanation for its decision to let the matter drop in much the same way that Niskanen dropped Crosby. The call provoked only a small amount of outrage, drawn along partisan lines. Washington fans perceived Niskanen's hit as a love tap entirely within the game's rules, and believed it would've been a raw deal for Niskanen to be whistled for a two-minute minor, never mind the major and game misconduct he received. The Capitals were on message. Coach Barry Trotz called it "a hockey play" and left it at that. Niskanen went into greater detail: "Super slo-mo looks really bad. I caught him high. I think he's coming across, trying to score. As he's doing that, he's getting lower and lower. And when it's happening that fast, my stick and his head [collided]. I hope he's okay. I certainly didn't mean to injure him. It's an unfortunate play that happened really quick."

First, an assault on Crosby, then an assault on our intelligence. It wasn't a matter of "looking really bad." It *was* really bad. That much was plain to the eye in real time. Slow-motion doesn't exaggerate things; it reveals what might have been missed. The idea that it just happened to be Crosby, that it could have been any other player, is a non-starter. Niskanen knew he was going to be out on the ice if Crosby was out there, as often as Trotz could get his preferred matchup. He knew he had been trusted with an important job, given how the line of Crosby, Jake Guentzel and Patric Hornqvist had torn up the Capitals in the Penguins' pair of road wins to open the series.

A Pittsburgh team in the postseason without Crosby seemed like the spring of 2011 redux. But then the series against the Capitals took a couple of strange turns. The first played out on the ice: Washington thoroughly outplayed the Penguins in Game 4, showering Marc-Andre Fleury with 38 pucks and firing another 24 shots that were blocked by Pittsburgh skaters. Not a great situation for any goalie, but even worse for the Penguins, given that Fleury was the ostensible backup to Matt Murray, who went down with an injury in the warm-up prior to Game 1 of the first-round series against Columbus. On the flipside, Capitals goalie Braden Holtby made only 15 saves and just 11 more attempted shots hit Washington defenders. The game could scarcely have been more one-sided, yet somehow Pittsburgh defied all the mathematics and won 3–2 to take a three-games-to-one lead in the series.

Attend a thousand games and something like that will happen with the frequency of total solar eclipses—rare, but inevitable. What was stranger, though, was a whisper circulating around the arena that Crosby had laced up his skates—not in the game, not in practice, but when the arena was otherwise dark. In fact, the story went, Crosby had stepped onto the ice in the dead of night after Game 3. It sounded unlikely, to the point of seeming apocryphal. How could it be that Crosby would even think about being anywhere but a dark room? It seemed a certainty that he was going to be shut down for the season, yet he wasn't even shut down for the *evening*?

And yet it made sense in the context of a conversation about recent advances in diagnosing and treating concussions that I'd had with Dr. Ted Carrick, the Florida-based chiropractic neurologist who had worked with Crosby back in 2011 and 2012. "The treatment of concussion years ago was basically 'rest and then you'll get better and tough it up a little bit and get back to things,'" he said. "That is nonsensical. Now we have equipment that allows us to put someone on the ice and have them do little turns to the left or the right. We can look at their efficiency. We can see if their stickhandling changes in one direction or the other. We can get their heart rate up to a certain rate and measure brain activity [through an electroencephalogram]. This is becoming just an exploding area, looking at technology that allows us to see things in real time."

The game had changed in the interval since Crosby's previous post-concussion woes, and so had physicians' ability to diagnose and treat brain trauma. Those assessing and treating Crosby back in 2011 didn't have much of a baseline to work with; in assessing Crosby in the spring of 2017, they were dealing with an athlete familiar to them, a very thick file.

As it turned out, Crosby would be back sooner than anyone could have expected.

I'll admit it: it seemed reckless to me. Needlessly so. Never mind whether it made medical sense, it didn't even make hockey sense. There was an unnecessary urgency, even a desperation, about Crosby's return to the lineup in Washington for Game 5. The Penguins were leading the series three games to one, which meant they had three chances to close out the series against Washington. Beyond that, however, they would need to win another eight games (out of 14, or fewer) if they were going to raise the Stanley Cup—a prospect that seemed very far away indeed.

The Penguins had been down this road before, had had the opportunity to meditate on the prospect of losing their most valuable asset. The risk over the long term, versus the potential reward: it seemed impossible to justify, but there he was. The blinkered stubbornness that had led him to disregard the warning signs after the Steckel hit in 2011 seemed to come to the fore once more. But who can say no to Sidney Crosby? Certainly no one in the organization. The franchise seemed obliged to accommodate the franchise player and his hypercompetitive streak once again, even if his instincts were questionable and dangerous.

That Crosby had been newly concussed on May 1, skated in practice with full contact on the 5th and played over 19 minutes on the 6th was a tribute to, well, you pick: advances in the treatment of concussions; the power of prayer; or pluck.

While it didn't reflect at all on neurological science, the Penguins' 4–2 loss defined the limits of devotion and resolve. For a long stretch in the middle of the game, it looked like Crosby's return would take the Penguins into the Eastern Conference final. Pittsburgh took a 2–1 lead early in the second period that had Crosby as cause and catalyst. The Penguins went on the power play when defenceman Nate Schmidt mugged Crosby behind the Washington net. No. 87 just ducked under a jab from the blueliner —Schmidt had to be the only one in the arena who didn't know that any play involving Crosby that coloured slightly outside the lines would be rewarded with a ticket to the penalty box.

The ensuing man advantage was something drawn on a coach's

erasable board, at least until his Sharpie ran dry—over the course of 48 seconds, a dizzying sequence of passes, every Pittsburgh skater touching the puck at least once. The last was Phil Kessel, who hammered the puck home on a one-timer from the weak side. Watching it, you wondered how anyone ever stopped these guys.

"That goal [the power-play unit] scored is an indication that they're a talented group, and when [Crosby] is out there with them they're that much more dangerous," Sullivan said. "I thought we had control in the second period."

If that was actually the coach's thinking, he was missing or ignoring a significant danger sign: that besides Kessel's goal, Pittsburgh managed only two other shots on Braden Holtby during the second period. Washington had outshot the Penguins through two periods, 18–10, and the play was shaking out much like it had in Game 4. The only real sustained advantage for the visitors was on the scoreboard, but they only needed the dark cloud to hold off for 20 more minutes. Hockey talk is rife with clichés, but the ripest, one that evolves slightly according to the situation, concerns the most dangerous lead in hockey—pundits might cite a two-goal lead, or maybe a three-goal advantage, as the most tenuous, or maybe they'll posit that it's 2–0 or 3–1 or whatever. The Penguins' lead, though, seemed particularly precarious despite Sullivan's gut —a one-goal lead on the road despite the inability to generate scoring chances or even shots at even strength. And Schmidt's penalty would be the last to be whistled against the home team that night.

The Capitals came storming back in the third period with three even-strength goals, and the Penguins visibly sagged after Nicklas Backstrom tied the game less than three minutes in. Backstrom finished off a pass from Andre Burakovsky, who was filling the left wing spot usually occupied by Alexander Ovechkin.

Everything at that point was trending the home team's way. The Capitals put the game to bed five minutes later on goals 27 seconds apart by Evgeny Kuznetsov, Washington's most consistently dangerous threat in this series, and the aforementioned Ovechkin, who silenced the Pittsburgh fans who had tauntingly chanted his name during Game 4.

The loss in Game 5 was a small setback for the Penguins, but still they were just a win away from once again knocking off the Capitals, with the advantage of home ice in Game 6. At the end of the game, though, you were left wondering about Crosby and this small miracle of a comeback. He didn't flash Hart Trophy stuff, but then again, the Penguins were poised to win with the game he gave them: three shots on goal, a few other scoring chances created, winning 15 of 23 faceoffs he took. Yet the Penguins couldn't hold on to that one-goal lead in the third period. There were echoes of November of 2011, when Crosby made a sensational return that proved to be premature.

Crosby said he was given clearance to play right before the game, even though he said he "felt good the last few days." Maybe, but it was hard to see how it would have been possible to satisfy even the most minimal of protocols—a week without any concussion symptoms—given that only five days had passed since Niskanen drove into him in Game 3. Crosby seemed at a bit of a loss to explain what type of message he was sending by playing so soon after a concussion. "[Attitudes towards concussions] have come a long way," he said. "Everyone is trying to do their best to be more aware. That's kind of the process for everybody."

This dubious message took me back a couple of decades, when the NHL and the players' association were sorting out standards for helmets and Wayne Gretzky was wearing an old Jofa lid that offered so little protection that Brian Burke, then a league vice-president, described it as "a cereal box." Gretzky was in no position to be a spokesman on the issue, attached as he was to his outdated helmet out of nothing more than superstition, but as the face of the league he really didn't have any choice in the matter—the questions were going to come. When he ducked and dodged, I asked his agent at the time, Mike Barnett, about Gretzky's position on new helmet standards from which he would be exempted. Barnett told me, "Wayne's position is that young players should do as he says, not as he does." Gretzky, of course, had identified Crosby as the kid who had a shot of breaking his records, but here Crosby was apparently challenging his predecessor in terms of mixed messaging about safety. No one should have been more aware of the risks. Through deed, such awareness seemed to apply to everyone else.

The situation grew even more awkward in Game 6. The fourth and fifth games had been fairly one-sided on balance of play, but the scores had remained improbably close. In Game 6, the dam finally broke and the Capitals routed the home team 5–2—a score that flattered the Penguins, who generated only one real shot on goal in the first period (of the three they were credited with) and nary a legitimate scoring chance among the nine shots they'd registered by the end of the second.

Five minutes into the first period, Crosby was chasing a puck behind the Capitals net and he got tangled up—again—with Niskanen. When his head snapped back after being hit with an errant stick, it looked as bad as bad can be. He was clearly stunned, and he made his way up to his feet and off the ice very slowly. On the bench he was in obvious distress, and the PPG Paints Arena turned into the world's largest waiting room, a crowd of more than 18,000 watching to see if Crosby would take that long walk down to the dressing room to be examined by the medical staff. He did not, and they let out a collective sigh of relief.

A few minutes later, Crosby skated straight up the middle of the ice to chase a puck that ended up behind the Washington net. This time his left skate appeared to clip the post as he cut through the goal crease, and Washington defenceman John Carlson seemed to lean lightly on the 8 and the 7 on the back of Crosby's jersey. Crosby's linemate Patric Hornqvist appeared to brush Carlson just enough that all three crashed into the boards, landing in a pile. This time, Crosby was even slower to get back up and to the bench.

Still, he stayed in the game. His frustration was plain, as evidenced by jabs and slashes away from the puck. At different points his temper seemed to boil over. He jousted with Jay Beagle for what seemed like an entire shift. He even gave defenceman Dmitry Orlov a forceful face wash. These were the highlights of Crosby's game until he picked up an assist on Jake Guentzel's goal with less than four minutes left to snap Braden Holtby's shutout. And if you were looking for anything else positive from Crosby's game, then perhaps it would be his ice time: he rolled out there three ticks short of 20 minutes, not missing a shift, even when Washington ran out to a 5–0 lead in the third period.

Crosby was okay if you interpret that as meaning he was good enough to play. Okay-ish, maybe. But he definitely wasn't playing at the level he did during the regular season, not remotely like he did in Pittsburgh's wins in Games 1 and 2 in Washington.

———

"Whither Crosby" became the prevailing storyline beginning with Game 3. Were it not for his concussion and his improbably rapid recovery, the narrative would have been (as it had been so many times before) the battle between Crosby and Ovechkin. And really, by Game 7, with Crosby's return from the sidelines only a few days in the past, it had become that once again.

It's not just that these two have been the most compelling players of their generation, nor that they have developed the greatest personal rivalry over that time. Fact is, their rivalry really has no precedent in the game. Other great players have come along at the same time, but no two have been so measured against each other.

What makes it all the more remarkable is the sheer number of times the paths of Crosby and Ovechkin have crossed. For comparables, you'd have to look back to the six-team NHL. Gordie Howe would've run up against Jean Beliveau and Doug Harvey many times over the courses of their long careers, given that their teams faced each other 14 times a year in the regular season alone and met seven times in the playoffs between 1948 and '58. But with every round of expansion, with the advent of divisions and conferences and an unbalanced schedule, meetings between a pair of superstars became an occasional thing. How much of a rivalry was there really between Gretzky and Lemieux, beyond media narratives or fans' imaginations? For Lemieux's first 11 years in the league, Gretzky was on the opposite side of the conference divide, playing in the west with Edmonton, Los Angeles and briefly St. Louis. The frequency might have spiked when Gretzky came east, signing with the Rangers, but soon thereafter Lemieux announced he was walking away from the game. By the time Lemieux came out of retirement, Gretzky was deep into his own. Their teams never met in the playoffs. In fact, in their most memorable game, not only were they teammates, but linemates, No. 99 setting up No. 66 for the series-winning overtime goal against the Soviets in the 1987 Canada Cup. They weren't rivals at all, and in fact they were kindred spirits of sorts—no one could appreciate their skills and their lives as well as one another.

With Crosby and Ovechkin playing their entire careers in the same conference—and since 2013 in the same division—they have met about as frequently as any pair of opposing players can in this era, although the league's current alignment pre-empts the possibility of them facing off in the Cup final, as Crosby did with Nick Lidstrom. Before the second-round series in 2017, Crosby and Ovechkin had met twice in the postseason, in 2009 and 2016, and both times Pittsburgh had gone on to win the Stanley Cup. By the time of that first playoff matchup, they were already the league's two biggest names, and if anyone thought the series was over-hyped such notions were put to rest early: in Game 2, Crosby and Ovechkin each scored hat tricks, with Washington winning 4–3. And while their personal stats for the series were a wash, Crosby won the day, with two goals and an assist in a 6–2 victory in Game 7 in Washington. In 2016, the drama didn't run quite as high, with Pittsburgh winning in six games.

What separates Crosby and Ovechkin from the pack of the game's greatest, though, has been the stage: on so many occasions when they met, the rest of the hockey world stood still and watched —and not simply because of their star power. Theirs were the biggest games on those days, the games with the highest stakes. And unlike all the others before them, their rivalry was not limited to the bounds of the NHL. It started before they arrived in the league and crossed over to an even bigger stage, to international play, to the Olympics. And really, if you dig down deeper, international play tilts the balance even more in Crosby's favour.

The first chance of a meeting of the two stars evaporated. They both played in the 2004 world juniors in Helsinki, but Canada and Russia were in separate pools in the opening round and didn't meet in the elimination round. Ovechkin's Russian team, the defending tournament champions, were a crashing disappointment, losing to the host Finns in the quarter-finals and finishing fifth. Meanwhile, Crosby as a 16-year-old had a limited role on a powerhouse Canadian team that cruised undefeated through the opening round and seemed headed to a gold medal with a two-goal lead going into the third period of the final against the US. A pair of goals by Patrick O'Sullivan, including a crazy carom of a puck mishandled by Marc-Andre Fleury, gifted the gold to the Americans.

Crosby and Ovechkin first collided, quite literally, in the finals of the world juniors in Grand Forks, North Dakota, in January 2005, and it was unforgettable stuff. I went out to the tournament after Canada's first two games in the opening round and talked to a couple of friends, veteran NHL scouts who had seen world junior tournaments going back to the early '80s. I asked them what to expect. As noted earlier scouts are skeptics and avoid hyperbole. Said one, "The other guys are beaten before they step on the ice and they know it." The bulk of the team was made up of players selected in the 2003 NHL Entry Draft, considered the richest and deepest draft class in history, the one against which all other years are measured. Arguably, at least five of the Canadian players should have been playing in the NHL that winter and unavailable for the under-20 tournament—Patrice Bergeron had already played a full season with the Bruins at that point—but that was the winter of the lockout that led to the cancellation of season. Thus was the

Canadian team loaded like none had ever been before and likely will never be again. Crosby had to shuffle over to right wing, playing on a line centred by Bergeron and the London Knights' Corey Perry, who would go on to win a Hart Trophy a few seasons down the line.

Ovechkin was front and centre for the Russian team in '05. He had played for Russia in the World Cup a few months earlier, the youngest player in the tournament among the best in the NHL. The Russian team in North Dakota also featured Evgeni Malkin in a supporting role.

Even though it was Canada versus Russia, the next biggest storyline was Crosby versus Ovechkin. The former was a source of mystery: Crosby had been little seen outside of the Quebec league. There were some hard feelings attached to the latter: the public's image of him had been formed in Halifax two years earlier, when he trash-talked and laughed at the Canadian team during the medal presentation, seemingly embracing the role of the heel. While the scouts were impressed with the 2005 Canadian team, they were somewhat less so with Crosby. "He's been *good*, but he's not their best player," one of them told me. In the media, there was still skepticism about Crosby—this wasn't *his* team, not in the way the Russian team's was Ovechkin's. If it wasn't quite a consensus on press row, there was at least a contingent who believed Ovechkin would put Crosby in his place. It didn't play out that way.

From the game's first minute, Canadian coach Brent Sutter matched the Perry–Bergeron–Crosby line against Ovechkin's line. Sutter also made a point of lining up defencemen Dion Phaneuf and Shea Weber against Ovechkin. Midway through the first period, with Canada out to an early 1–0 lead, Ovechkin carried the puck down the left wing and pulled up at the Canadian blue line, where he cut towards the middle of the ice, cautious about approaching the punishing Canada defence. He looked for his linemates to skate into the frame, but he didn't see Crosby, coming at full speed on the backcheck. Though he was giving away four inches in height and at least 25 pounds to Ovechkin, Crosby didn't hesitate to lay hip and shoulder into him. It wasn't quite a knockout punch, but Ovechkin was dazed. When he managed to get back up on his skates he shook his head in disbelief. He played a few more ineffective shifts before pulling himself out of the game. At the press conference after the game, his right arm hung in a sling. He had reportedly suffered a shoulder separation, though he didn't identify the blow that had done the separating—Ovechkin had already taken a few heavy hits by the time Crosby dropped him.

With Ovechkin on the sidelines, Canada rolled to a 6–1 victory, a game that wasn't as close as the one-sided score. Bergeron led the tournament in scoring and came away with the most valuable player award. Phaneuf was named the tourney's top defenceman. In the press conference after the gold medal game, Crosby was content to sit off to the side and let Bergeron and the others take centre stage—even Jeff Glass, the virtually untested goaltender, sat up front—to his seeming dismay, as he faced more testing questions from the media in a single session than scoring chances in the entire tournament.

Crosby didn't score in the finals, but make no mistake: he made the most important play in the game. An almost reckless but completely legal open-ice bodycheck. Canadian fans had packed the University of North Dakota arena for every game and had come with expectations of seeing some sleight of hand, puck skills and flash from Crosby. Instead they saw him make a play that didn't evoke Lemieux and Gretzky so much as Gordie Howe.

Crosby didn't miss a shift, but the hit had taken something out of him. It was exactly as Tim Burke had told me back in Breclav, that Crosby "fights his own battles and looks after himself."

That was true before he went to Rimouski, and more so by his draft year. "Sidney was so much stronger on the puck," said centre Mike Richards, who would go on to play in the Stanley Cup final with Philadelphia and raise the Cup twice in Los Angeles. "It was unbelievable, the difference in his strength. And he was a lot more aware of what was happening on the ice. He had a better under-standing of what it was going to take for us to win. It was strange. It was like a carry-over from Finland. We had a bunch of players that knew each other so well from over the years coming up, and in North Dakota Sidney was now one of those players. [Brent Sutter] didn't have to bother with the team-building exercises. On the ice and off the ice we picked up where we left off the year before."

Crosby admitted later that it wasn't a coincidence that he found Ovechkin in the crosshairs. "Yeah, I knew it was him [Ovechkin]," Crosby said. "And really, it was a situation that we knew to look for. We knew that nobody was challenging Dion [Phaneuf] in this tournament. No one beat him wide during the tournament and everybody had stopped trying. And from watching him and from the scouting reports, we knew that Ovechkin liked to pull up at the blue line and skate towards the middle."

Of such things are bitter rivalries forged. It wasn't renewed at the 2006 Olympics in Turin, however, since Crosby was not in Team Canada's lineup. But Ovechkin did get a measure of revenge when he beat Marty Brodeur with the eventual game-winner to eliminate Gretzky's team. And he burnished his reputation by earn-ing a nomination to the all-tournament team alongside Teemu Selanne—the only player who scored more than Ovechkin in

Turin. The Canadian team's general manager, Wayne Gretzky, passed over Crosby, then in his rookie season, deciding to go with a lineup long on experience and role players, but No. 87's omission would be second-guessed. Though the Russians would themselves get shut out by the Czechs in the bronze medal game, Ovechkin's play in the Olympics fuelled the media and fans who maintained that Crosby had been overhyped. Likewise did they consider Ovechkin beating out Crosby for the Calder Trophy as the league's best first-year player to be a validation.

The dynamic, the narrative, was obvious and it sorted itself out before the pair's sophomore NHL season. The league recruited them to take the leading roles in a commercial, along with an ensemble of established and emerging talent. The premise of the commercial was light-hearted: showing fun-loving stars fooling around in a hotel, boys acting like boys. Veterans such as Joe Thornton and Brendan Shanahan were in the mix, likewise the Staal brothers, Eric and Jordan. Nonetheless, Ovechkin and Crosby had the most memorable roles. The commercial opened with Ovechkin calling room service and ordering a long list of items from the menu; it closed with a waiter knocking on Crosby's door with a line of food carts, prompting him to mutter, "Ovechkin" through gritted teeth. The script was written with a wink and a nod to the greater narrative, the construct of the media and fans alike —that the sober, all-too-serious Crosby was irked by fun-loving Ovechkin, who took unconcealed delight in irking him. The commercial played midway through the season in which Crosby became the youngest-ever winner of the Art Ross and Hart Trophies, but even with that performance he couldn't win over the doubters. Consider a column by Evan Grossman on NHL.com, the league's own website:

Please don't base your entire Crosby-is-better argument on how much he's accomplished at such a young age, because that doesn't wash. No disrespect to either guy, but there's something you people need to wrap your minds around . . . [Crosby] is not as good as Alexander Ovechkin. That's right. I said it. Crosby might be the face of the NHL, might have all those endorsements and that brand new "C" stitched into his uniform system, but in no way shape or form is he better than Ovechkin and his tinted visor. Crosby will be the first to tell you that, but maybe humility is Crosby's only winning character trait in this argument. Ovechkin is good—and he knows it—and that room service commercial gag is but the first of what will be many last laughs No. 8 has over No. 87.

Of course, Ovechkin had his share of shining moments in games against Crosby, but there was never anything like a balancing of the books. The hope that he would lead the host Russians to redemption against Canada at the 2014 Olympics in Sochi came undone when his side crashed in the quarter-finals against Finland. With the NHL taking a pass on the 2018 Games in South Korea and the league's future participation in the Games uncertain at the time of this writing, it may be that we have already seen the only matchups between Crosby and Ovechkin on the biggest international stage. In the interim Ovechkin would have to look for a measure of payback wherever he could, and Game 7 of the second round in 2017 seemed like his best opportunity. And with the Penguins standing as the defending Stanley Cup champions, their elimination would at least be *something* on Ovechkin's side of the ledger.

For the first five minutes I thought Crosby and the Penguins had no shot at even keeping it close. In the early going they couldn't get the puck out their zone, couldn't get a change, couldn't really draw a deep breath. There was only one thing that Washington couldn't do, but it turned out to be the thing that matters most: they couldn't put the puck past Marc-Andre Fleury, not in those first five minutes and not for the last 55 either. Twenty-nine shots, 29 saves. Pittsburgh 2, Washington nothing to show for all the toil again.

In the dressing room after the game, the Penguins heaped praise on the goalie. "He stole us a couple of games in this series and kept us in a couple of other games," centre Matt Cullen said. "Flower has been our best player in the playoffs."

Fleury was the Penguins' best story on a team with a lot of them. The previous spring, he wound up with a second Cup ring, but watched the games from the bench with a towel around his neck, backing up Matt Murray, a kid as green as a cucumber who stood in the crease in his stead. Fleury wasn't even going to play in the spring of 2017: the chores were supposed to fall to Murray once again. But when Murray tweaked his knee in the warm-up before the Penguins' playoff opener against the Blue Jackets, the Penguins had to turn to Fleury, who had been the subject of much discussion during the season, none of it confidence-building. All the talk focused on the likelihood that, with the Penguins able to protect only one goaltender in the upcoming expansion draft, Murray would be their choice and Fleury would be bound for Las Vegas in June. (The situation was made all the more awkward because Fleury's contract contained a limited no-trade clause.) As the Penguins' season began back in October, none of the pundits could have foreseen that he would be what he was right now: the team's saviour.

Washington's energy ebbed after the electrifying start, and for the Penguins it was a slow build towards playing on somewhat level terms until the midpoint of the game. Fleury had put the defending Stanley Cup champions in the ideal position in Game 7 against the Caps—that is, needing only a single goal to win. Enter Crosby.

Crosby wasn't the best story in this series, but without a doubt he was the biggest. Pittsburgh coach Mike Sullivan shuffled Hornqvist off Crosby's line and brought in Bryan Rust. For the coach, it wasn't a small move at this juncture. But Game 7 marked a near-complete return to form for Crosby—he has had many clutch moments but maybe none bigger than this one.

The first and really only necessary goal came midway through the second period, and it came off the stick of Rust, as these things seem to do—the previous spring he had scored a pair of goals in the Penguins' Game 7 win over Tampa Bay. Crosby was credited with the second assist, but it was a piece of skill that outstripped Rust's finish. Crosby found Guentzel with a feathered pass and then went to the net, throwing a moving pick on Niskanen (a measure of payback in itself), allowing Rust to find the open ice and enough of an opening to beat goalie Braden Holtby.

When asked about his return to form from the hit on Niskanen, Crosby wanted to move on and only wanted to talk about the game in the team context. "We knew we had to be more aggressive than we were the last couple of games," Crosby said. "We got through that first wave there. We were much more on our toes. We got the goal and had some great looks to add on it."

Eventually they did add to that goal, and you could see the Capitals break into a thousand little pieces after it. Five minutes into the third, only trailing 1–0, Ovechkin lost a footrace to defenceman Justin Schultz for a loose puck at the Washington blue line. Schultz threw the puck over to Patric Hornqvist, who beat

Holtby just under the crossbar—it wouldn't be fair to call it a shot so much as a backhand lob from the slot, a complete whiff.

That was the Capitals' series in a nutshell: Ovechkin relegated to the third line and yet still a liability there; Holtby, for all his regular-season heroics, looking vulnerable against the Leafs in the first round and effectively letting the air out of his teammates in the third period in Game 7. The Capitals managed but five shots in the last 20 minutes and boos rained down on them from fans who thought this was the year Ovechkin et al. would finally make it to the third round.

The Penguins moved on to face the Ottawa Senators in the Eastern Conference final. Crosby had more hockey to play, more opportunities to put questions about his concussion or Ovechkin at a greater distance. In the end, though, he would leave no question about his place in the game—only a few weeks after it seemed like his career was once again threatened, he would play the very best hockey of his career.

CHAPTER 13

"HE SAID, 'FOLLOW ME.'"

A bit more than a calendar year before Pittsburgh's second series win over the Capitals in as many seasons, many wondered whether Crosby had passed his peak. Many wondered if he was in fact in decline. Many floated opinions like these out loud or on the printed page. And by "many," I must include myself. I don't intend to throw anyone under the bus to keep me company—I'll leave names out. Let me just say that I wasn't alone in going out there on the record musing about Crosby's struggles, and my take wasn't exactly scalding hot. "Crosby at 28 is < 87," I wrote, painfully too cute.

In the first half of the 2015–16 season he was much in the news, mostly because it wasn't him making news, at least not in the usual way. That was Connor McDavid's rookie season, and he had fairly exploded onto the scene in Edmonton—having been the most hyped first-overall pick since Ovechkin and Crosby and also having been tagged as a "generational talent." Even by the time McDavid was entering the second month of his professional career, he was regarded as the fastest skater the NHL had ever seen, more dynamic in that way than Crosby had ever been. Comparisons were being drawn between McDavid at 18 and Crosby at the same age, and again I put it out there: "97 > 87."

The talk died down when McDavid took a hard bump—he crashed into the boards in a game against Philadelphia and was sidelined by a separated shoulder. Some seemed to take a measure of satisfaction in his injury, suggesting that this proved he would have to make an adjustment to play in the NHL, that he couldn't get away with what he'd been accustomed to in junior, that he'd have to draw his game back to survive in "the men's league." Of course there were the knockers—even Gretzky had been targeted by critics when he came out of junior at 17, and then a season later when the Oilers and the three other WHA teams came over to the NHL in the merger. And yes, Crosby had them, too, as an 18-year-old rookie.

Only with McDavid on the sidelines did people really turn their attention to Crosby's struggles.

Expectations had been high in Pittsburgh at the start of the season. Mike Johnston, a much-decorated hockey man in the junior and international ranks, was in his second season behind the Penguins bench; in his rookie year as an NHL head coach, Johnston had the team off to a 22–6–4 start before a spate of injuries exposed some holes in the lineup, holes that seemed to have been addressed over the summer. The acquisition of Phil Kessel from Toronto was supposed to give Crosby an opportunity to skate with a winger who possessed elite skills—if Chris Kunitz became an all-star playing beside Crosby, then surely Kessel, owner of one of the league's best releases, a pure scorer, could break out for a 50- or 60-goal season. Two months into the season, the expectations were sharply downgraded. Ten seasons after his NHL debut, Crosby was mired in a slump unlike any in his career. With just five goals and 10 assists through 24 games, his stats line would put him in the league's middle ranks—a fall from First All-Star to second-liner. In the bleakest patch, he went 11 games without a goal. The Penguins were sputtering along at 15–10–2 when general manager Jim Rutherford fired Johnston and replaced him with Mike Sullivan, who had been coach of Pittsburgh's American Hockey League affiliate in Wilkes-Barre/Scranton.

Upon the firing of Johnston, I wrote:

> Look, I'm not here to bury Crosby. I don't imagine that it's over
> for him. Still, it does seem like he's moving into a different stage
> of his career. Something like an athlete's mid-life. Whether this
> is the proverbial crisis or not is another thing. It might turn out
> that he wins more Stanley Cups on the back nine than on the
> front. It might turn out that he can reinvent himself as a player,
> becoming less spectacular but more effective overall than at his
> physical peak. That's exactly the career path of his favourite
> player growing up, Steve Yzerman. There's no doubt that Crosby
> understands the game well enough to find a different game to
> play. But will he prove too proud to do anything but be carried
> out on his shield?

I don't keep a scrapbook or a file of my clippings. I'm not one to look back on what I've written. I didn't keep a copy of the magazine where this appeared. It should come as no surprise that I don't even own a copy of the book I wrote about Sidney Crosby back in

2005. I was able to find this passage online, though. I remember being ambivalent about it—I know for a fact that at some point I had worked *malaise* into the text and then deleted it, thinking that it struck a little too close to the bone. Not that I was reluctant to inflame. Not that I wanted to soften the blow. Just that I thought *malaise* was unfair.

It was hard to question Crosby's commitment when he had worked so hard for so long. He came back from his time on the sidelines with post-concussion syndrome, even though he would have had the financial wherewithal to walk away and could have done so blamelessly. Having accomplished so much already, having reached the summit of the game, he had nothing to prove to anybody, especially so given the awful risks he was assuming by continuing. He had emptied his tank so many times; maybe it couldn't be filled all the way anymore. If that were so—*if*—that might be a failure, but not a failure of will.

Okay, thank God I didn't go with *malaise*.

In the 18 months between the time I wrote that column and the time I dug it out to wave in my own face, Crosby had what I have to admit was a better-than-decent run. First, he won the Conn Smythe Trophy by leading the Penguins to victory in the 2016 Stanley Cup final. Then he won MVP honours after leading Canada to an undefeated run through the World Cup of Hockey. And finally, the day that I pulled out the column, the Penguins were just two games away from a second Stanley Cup in as many seasons—the final against the Nashville Predators was tied at two games apiece, with Game 5 to be played in Pittsburgh.

To whatever degree he had reinvented himself or rebooted his career, he had become "less spectacular but more effective overall than at his physical peak," but even as I had written it, I was imagining a transformation like Yzerman's, one that played out over the course of several seasons and with a few bumps and setbacks along the way. Though some of it was close to the mark if not prescient, I was thankful that sportswriters don't have to take vows to eat misbegotten opinion pieces. We're not even obliged to issue *mea culpas*. Still, I think I should have been able to put it together. I had watched more than a decade's worth of Crosby—not with the frequency of the Pittsburgh beat writers, to be sure, but with the benefit of a measure of context. He had reinvented the game itself along the way, so how could anyone really put it past him to reinvent his own game? He understood better than anyone that the league was evolving independently of him, and as a result of all manner of influences: the arrival of McDavid, MacKinnon and other young talents accelerating play; new coaching schemes turning the game ever more towards puck possession; the distribution of talent as a function of the payroll cap; the virtual extinction of the fourth-line enforcer; and sundry other developments.

NHL games when Crosby won his first scoring title a decade before looked very different than when he slumped early in the 2015–16 season; then again, so too did that slumping Crosby look very different than when he was deep in his run for a third career Stanley Cup—in those last three games of the Washington series when he came back from the blow levelled by Matt Niskanen, in the tense seven-game Eastern Conference final against the Ottawa Senators and in splitting the first four games of the final against the Predators.

Still, as noted, at that point the Penguins had won 14 playoff games that spring, 13 of them with Crosby in the lineup. Nashville was still in position to flip the script, as they had done with everyone else standing in their way—they had entered the playoffs as the eighth seed in the Western Conference, the playoff team with the fewest regular-season points, a franchise with no previous play-off successes to build on. They had fallen behind, three games to two, against Anaheim in the Western Conference final and lost their ostensible first-line centre, Ryan Johansen, in the process and still figured out a way to reach the final.

As of this writing, Game 5 against Nashville might go down as Sidney Crosby's greatest performance in a Stanley Cup final game. It's not going to define his career—there's no eclipsing his gold medal goal in Vancouver, let's face it. Nonetheless, Game 5 of the 2017 final will rank up there with a few other moments when he displayed his skills and will to their best effect on the biggest stages. Crosby took possession of the night on the very first shift, splitting the Predators defence at the blue line and pouring in alone on goaltender Pekka Rinne, only to put the puck off the post. No matter. The Penguins had been flat in long stretches of the first four games against Nashville, seemingly spent after back-to-back seven-game series. They had fallen into a counterpunch-ing mode. Not in Game 5, however; they dictated the play from the drop of the puck and Nashville reeled. And Crosby hitting the post in the opening seconds seemed to have a Pavlovian effect on Rinne—in his career he had given up an average of more than five goals per game in Pittsburgh. That average would climb by night's end.

Not even 20 seconds after hitting the post, Crosby drew a hold-ing penalty on defenceman Ryan Ellis. Inside the two-minute mark, Nashville trailed the home team 1–0 after a shot from the point by Justin Schultz, who had emerged as the team's key blueliner after Kris Letang was ruled out for the entire postseason because of neck surgery. Five minutes later, Bryan Rust made it 2–0 on a backhand that went by Rinne's glove and in off the post. To put it in boxing parlance, the Penguins hit the Predators with their Sunday punch in the opening seconds and never gave them time or opportunity to draw a breath and clear their heads.

But neither those goals nor the half-dozen breathtaking plays Crosby made across 60 dominant minutes would be replayed as often as a sequence that took place late in the first period. It started after P. K. Subban rushed the puck deep into the Pittsburgh end. The Predators defenceman battled for possession with Crosby behind Matt Murray's net. They grappled and Subban lost his balance. Crosby wound up standing over Subban, straddling him. He put his glove up against the side of Subban's helmet and bounced his opponent's head off the ice, five times at least, as if he was trying to drive a nail into the cold surface with Subban's left temple as his hammer. It might have looked like a variation on a face wash —because it was beside the net, most people in the arena didn't have a clean look at it. But then, when you watched the replay, you saw that these weren't love taps. Crosby could easily have wrenched Subban's neck. Worse, as he straddled Subban, his skate blade was just inches from the Predator's exposed neck. It was unnecessary, petty and reckless.

If there had been an enmity building between the two, the history of it was lost or missed entirely and the principals hadn't let anyone in on it. They had been teammates on the Canadian Olympic team that won gold in Sochi, although Subban, then the defending Norris Trophy winner, was controversially left out of the lineup in the games that mattered most. And perhaps even more controversially, he hadn't been selected for the World Cup team the previous fall.

Crosby's shots at Subban seemed out of character—maybe one shot would have been understandable, but this went beyond the pale. Some on press row ran with the idea that Crosby didn't like Subban's style—that he was the anti-Crosby in the way that he courted the media and seemed to enjoy the spotlight. It sounds like a plot lifted from a novel, I suppose: someone so serious-minded as to resent anyone who has fun or takes unbridled joy in the game the way Subban does. I don't imagine that Crosby had singled out Subban for special sanction to defend old-school values against a "big personality." Might that kind of thinking have contributed to the Montreal Canadiens' decision to trade Subban to Nashville? Sure, doubtless a factor. But in Game 5 of the Stanley Cup final, Crosby just had too much at stake to indulge in any score-settling of any description.

The Pittsburgh fans who cheered as Crosby drove Subban's helmet into the ice have short memories or no memories at all. Or embrace double standards in the extreme. Crosby has taken more physical abuse than any great player in history, but that shouldn't grant him licence to cross lines. And yet when referee Brad Meier finally blew the whistle, he dealt out minor penalties for holding to both Crosby and Subban—and no one could tell exactly what Meier thought the latter was holding. Just more fuel for the belief of fans in Nashville, Washington and elsewhere that the NHL is engaging in some sort of vast pro-Penguins conspiracy.

Because less than two minutes remained in the first period, the pair skated off the ice to their respective dressing rooms. Thus, they missed Evgeni Malkin's goal with 10 seconds left. And just over a minute into the second period, with Rinne pulled in favour of backup Juuse Saros, Conor Sheary made it 4–0. The Predators knew there was going to be no rally like the one they had mounted in the opening game in Pittsburgh.

Crosby didn't score, but he did end up with three assists. He might have added a goal if Sullivan had sent him out in the last minutes, but the coach decided that, at 6–0, things were getting too ugly to take any unnecessary risks. The game featured dozens of heavy hits, many of them borderline. Every shift ended with scrums that led to fights. The action achieved an awesome level of absurdity when 40-year-old Matt Cullen got into his first fight in 18 years, taking on Roman Josi—who, if the websites that track these things are to be trusted, has dropped the gloves precisely once before. It wasn't all comedy, though. The game reached its nadir when, near the close of the hostilities, Colton Sissons was kicked out for cross-checking Penguins defenceman Olli Maatta in the face.

On the next-to-last night of the season, with so much skill on display and players gunning to have their names engraved on the Cup, the last five minutes looked like something you'd see in the minor-pro bus leagues. If the Predators thought they could intimidate the defending champions, they had it all wrong, per Malkin in the dressing room afterwards: "So many fights after whistle. They understand they lost. We understand we win. But there's still 15 minutes left. We still play. I think they're upset. They don't like what they do tonight. They start extra hit, extra fights. We're ready. We understand it's coming."

It's fair to say that the officials let the game get away from them, and Crosby's mugging of Subban was a sore spot for Nashville coach Peter Laviolette. "I really don't understand the call [of offsetting holding penalties]," the coach said. "I saw my guy get his head cross-checked into the ice 10 times. I don't even know what he did. I disagree with the call."

Taking unusual pleasure in Subbanning Subban, Crosby said his foil "lost his stick and he was doing some UFC move on my foot there. I don't know what he was trying to do."

Subban didn't swallow the bait. "It's hockey, man," he said.

Subban brushed off further questions about the incident, but consider this: what would the fair-minded people think of Subban if he had jammed Crosby's head into the ice? Well, for a start, I'm betting that Brad Meier wouldn't have called coincidental minors. It would get labelled a mugging. Some would call it an attempt to injure; others, felony assault. Such is the double standard, a perspective generated by reputations—in this case Crosby as patron saint of the game's traditions, and Subban as nemesis, cast out of Montreal for not being suitably Canadien.

When I heard that NBC commentator Mike Milbury had said Subban "had it coming," well, it's at times like this that I wish there were an emoticon for "sigh." Milbury, who previously had called Subban "a clown," seems to possess a vision of the game that has not evolved from the days when he climbed out of the Bruins bench to slap around a fan and bang him upside the head with his own shoe. Meanwhile, the same fans who had booed Niskanen's hit delighted in the number Crosby did on Subban.

Regrettably, in 2017, that's still hockey. As much as Sidney Crosby changed so many aspects of the game over the years, in the NHL and beyond, a few ugly aspects of it are as permanent as granite.

Matt Cullen just drank it in, a moment that he wished could last forever. He sat in front of his stall, sweat still pouring off him. His 11-year-old son, Brooks, was sitting beside him, looking around with eyes as big as pucks. Brooks's T-shirt featured a graphic treatment of a hockey player standing over a fallen opponent. The bold type framing the artwork summarized Cullen family values: IF YOU CAN'T SCORE, DROP SOMEONE WHO CAN. To his three young sons—Brooks being the oldest—the 40-year-old centre imparts life lessons and espouses play without the puck, things that have put food on the table and a roof over their head. To the media, he tried to put into words a teammate's appreciation of Sidney Crosby—not the guy who jammed Subban's head into the ice but the talent who dictated every shift from the opening faceoff.

"He has that drive and determination," Cullen said. "It was one of the best games [I've seen him] play. Right from the beginning. He did the same thing last game in Nashville. When he plays like that, our whole team picks up. I've been here for a couple of years and played against him for years, but I just love how he steps up . . . really everything about his game. He's one of those rare players who has that sense of [recognizing] when it's that time to step up, like he did at the start of the game. He put the team on his shoulders. He said, 'Follow me.' He's one of the very few that can raise his level that high. It's just fun to see it."

I asked Cullen how the young players in the Penguins' lineup and others around the league have gone to school on Crosby. Cullen, one of the last players in the NHL who had played against Wayne Gretzky, said his teammate's influence wasn't limited to younger generations. "I've played this game a long time, but I learn stuff from Sid all the time," he says. "I pick up something that I'll see him do. And the work he puts in, that really sets the standard here. The way he prepares, you have to fall in and get with the program, for the good of the team and really for your own good too. I'm convinced that being here, being around Sid, that's been a factor in stretching my career."

I've been told umpteen times that, unless you've drawn an NHL paycheque, you'll never understand the pain that players endure. I've never doubted it. I've seen it too often: players who suited up despite bone breaks and muscle and tendon tears that would put the bravest of us on the sidelines for a long time. And while that might be true on a fairly regular basis in NHL play, it reaches its extreme in the playoffs. No one in a dressing room wants his sweater and equipment to hang in the stall while his teammates play on.

The stories figure prominently in the lore of the sport, but only a few become NHL heritage moments. Most fall into the category of "What happens on the bus stays on the bus." Only by proximity to the dressing room have I caught glimpses of broken men tapping into something beyond courage. One player I count as a friend played through a torn ACL because he was retiring at the end of the season and thought that leaving the game while his teammates played on would be far more awful than being carried out on his shield. And 20 years back, I remember seeing Mikael Renberg, not anyone's idea of a lion-hearted warrior, moving around the hotel lobby on crutches with a cast on his foot on the morning of a playoff game—done for the remainder of the playoffs, I thought, but of course he was in the lineup that night.

I saw it again in Nashville, in the next-to-last minute of the last game of the season.

It wasn't news on game day that Predators defenceman Ryan Ellis was banged up. He had left Game 5 after a hit by Chris Kunitz and didn't return to action—whether Kunitz's hit was the cause or it merely compounded a pre-existing wound, we may never know. The official word was that Ellis had an upper-body injury. The best guess was a fractured or broken rib. That wasn't his only ailment. Ellis was also wearing a heavy knee brace and would require surgery on the joint over the summer. In the days before the game, Ellis was seen around the dressing room, but when he skipped the game-day skate, teammates suggested to the media that he wasn't going to be available. Ellis was a game-time decision: his own. When it came time to make it, he was in. Of course.

I winced with him when the Penguins lined him up. Over the course of 58 minutes, Ellis struggled to get back to the bench after Pittsburgh players ran him. And they did run him, targeting him conspicuously. Defenceman Trevor Daley took a minor for roughing up Ellis, which gave Nashville a brief five-on-three power play in the second period.

Was Ellis at 70 percent? Maybe he could convince himself of that. No doubt Laviolette had calculated that whatever fraction of Ellis's game was lost, he still possessed more than anyone who might take the ice in his place. Ellis's 34 shifts tied him with Subban for the most on the team. He logged more than 24 minutes of ice time as Laviolette leaned on his top four blueliners— the third pair, Matt Irwin and Yannick Weber, saw less than 10 minutes of ice time. Still, Ellis strained to make what would have been routine plays. I didn't think there was any way he was going to finish the game, but by the third period I realized that he was bound and determined to see it through. By the last minutes of the third period, when it was clear that one thin goal was enough for the win, I was overtaken by dread. It wasn't that I had a problem with the Penguins winning the game; I just didn't want a

Nashville loss in Game 6 that could be pinned on Ellis—or that Ellis could pin on himself, telling reporters after the game something like "I don't think you ever get over something like this, the way it went down."

Awful dread became a more awful reality. With less than two minutes left in regulation time, Kunitz carried the puck into Nashville's end for what looked like a cautious buildup with no immediate threat. The Predators had men back. They had the advantages of numbers and position. Ellis was in front of the net, as was Patric Hornqvist. The puck came back to the blue line and Justin Schultz let fly with a slapshot that was wide right by at least a couple of feet. A carom off the end board landed on the stick of Hornqvist, who was between Ellis and the puck. Hornqvist had no angle at all, but played a second carom, this one off the back of Pekka Rinne —one bank and in. While Rinne flailed, trying to recover, the shaft of his stick caught Ellis in the face and snapped his head back.

With 95 seconds left, there was going to be no tying the game. With Rinne pulled in favour of an extra skater, there was going to be no solid scoring chance. With Carl Hagelin's empty-net goal with 14 seconds left in regulation, there was nothing but suffering in absolute terms for Ellis and the Predators—that and the handshake line.

When I saw Ellis and Crosby shake hands and exchange words I thought about the risks they had taken to stay in the lineup with a Stanley Cup on the line. I could fully respect and admire Ellis's commitment but it didn't take calculus for him to figure out the odds—going into Game 6, he was two games away from a championship, two games of intense pain with the risk of worsening a fracture into a full break. Something more severe—a displacement of a rib and a puncture of the lung—couldn't be ruled out. As for

Ellis's knee, perhaps not the same level of pain, but a greater risk of exacerbating the injury—just one bad turn, not even contact, could turn a partial tear into a full one.

Crosby's situation provided a sharp contrast. When he returned to the lineup after Niskanen's head shot left him concussed, the Penguins were 10 wins away from a championship. That is to say, they were in the hunt and, even if they didn't quite need a telescope to see the trophy, they were still a very long way off indeed. The specialists treating Crosby gave him a green light to return to the lineup, presuming he was recovered, but no neurologist offers guarantees, not even with the most thoroughly examined grey matter in the game—they had prematurely cleared Crosby for a return before. Crosby was looking at far longer odds than was Ellis, and was really putting himself at far greater risk.

There's much to admire about the greatest players in the history of the game, many of whom played through pain and injury. Orr, of course, played until knee injuries robbed him of his game. Lemieux came back from debilitating back injuries and treatment for lymphoma. Brain injuries, though, are an entirely different matter; they represent life-threatening risks. Other than Crosby, the only era-defining player who suffered a brain injury was Gordie Howe, in Game 1 of the first round of the 1950 playoffs. Accounts of the incident vary—some say it was just an unfortunate fall, others say it was the by-product of a butt-end from Toronto's Teeder Kennedy—but Howe's unhelmeted head struck the boards at the Olympia and he had to be rushed to hospital. There, doctors drilled a hole in his skull to relieve pressure on his brain. Howe was out of hospital and on the ice in street clothes to celebrate the Wings' Cup victory a few weeks later, but the only concession he made to his brain trauma was a brief stretch when he wore a flimsy helmet, which he soon discarded. What Howe and physicians in his era didn't know about brain injuries didn't hurt him any further —or so it seemed, anyway. It may be that only Crosby would have been so bound and determined to return from post-concussion syndrome while being fully aware of the risks. There may be a few players who rank higher on the list of the greatest of all time, but none ever had to make so tough a call.

ACKNOWLEDGMENTS

The first feature I wrote about Sidney Crosby was a significant leap of faith of my friend Derek Finkle. Back in the summer of 2003, I managed to convince Derek, the editor of *Toro*, that a kid who had yet to play a major junior game was the next big thing. That was a tough sell and I made it harder by suggesting that the story would be best covered at a tournament few knew about and nobody saw: the summer under-18s in the Czech Republic and Slovakia. *Toro*, a men's magazine that was an insert in the *Globe and Mail*, was still very new and to that point I'd only written one story for them. To my shock, Derek gave the story the green light when 99 44/100 percent of editors would have balked and laughed. I lucked out not just with Sidney Crosby living up to his billing but also finding an editor who trusted me.

I next wrote extensively about Crosby in the junior ranks for *ESPN The Magazine*. There, my champion was the late Mark Giles, a wise and impossibly likeable editor who had all kinds of time for hockey, though his enthusiasm wasn't necessarily shared around the office. Again, I had written one story for Mark when I convinced him it was worth going to small town Quebec and the world juniors to stake out this kid who hadn't yet registered with the US media. Mark died almost ten years ago but I really do think of him daily—I never learned more and had more fun than working with him. Also in my corner on East 34th Street was Gary Belsky, whose judgment and instincts were at once unerring and unnerving. Again, working with Gary was like going to grad school in magazine writing, something I've tried to thank him for whenever we get together . . . so here it is in writing.

This might seem hard to believe but back before the 2004–05 hockey season (and a NHL season that would be gassed due to a protracted labour impasse), I tried unsuccessfully to sell a book on Sidney Crosby to a bunch of the biggest publishers in Canada. Tried and failed. They couldn't get their minds around a book about a teenager who had yet to play a game in the NHL. Only one publisher, late in the day, warmed to the idea: Fitzhenry & Whiteside. Richard Dionne, a friend and editor there, backed me and the book, *Sidney Crosby: Taking the Game by Storm*, wound up on the bestseller list. That we managed to get the book out in October 2005 was a small miracle, given that the entry draft was delayed until mid-summer. Richard went the extra mile backing me and then working to grind it out and I'm forever appreciative of his support and hard work.

In the time I was working for ESPN, I also wrote about junior hockey for Sportsnet's website with Pat Grier being the point man. The late Jim Kelley introduced me to Pat and paved the way for me there. I wrote about Crosby's run through the playoffs and the 2005 Memorial Cup for the website. I owe Pat and Jim for supporting my junior hockey jones.

In 2011, I left ESPN and went over to Sportsnet full-time when the folks at One Mount Pleasant were launching a biweekly magazine. In its hundred or so issues, *Sportsnet Magazine* pulled down all kinds of awards and was one of the most exciting experiences I've had over my long career. At times, it felt like I was writing about Crosby every third issue, but my memory here is unreliable. He was, however, on the cover of our debut issue, at that point the hanging question was whether he'd ever play in another NHL game because of his post-concussion woes. I'm still at Sportsnet — we, like so many, do our business strictly online and, yeah, I'm still unofficially on the Crosby beat, which has included his playoff and Stanley Cup runs. I'd like to thank everyone involved at *Sportsnet Magazine* and Sportsnet.ca for their support, including: Steve Maich, who basically founded the magazine and probably against his better judgment hired me; John Intini, who inherited the corner office from Steve and was maybe the sharpest, most cerebral editor I've ever worked with; John Grigg, who manages me these days on the website and whose patience I try on a daily basis; Evan Rosser, who handles my copy with a deft touch and infinite good cheer; and Dan Tavares, who suffers me but supports our group's feature writing unlike virtually any media outlet these days in Canada and beyond.

Among those in the ranks who've helped me out over the years, I'd like to thank: Dave Molinari, a Hockey Hall of Fame report who recently took vast knowledge and deadpan delivery from the Pittsburgh *Post-Gazette* to dksports.com; Terry Koshan, the linchpin of the *Toronto Sun*'s junior hockey coverage, with whom I have spent countless hours in rinks great and small and occasionally both; and Andre Brin, the former head of Hockey Canada media relations, who helped me out back at the summer under-18s in 2003 and was a great resource ever after in all things Sidney.

I can't count all the scouts I've talked to over the years about Sidney Crosby but they include among them: San Jose's Tim Burke; Tod Button of the Flames; Daniel Dore who's with the Rangers these days; and Tim Bernhardt, who earned a ring with the Dallas Stars back in 1999. Every one of them told me about aspects of Crosby's game that I might easily have missed.

I'd like to thank my agent, Chris Bucci of CookeMcDermid, for his belief and support. In publishing, a writer is ever the unrestricted free agent coming off a bad season and a back injury and yet Chris manages to land me a deal, although not always on July 1.

I'd like to thank my friend and editor Nick Garrison at Penguin Random House Canada. We go all the way back to 2005 and I owe too much to him to fully catalogue here. Suffice it to say that when I'm on a project with Nick, work never feels like work. He's made everything I've ever done for him better and such is again the case here. Also in the Penguin Random House house: I'd like to thank Justin Stoller, who helped me through first and second drafts, late changes and nitty-gritty stuff when others would have thrown in the towel. I'm sure when I came down with pneumonia this past spring, Justin must have felt he was coming down with something, too.

As ever, I owe an unpayable debt to my daughters, Ellen and Laura, and my partner Susan, without whom none of this would be possible and none of this would have any meaning.

INDEX